WITCHCRAFT
DISCOVERED

T0035208

Josephine
Winter

Magic, Ritual & Enchantment
for Head, Hands & Heart

Llewellyn Publications | Woodbury, Minnesota

FIRST EDITION
First Printing, 2023

Book design by Samantha Peterson
Cover design by Shannon McKuhen
Interior art by Llewellyn Art Department

Photography is used for illustrative purposes only. The persons depicted may not endorse or represent the book's subject.

Llewellyn Publications is a registered trademark of Llewellyn Worldwide Ltd.

Library of Congress Cataloging-in-Publication Data (Pending)
ISBN: 978-0-7387-6916-5

Llewellyn Worldwide Ltd. does not participate in, endorse, or have any authority or responsibility concerning private business transactions between our authors and the public.

All mail addressed to the author is forwarded but the publisher cannot, unless specifically instructed by the author, give out an address or phone number.

Any internet references contained in this work are current at publication time, but the publisher cannot guarantee that a specific location will continue to be maintained. Please refer to the publisher's website for links to authors' websites and other sources.

Llewellyn Publications
A Division of Llewellyn Worldwide Ltd.
2143 Wooddale Drive
Woodbury, MN 55125-2989
www.llewellyn.com

Printed in the United States of America

WITCHCRAFT

DISCOVERED

© Kylie Moroney Photography

About the Author

Josephine Winter has been a Pagan and witch for over two decades, beginning in Norse-inspired heathenry and later the Alexandrian tradition of Wicca. She holds degrees in education, literature, and the arts, and she works as a literacy and language acquisition specialist. For the last decade she has been a regular volunteer and organiser at various Pagan events around Australia and is the founder of Lepus Lumen, a teaching collective of covens, outercourts, and solo practitioners.

Other Books by Josephine Winter

Fire Magic

CONTENTS

Part III: The Heart

Part IV: Going Deeper

EXERCISES

Basic Skills

DISCLAIMER

In the following pages you will find recommendations for the use of certain herbs, essential oils, incenses, and ritual items. If you are allergic to any of these items, please refrain from use. Each body reacts differently to herbs, essential oils, and other items, so results may vary person to person.

Essential oils are potent; use care when handling them. Always dilute essential oils before placing them on your skin, and make sure to do a patch test on your skin before use. Perform your own research before using an essential oil.

Never self-medicate, even with herbal remedies. Herbal remedies can be extremely potent; some are toxic. Others can react with prescription or over-the-counter medications in adverse ways. Please do not ingest any herbs if you aren't sure you have identified them correctly. It is worth mentioning that some herbs have different names in different countries, so researching them is important. If you are on medication or have health issues, please do not ingest any herbs without first consulting a qualified practitioner.

ACKNOWLEDGEMENTS

This work would not be possible without the support and love of many, including my various families; the teachers, students, and graduates from Lepus Lumen; and others in this wonderful community that I feel so blessed to be a part of.

Thank you, from the bottom of my heart and with everything that I am, to my partner Mark, to my mum Fiona, to Jason, to Tim, Leathy, Hughie, and Augie, to aunty Chris and Sue. To Andrew, Julie, Melliee, Drew, and Ryan. To Jasper, Fiona, Kerry-Ann, Tim, Lee, Shannon and Anna. To Eryk. To James, Peter, and Gi. I love you all.

—Josephine Winter
Summer Solstice, 2022

"The lyf so short, the craft so long to lerne." —Chaucer

INTRODUCTION
Start with This

I was a teenager in the late 1990s when I first started looking into witchcraft. My hair was shaved down to almost bald and dyed sunflower yellow. I'd had a friend use a stencil to spray-paint—yep, actual paint in an actual spray can—a big red heart on one side of my head. Among my most treasured possessions was a pair of pants made from a shopping centre banner that my friends and I had stolen from a rooftop.

Things have changed a bit since then.

The witchcraft in this book is the witchcraft I am practising now. It is informed by everything I have done and been involved with up until now—eclectic witchcraft, Norse-inspired paganism, Alexandrian Wicca, lots of pagan community building work, and other bits and pieces including stolen banners and DIY hairdos—and that's what makes it uniquely my own. It won't be the craft I am practising in ten or even five years' time, as witchcraft is—as you'll find, if you persist with it—quite a fluid and unexpected journey most of the time. And more than you know, it's tempered by what you do and who you do it with as you go along. A lot has changed, but I can sew my own clothes with ease, even though they're made of tamer, more legal stuff these days.

Getting Started: Doing the Thing

This book has been put together with the intention of inspiring the reader to experience witchcraft with the head, the hands, and the heart, with activities to get you thinking, learning, doing, and reflecting.

Many new witches have trouble making the transition from reading and learning about witchcraft to actually practising it. This shouldn't be the natural order of things: it's normal to have reservations about trying a new thing, but don't let it get to a point where you are holding back because you don't feel you "know enough." *Enough* is a nebulous term and is almost impossible to define in this context; just how much knowledge is enough, anyway? I don't think I've met a witch or Pagan anywhere who felt they knew or had read enough. Amateur or ace, we're all learning, all the time. And one of the best ways to learn is by actually doing and experiencing. Consider this your permission slip, not that you need one.

It Doesn't Cost Any Money to Practise Witchcraft

More often than not, the witchcraft we see on social media and elsewhere on the internet is geared toward getting you to pay for something, whether it's a workshop, a lecture, or shiny, pretty things for your altar. We're told that witches need to look a certain way or own a certain number of books, crystals, or miscellaneous jars of spooky shit to be authentic. It's just not true.

It's not tools, accessories, or books that you need to be a witch. All you need is to *do* witchcraft, rather than just reading about it or viewing content about it online.

The Worst That Can Happen

Something that seems to be quite paralysing for a lot of new or would-be practitioners is the worry that they will somehow get things wrong—that they will say the wrong words, make the wrong gesture, or otherwise mess up in such a way that has catastrophic consequences or, worse, brings magical nasties into their lives.

Let me be very clear here: *the worst that can happen is nothing at all.*
Seriously.

If your spell or working fails in some way, it will not work. The worst that will happen is that you won't bring about the thing or change that you set out to.

If witches and occultists really could bring about evil spirits, "dark" magic, or three-headed beasties from the dungeon dimension just by flubbing part of our workings, don't you think there would be more of these things wandering around the place? My front yard would be overrun with the amount of things I've tried and failed at over the years, and I don't mean just as a beginner either. Some folks I know would have been incinerated by dragons three times over.

The worst that can happen is nothing. And you've got nothing to lose.

You Will Probably Feel Silly

Witchcraft is more than an aesthetic. Witchcraft is often ugly and deeply uncool. Witchcraft can be inherently silly at times, and practising it can feel ridiculous. Feeling silly is normal. Feeling silly is how we relax and know that, under the funny costumes and weird names, we are human beings just trying to make sense of the world around us. Witchcraft, ritual, and magic are a few of thousands of different languages we employ to do that.

It's okay to smile or laugh in ritual. It's okay to feel—or be—a bit daggy at times. It's the practitioners who take themselves too seriously that I'm wary of.

Using This Book

Throughout the book, there are practical exercises and basic skill entries to get you actually *doing the thing* rather than just reading about it. Any technical, specific, or unfamiliar terms used have been defined in the glossary at the back of this book.

At the end of each chapter, I've included journal prompts as suggestions to get you writing and reflecting on your thinking about witchcraft, your research, and your practice. Consider starting a journal, whether it's a raggedy old notebook, a digital notebook on your phone or another device, or a fancy bullet journal with all the trimmings. Your journal doesn't have to be anything fancy or complicated. Keeping any kind of journal about your craft is an invaluable skill and practice to get into. I wish I'd started years before I actually did. If journaling is completely new to you or if you want some ideas, I've included some material on journaling in chapter 15.

There is also a suggested reading list at the end of each chapter. These are intended to give you a bigger, more detailed picture of the content covered in the chapter. I don't believe any one book of witchcraft can be "complete," and there is no way I could say everything there is to say on a topic without each chapter becoming a book in and of itself. These lists are optional, of course—obviously you aren't going to go out and purchase hundreds of brand new books—but even if you only check out one of the sources listed, you might broaden your understanding.

EXERCISE
A Rite of Beginnings

I've included this ritual here as an intentional, obvious beginning to your working with this book (or maybe with witchcraft itself?).

Before you begin, have a candle and a means of lighting it handy. If you're working outdoors, you might want to use a lantern or container to keep your candle from blowing out. Figure out which direction is east, either by working out where the sun rises each day or by using a compass or app. You might want to try responding to the journal prompts at the end of this chapter and keeping these ideas in your mind as you begin.

1. Find a place where you feel comfortable, either indoors or outdoors, that is quiet and free of distractions. Dawn would be a great time to do this, but any time of day is perfectly fine.

2. Stand or sit facing east. This is the direction of the rising sun, often associated with new beginnings, the springtime, birth, and awakenings.

3. Light your candle and spend some time focusing your thoughts on the task at hand: really figuring out what it is you want to learn, do, or achieve by reading and using the information in these pages. Take some deep breaths to relax if you need to. Think about why you set out to do this.

4. Say aloud:

   Between the land and the sky
   Amidst the cycles of nature
   Between history unfolded and unfolding

Beneath the eternal sun and moon
I, (name), take this step
Small, but intentional
The first step on my journey

5. Spend some time sitting in quiet contemplation before extinguishing the candle.

Afterward, write a journal entry about this rite. Include how it made you feel and what you experienced, if anything. Keep the candle; you might like to use it when you're reading or writing about witchcraft as a reminder of the rite you just conducted and the journey you've embarked upon.

☽ ☽ ☽ ● JOURNAL PROMPTS ● ☾ ☾ ☾

You might be new to witchcraft, but that doesn't mean you're new to life, knowledge, or learning. Before we go any further, write a sentence or two about what you already know about the following:

- How old is witchcraft? How old is Wicca?
- What is the difference between the two?
- Who was Gerald Gardner, and what was his contribution to modern witchcraft?

PART I
The Head

Quiet contemplation. Loud postulation. History and myth; folklore and fakelore. The road to now, and what comes next. Asking the questions; viewing versus looking. This is the witchcraft of the head.

CHAPTER 1
Orientation

Nobody is a blank slate. You're bringing something to the table here as you read this book. Maybe your ideas and curiosity about witchcraft come from TV shows, films, or books. They might come from something you've seen online or people you follow on social media. Maybe you know practising witches and have decided to look into it more. You might be already well-established in your craft, in which case I hope this book encourages you to examine some of it with fresh eyes, or maybe to try or research something you never have before. Regardless, you are not coming at this with nothing. Remember that as we go forward.

In this chapter, I'll share some different definitions of witchcraft, share a smattering of history, and have a go at unpacking and examining what it is that modern witches do.

Definitions

I'm a word nerd. I need to tell you that from the outset. Out in the "real" world I help upskill teachers of English and work with young people who have diagnosable issues with their language and literacy. This tends to spill over into my witchy life, as you'll see in the various dives into etymology and definitions throughout this book.

Dissatisfying Dictionaries

Look up *witch* in the dictionary and you get some pretty specific meanings…very few of which give any information about what it is that witches today actually do. Allow me to demonstrate:

> Witch (noun):
> 1. a female sorcerer or magician;
> 2. a being (usually female) imagined to have special powers
>   derived from the devil;
> 3. an ugly evil-looking old woman;
> 4. a believer in Wicca.[1]

Are you seeing a theme here?

Witch in modern English still has negative and gendered connotations because it is a word that has been used as an insult (or an accusation) toward women for centuries. It's from these negative connotations that we get the classic archetypes of the witch: the vile old woman in a black pointy hat casting spells, the spooky teenager with magical powers—sometimes evil or devilish—and so on. This is, unsurprisingly, a long way from the truth.

Because of its history as a word to oppress women especially, some modern feminists have reclaimed the words *witch*, *coven*, etc. for use in the general context of activists and activism. And that's pretty damn cool. But that isn't the witchcraft we'll be looking at in this book either.

That final definition (and the only one that isn't specifically about women) mentions "Wicca." That's starting to sound more like it. Let's see what the dictionary has to say about this word.

> Wicca (noun): the polytheistic nature religion of modern witchcraft whose central deity is a mother goddess; claims origins in pre-Christian pagan religions of western Europe.[2]

Okay. This is a bit better, but still only partially true.

---

1. Vocabulary.com, s.v. "witch (*n.*)," accessed September 1, 2020, https://www.vocabulary
.com/dictionary/witch.
2. Vocabulary.com, s.v. "Wicca (*n.*)," accessed September 1, 2020, https://www.vocabulary
.com/dictionary/wicca.

There are a few bits and pieces that I'll unpack later in this chapter, but for now, let's look at the differences between the words *witchcraft* and *Wicca*—a word that, while old, has only been used to describe a practice of witchcraft since the mid-twentieth century.

Witchcraft versus Wicca

The word *Wicca* as it's used today is often used interchangeably with the word *witchcraft*. It first appears in published witchy material with this spelling in the early 1960s. Around a decade before, Gerald Gardner (who you'll read more about later in this chapter) and others used it only to describe the actual *practitioners* of witchcraft. The word is thought to be related to—or more likely a reconstruction of—the Old English words *wicce* and *wicca*, which refer to female and male magicians respectively, especially in the same evil/devilish sense as many of modern society's definitions of a witch.[3]

The word *Wicca* was also used for some time in the late twentieth century to differentiate between lineaged, initiatory, oathbound witchcraft (like Gardnerian or Alexandrian witchcraft) and the more eclectic practices that were becoming more and more popular during that time. As the word has become more widely adopted to describe many kinds of witchcraft, members of these initiatory traditions have begun using "Traditional Wicca" to describe their paths. Some North American practitioners refer to it as "British Traditional Wicca."

Generally, dictionary definitions of the word *witchcraft* will talk about sorcery and spells. In modern witch spaces, the word can mean the same thing, or it can be extended to cover just about anything modern witches do. Many witches talk about their "craft" or their "art," meaning their practice, their way, and what it is they actually do.

So far, I've done a lot of dismissing of definitions and not much clarifying. But what makes a witch a witch these days?

In an interview with the American Academy of Religion, Professor Ronald Hutton described the figure of the witch as being one that is very attractive to people who might feel out of place in contemporary society for some reason.[4]

---

3. *Online Etymology Dictionary*, s.v. "Wicca (*n.*)," accessed September 1, 2020, https://www.etymonline.com/word/Wicca.

4. Applewhite, "Author Interview."

He also gave four very workable definitions of witchcraft. The first two are quite old, and two others are newer but have still been in use for a few centuries:

- A witch is somebody who uses magic to harm others.
- A witch is somebody who uses magic for any purpose, not necessarily "evil": for example, to heal or to see the future.
- A witch is a woman persecuted by men (and the women who support those men).
- A witch is a practitioner of a pagan religion.[5]

Modern witches, then, can be any or all of the above: they might practise magic; they might not. They may practise witchcraft or even be attracted to it because they feel marginalised or othered in some way; they might not. They might also identify as Pagan or worship deities; they might not.

Even within witch communities, *witch* can be a tricky word to define. There's not necessarily a clear line we can use as the cutoff point for what is and isn't witchcraft, but Hutton's definitions certainly come close.

A lot of folks starting out worry that they aren't doing things "right," or that they aren't witchy enough to walk this path. Please don't. Outside of particular traditions, there is no centralised organisation, no priesthood or ruler who dictate the way things should be. There are no bands of witch enforcers who will kick in your door because you aren't doing things like a "real" witch, because only you know what's real to you.

Witchcraft versus Paganism

Theistic witches—witches who worship or work with deity or spirits—often identify as Pagan as well as witches. *Paganism* is an umbrella term that covers a huge range of spiritual and religious paths that may be nature-based, ancestor based, animistic, modern approximations of pre-Christian paths, or completely new paths in and of themselves. Witchcraft is just one of the many, *many* "denominations" that fall under this umbrella.

As one author explains:

5. Applewhite, "Author Interview."

There are many different paths of paganism, just as there any many different traditions within Christianity, Islam, etc. Pagan religions, for example, include Wicca, Druidry, Heathenism, Hellenism, and witchcraft. Paganism does not claim to be the one true way, nor does it suggest that other religions are somehow wrong, or misguided, or inappropriate in today's world. All spiritual paths point to a divine source.[6]

In his book *The Path of Paganism*, author and blogger John Beckett defines contemporary Paganism as not being a single path but a collection of many concepts, practices, values, and beliefs—thousands of belief systems and ways of worship under one big "tent" that is supported by four "poles" or centres of Paganism: Nature, Deity, Self, and Community. Some Pagans are so close to one pole that they don't pay much attention to the other three. Others are close to two, three, or even all four centres.[7]

The Not-So-Old Religion

Witchcraft today is multifaceted and vibrant in its histories and origin stories. The following is intended as a rough outline of how modern witchcraft came about, rose to popularity, and evolved to influence what is practised today.

When I say "modern" witchcraft, I mean eclectic witchcraft as it is practised today, in the twenty-first century. Remember, the word *witchcraft* had some pretty ghastly connotations a century ago, and it was used to describe any number of folk practices, traditions, and customs considered "ungodly."

Before Wicca

Margaret Murray (1863–1963) was a historian, folklorist, archaeologist, and anthropologist who wrote and published *The Witch-Cult of Western Europe* in 1921. In this piece, Murray hypothesised that medieval witchcraft wasn't Christian heresy but an organised fertility cult that had survived through the Middle Ages and into the present day.

While this story had fantastic romantic appeal, Murray had no proof and her theories were later discredited. Critics pointed out that it was highly

---

6. "What Is Paganism?"

7. Beckett, *The Path of Paganism*, chap. 2.

unlikely that such an organised cult could exist without communication, transportation, or even a common language between the supposed "covens" around Europe.[8]

Even though Murray's theories have long been discredited, several of them persist in modern witchcraft today, thanks in part to a man named Gerald Gardner.

The Birth of Wicca

In England, the last laws that made witchcraft illegal were repealed in 1951. This allowed Gerald Brosseau Gardner to publish two nonfiction books that would have a huge impact on witchcraft for the remainder of the century and beyond: *Witchcraft Today* (1954) and *The Meaning of Witchcraft* (1959).

Gardner was a retired civil servant who had spent much of his life overseas in places such as Borneo, Malaysia, and Ceylon (which is now a part of modern Sri Lanka). He had a keen interest in foreign culture, and through his research he became an expert on the *kris*, a Malaysian ritual knife.

Upon his retirement and return to England, Gardner looked for people who might be interested in esoteric teaching and study. This led him to a Rosicrucian (a European spiritualist and cultural movement) theatre group. While Gardner didn't get much out of the group itself, a few of its members intrigued him. This group later befriended Gardner and took him into their confidence. Gardner claims that these people told him they were witches and, after some time, initiated him into Wicca.

Gardner believed at least some of Margaret Murray's theories about witchcraft; Murray even wrote the introduction to *Witchcraft Today*. He claimed that the material given to him by his teachers and initiators was only fragmentary, with many pieces being lost over time.[9] He used his research and knowledge of other occult traditions—including ceremonial magic traditions such as the Golden Dawn and Ordo Templi Orientis, fraternal orders like the Freemasons, etc.—to fill in the gaps.[10]

---

8. O'Brien, "NeoPaganism."

9. Biographical information about Gardner was found in Mankey, *Transformative Witchcraft*, chap. 1, and Heselton, *Witchfather*.

10. O'Brien, "NeoPaganism."

Ceremonial magic is a term that covers a wide variety of practices that are characterised by their rituals, symbols, and ceremonies that are used as a way to represent the supernatural and mystical forces that link the universe and humanity. It's sometimes called "high magic," "ritual magic," or even "learned magic," and it draws on several different schools of occult and philosophical thought. Some of the most well-known orders, groups, and organisations that practise ceremonial magic include the Hermetic Order of the Golden Dawn and Ordo Templi Orientis, sometimes called the OTO.

The rituals of ceremonial magic orders often include costume, dramatic invocations to gods or spirits, incense, and dramatic-looking tools or props. Author and academic Nevill Drury describes it in its highest sense as "a transcendental experience, transporting the magician beyond the limitations of the mind toward mystical reality."[11]

These orders and their rituals certainly influenced Gardner as he went about reconstructing and adding to the material he claimed he received from the people who initiated him, and these reconstructed rituals are still used by Gardnerian Wiccans today. Wherever it came from, Gardner's work had a marked effect on the witchcrafts that have appeared since it was published.

Wiccan Roots

Much of the eclectic witchcraft written about and practised today has been influenced in some way by the witchcraft first written about by Gerald Gardner, or it features customs that made their way in via traditional Wicca.

Your witchcraft has likely been influenced by early traditional Wicca if you:

- Cast or use a magic circle.
- Wear a pentacle or use one in ritual.
- Wear ritual jewellery, especially necklaces.
- Call watchtowers/guardians/elements/spirits/quarters.
- Use a ritual knife/dagger/athame/sword.
- Raise energy, especially by dancing/chanting in a circle.
- Have representations of the four elements on your altar or in your circle.

11. Drury, *The Watkins Dictionary of Magic*, 174.

- Use the Witches' Rune ("darksome night and shining moon...").
- "Draw down" the moon or any other deity.
- Use terms like *skyclad*, *Book of Shadows*, *esbat*, *merry meet*, *blessed be*, *cakes and ale*, *meeting dance*, *athame*, etc.
- Have initiations and/or degrees in a hierarchical structure.
- Use the Witches' Rede ("An it harm none, do what ye will").
- Worship a God and a Goddess (especially the Horned God and/or a moon goddess).
- Use magical names.
- Celebrate eight sabbats (two solstices, two equinoxes, and the cross-quarter days).

Remember that the witchcraft Gardner wrote about was partially sourced from other material, such as that from ceremonial magic traditions, groups, and organisations. Quite a few of the things listed have come to us via those traditions, but it is through Gardner and his early Wiccan material that they are associated with witchcraft as we recognise it today. And while Gardner's contributions to today's witchcraft are among the most notable, there are many others who helped pave the way.

Some Paganism and Witchcraft Hasn't Aged Well

Books and other modern witchcraft material are always products of their time. Outside of very specific traditions, not a lot is static or remains totally unchanged in our craft, and this is as it should be: if my witchcraft was indistinguishable from the witchcraft practised in the 1960s, '70s, or '80s, I would be ignoring a lot of the work that has been done not only in academic fields like history, anthropology, and archaeology, but also the work of those who have made this world better, fairer, and safer for many different people who were otherwise marginalised.

Paganism as it was presented in the most popular witch books of the 1990s and 2000s (often called Neopaganism back then) was very heteronormative, it was very white, and almost anything went: cultural appropriation wasn't really a thing, and as many folks came to Pagan faiths from more strict mainstream paths and cultures, the Pagan community was seen to be a bit of a free-for-all in terms of their values.

This isn't to say that we should ignore books written during that time—many of these authors are the giants upon whose shoulders I and many others stand. What's important is that when we read older books or recommend them to others, we do so with some knowledge of what the Pagan/witch scene and wider society was like at the time they were written, and with the understanding that not all of what is written will apply to witchcraft as we know it today. And hey, I'm sure there are aspects of today's witchcraft that aren't going to age well either. Times change, and art will always be a product of the time it was created.

On the Burning Times

"The burning times" was—and still is, in some spaces—a term used to describe the witch trials in Europe. Stories and mythology from this time were popularised throughout the twentieth century (and even the early 2000s) as a means of legitimising witchcraft and to make it seem more ancient and romantic. A lot of the stories were presented as fact in witchy books of the time; they made claims about millions of women killed and the survival of the "Old Religion."

But while the witch trials were certainly a horrific and ghastly time that saw thousands killed, many of the figures given by modern witchy books are not factually accurate, and the stories simply untrue: most who died were not witches—not in any way that we would define witches—and would have been horrified to be labelled as such.

No, we are not the granddaughters of the witches they couldn't burn, and that's okay.

Antiquity Is Not Authenticity

Ancient isn't the same as *authentic*. We're not making wine or selling antique furniture here.

Witchcraft as we know it is not ancient; it might have some nods to ancient culture and roots in the history and mythology that has shaped it, but it isn't an undiluted (whatever that means) line of witches back to the mediaeval witch trials and beyond. And that's okay. In her fantastic essay "On Paganism,

Fakelore, and Tired Conversations about Authenticity," anthropologist and author Amy Hale points out that totally "pure" cultural practices aren't really a thing anywhere. She writes:

> Perfect unbroken transmission is nearly impossible to find with any cultural expression. I will bet you dollars to doughnuts that a little digging into the history of any longstanding and beloved tradition will reveal a beautiful, complicated, vibrant, hot mess. Focusing on cultural purity and origins leads to disappointment at best and Nazis at worst.[12]

Human beings haven't been on this earth for an especially long time in the grand scheme of things. And in the time that we have been here, we have used story and myth to try to make sense of the world around us. And those stories and myths change as we change. They move around as we move around…and throughout all of history, humans have a pesky tendency to not stay in one place for too long.

It's one thing to love the mythology and stories of a culture and to feel special when you read them. It's another to try to use those stories to justify being crappy toward other people, or to ignore empirical evidence because it doesn't fit a narrative you insist is true and complete.

Read about Paganism and witchcraft in books or online and you'll see it compared to tents and umbrellas. The phrase *melting pot* will likely come up. And while these comparisons are all grand, I think my preferred (if a little unorthodox) way to look at it all is to compare it to the 2001 film *A Knight's Tale*. Is it based on something old? Well, yes, technically. But that source material isn't always immediately visible or even referred to. It's embellished upon with whacky costumes and language (and hairstyle) quirks that are well and truly a product of their own time. Bits of it have *not* aged well. It involves some amazing talent, as well as some whose misdeeds later came to light. It's daggy—oh *man*, is it daggy in places!—and those who love it know that and debate that with others who love it. But those same people are the ones who will defend it the most earnestly from its critics. Nobody actually believes it to

12. Hale, "On Paganism, Fakelore, and Tired Conversations about Authenticity."

be a factual replica of ancient times, and those who insist that it is despite all the evidence to the contrary just end up looking a bit silly.

Your witchcraft and mine may not be entirely ancient, but the feelings they evoke certainly are. The words I said under the full moon the other night might be less than a century old, but how long have humans looked up at the moon on a clear night and felt a sense of awe or wonder? How many millions of humans over the years have felt that washed-clean feeling of standing in the rain after weeks of hot and dry weather? How many have eaten fruit and had the juice run down their arms, or hunkered down by a fire on a long, cold night?

These moments are some of the most human, and also the most natural. And what's history if not a series of moments all lined up together?

BASIC SKILLS
Finding Stillness

These first two chapters are going to provide you with lots of back-ground info before I get into the doing of witchcraft—witchcraft of the hands—in chapter 3 and beyond. But that doesn't mean you can't get started on building up (or revisiting) the most important skills a witch possesses: the ability to find stillness in oneself, to work consciously within your own body, and to visualise.

Each of these exercises builds on the next, so start here. It might seem simple, but you may find it's harder than it sounds. Persist anyway. You will need to have a good handle on these skills to get the most out of the rest of the exercises in this book.

1. Find a place that is warm and quiet where you can sit or lie comfortably. Switch off devices or notifications, and make sure you won't be interrupted. It helps to have a clock/watch nearby for this exercise, but it isn't super important.

2. Sit or settle yourself in a comfortable position. If you're lying down, you might want to lie on a rug or yoga mat for comfort. If you're sitting, make sure your head and neck are supported and your feet are flat on the floor or supported in some way.

3. Breathe gently and slowly, and let yourself relax. Close your eyes if you're comfortable doing so. Try to sink into stillness and not move at all.

4. If your mind starts to wander, mentally take note of how much time has passed, then start again.

5. Notice and make a mental note of any sounds and smells in the room around you.

6. Notice what sensations you feel on your skin and immediately close to your body: Is it warm or cool in the room? Is there a breeze or draft? What do your clothes feel like against your skin? Where is your body making contact with the floor or furniture?

7. Take the time to do an internal scan of your body and make a mental note of any sensations: tingles, twinges, discomfort, or other distractions.

Keep at this exercise daily if possible. After you complete it each day, make a note of everything—noise, feelings, anything else—you noticed. Try to keep going for a week, or until you are able to find stillness for at least five minutes.

Modification: If you have trouble sitting or lying silently to begin with, try starting lying flat with some music on. The music shouldn't be too loud or distracting, and ideally you should be listening with headphones. You could try a playlist of relaxing soundscapes, like rain or ocean waves. Breathe and check in with the body/room as above. Try to set the volume a little softer each day until you can complete this without music.

BASIC SKILLS
4:4 Breathing

Once you are able to sit or lie in stillness for around five minutes, try adding some 4:4 breathing.

1. Repeat the previous exercise, but this time focus on your breath and breathing in addition to everything you had been before.

2. Once you are relaxed, make your breaths deep and conscious. Breathe in through your nose for a count of four, then out through your nose for a count of four.

3. Make notes in your journal about the differences you notice in this activity and in yourself as you complete it. What difference does adding 4:4 breathing make?

Experiment with different factors and make notes: Does doing this at a different time of day change what you notice, or your ability to be still? What about trying it in a different room? Outside?

Modification: If you have trouble breathing in and out through your nose, try breathing in through your nose and out through your mouth to begin with. Once you're comfortable, try doing one rotation of in/out this way, followed by one rotation with your lips sealed, in/out through your nose. Take it slow and build upon this pattern until you're comfortable breathing in and out through your nose.

If you suffer from hay fever or allergies, you might find this easier if you take a dose of your preferred medication before you begin, or if you have an inhaler handy. Do what your body needs you to do.

❯ ❯ ❯ ● JOURNAL PROMPTS ● ❰ ❰ ❰

- Explore the definitions of witchcraft in this chapter and compare them to your own understanding. What surprised you? Are any of these definitions close to the type of witch or witchcraft you wrote about in the first journal activity in this book?

- Newcomers to the craft are often surprised or even disappointed that the actual history of the craft as we know it is often vastly different from what we originally thought, were told, or even read in books. How do you feel about it? Sit with what you are feeling right now and examine those feelings. If you're feeling disappointed that what we're practising isn't as "ancient" as you thought, try to work out why that is so important for you. Why does "ancient" equal "more authentic" to so many? Give examples.

Further Reading

Transformative Witchcraft: The Greater Mysteries by Jason Mankey (especially the introduction and chapters 1–3)

Wicca: A Comprehensive Guide to the Old Religion in the Modern World by Vivianne Crowley (especially the introduction and chapters 1–3)

Author interview with Ronald Hutton, author of *The Witch: A History of Fear, From Ancient Times to the Present*, by Courtney Applewhite

"Neopaganism: A Brief History of our Modern Pagan Religion" by Lora O'Brien

"On Paganism, Fakelore, and Tired Conversations about Authenticity" by Amy Hale

CHAPTER 2
What Witches Do

So far we've looked at some definitions of witchcraft and at where some of the most well-known ideas and traditions come from. But what do witches actually *do*?

The answer to this question will be different depending who you ask and in what context. Witchcraft looks and feels different to different practitioners: there isn't a "right" way to do it, unless you're practising a specific tradition. In this chapter, I'll look at the hows and whys of some common witchcraft practices and how they might vary from tradition to tradition, or even person to person.

My own witchcraft is flavoured by the tradition I was initiated into—Alexandrian Wicca has specific rites and practices that are done within the context of a coven, especially—but it is also more than that. In British Traditional Witchcraft traditions, practitioners have the autonomy to have their own spiritual practice and associations outside of coven work. As a high priestess and coven leader, I meet with my coven or certain members thereof at different times of the year and month: usually around once a fortnight, on average. But I also teach eclectic witchcraft to beginners in the form of a loose "outer court" situation.

I have my own devotional practices too, including meditative walks in the forests and native bushland near my home, and more structured offerings to deity that are influenced heavily by the time I spent in a Norse-inspired pagan group. While the acts in this collection of practices aren't especially out of the ordinary, there is no other witch with the exact same practice as me—what witches do is unique and deeply personal.

Because it is unique and personal is a good reason to explicitly point out that there is absolutely no hurry to start defining what your witchcraft is or isn't. While we will look at examples of what different kinds of witches might typically do, it isn't intended as a shopping list or a menu that you have to choose from. There is no rush to start labelling your craft or what it might or might not involve, I promise! The best thing about being new to this is that you get to be a sponge: listen, soak up what you can, try things out…If you approach these living, active traditions (and the people who practise them) with respect, you will be able to ask questions and learn even more.

Being new is license to try anything that interests you without feeling "locked in" to anything. It's *great*.

Operative versus Ritual Witchcraft

Well, for starters, witchcraft doesn't look much like it does on television— we can't fly. (More on that a bit later.) Most of what witches actually do can be categorised as either operative or ritual witchcraft.

Operative witchcraft and *ritual witchcraft* are terms originally coined by Margaret Murray, and they're used today as general terms for describing different types of ritual performed by witches and Pagans. Some of today's witches and Pagans tend to do both of these types of witchcraft in different amounts. The work of some practitioners could only be defined as one or the other. One or both are fine: there is no uniform "right" amount of either type of work to incorporate into your practice. Put simply, not all witches do all of the things listed in this section, and it doesn't make them any more or less witchy.

Operative Witchcraft

Operative Witchcraft refers to rituals and workings done with the intention of altering the external universe in some way: spells, charms, curses, blessings, divination, etc. It's operative witchcraft that we see most often on social media feeds. Operative witchcraft can include:

Spells and Charms: Magical or ritual acts done to bring about change of some kind. For example, a spell from a published book to quiet noisy neighbours, ritually crafting a bracelet to protect the wearer from bad dreams, or getting together as a coven to perform healing magic for a sick friend. There is an introduction to these types of witchcraft in chapter 10.

Self-Work or Self-Care: Intentional magical or ritual acts done to work on one's self. These could be workings that address internal conflicts or roadblocks you've been coming up against, ritual acts such as a ritualised bath or tea ceremony to heal or calm the self, or spells aimed at self-improvement. The ritual you performed from this book's introduction falls into this category.

It's important to note here that witchcraft is not ever an alternative to proper physical or mental healthcare professionals or their advice. Sadly, the self-care side of witchcraft is often one that is exploited by those out to make a quick dollar. Be careful out there.

Curses and Banishing: Acts performed ritually or magically to bring about harm or misfortune upon others, or to drive them away. Yes, these actually exist, but no, they aren't like in the movies. Examples of these could include banishing an abusive or toxic person or performing magic to thwart someone's plans.

Ritual Witchcraft

Ritual Witchcraft, on the other hand, refers to the rituals and workings done to bring us closer to deity, to benefit deity, or to otherwise alter the relationship between human and deity (or spirits) in some way: prayers, devotionals, seasonal celebrations, etc.[13] Not all witches are theistic (work with deity/spirit), though. Ritual witchcraft could include:

Prayers and Devotionals: Work done to honour and worship gods, spirits, or ancestors. This could include formal or informal prayers or offerings made to these entities, words or work done in their honour, and so on. There is a lot more detail on deity and how witches work with and honour them in chapter 6.

---

13. MacMorgan, *All One Wicca*, 244–45.

Rituals and Celebrations: Celebratory work done at a specific time or to celebrate a specific event. This could be, for example, a working to honour your god(s) at the winter solstice, celebrating the moon in its fullness, or inviting deity, spirits, or ancestors to bless a house or bestow good fortune on a baby.

Meditation and Pathworking: Meditation is achieving a calm, controlled state of mind through profound physical relaxation. Pathworking refers to a visualised journey, usually undertaken in a meditative or altered state of consciousness. The term was originally used to describe the process of mentally projecting up and around the paths of the Tree of Life in order to gain information or instructions, meet entities there, and ask favours of those entities.[14] When done purely for the self, these practices fall more neatly into the category of operative witchcraft, but when these involve deity or spirit, they are ritual witchcraft.

Remember that this isn't a one-size-fits-all situation. Not all witches do all of these things, but a fair chunk of witches practising today do some of these things.

Rituals of Celebration

Many solitary or group practitioners have significant days, times, or seasons that they mark ritually. These vary from person to person, group to group, and tradition to tradition. Factors like where and how someone lives also greatly influence their craft.

Full Moon

Full moon rituals are probably the most well-known practice among the wider public. The image of witches dancing around a blazing fire, conjuring up god-knows-what under an impossibly huge moon is iconic. While for some practitioners I know, this isn't far from reality, the image has its roots in mediaeval folklore about the terrors of the night: conformist propaganda and politicised warnings against wicked women and the dangers of straying beyond the stric-

14. Llewellyn, s.v. "Term: Pathworking," accessed April 1, 2020, https://www.llewellyn .com/encyclopedia/term/pathworking.

tures of a highly controlled and fearful social system. Political folk horror, if you like.

All that said, the full moon is considered by many modern witches to be a time of great power, and often of great reverence, too: in Traditional Wicca and many eclectic and Wiccan-based traditions, this is the time when the Goddess is at her most powerful and is worshipped and revered during a ritual (sometimes called an *esbat*) performed on or around the full moon. Some witches also use this powerful time to perform spells and magical workings, or to make offerings or perform devotional work to other deities.

Full moon rituals can be performed inside or outside. They could be as simple as someone sitting quietly and contemplating the moon for a while, or as complex as a full ritual with multiple speaking parts, props, and more. This is the time of the month when I and many practitioners around me are the most busy; I often organise specific teachings or workings for my coven to coincide with a full moon.

Seasonal Changes

Sabbat rituals are another common practice. Many witches follow some approximation of the Wheel of the Year, which is made up of eight sabbats, or holy days: four seasonal celebrations, two solstices, and two equinoxes each year. As it's a wheel, it is as eternal and as cyclical as the seasons themselves.

There is an entire chapter in this book dedicated to the wheel and its festivals, but for now it's enough to mention that these festivals are significant to many witches all over the world, and they are the foundations of our year. In the witchy spaces I am active in, sabbats are more celebratory, while the moons are often set aside for more serious ritual work. Often, sabbats I run are more open for this reason: my covenmates' partners or interested friends may be invited along, or I might open the celebration up to new seekers who are curious about experiencing ritual.

Sabbat rituals usually involve symbols of the season in some way. Winter solstice rituals, for example, might have holly on the altar for decoration, use candles to celebrate the slow return of the light on the longest night of the year, or mention the cold or dark in some way. A spring equinox ritual might have flowers involved or focus on the "blooming" of new ideas and undertakings. Depending on the time of year being celebrated, there might be singing, chanting, music, dancing, games, gift giving, or other frivolity. Or things could be more sombre and solemn, depending on what is being celebrated and why.

As with full moon rituals, sabbat rituals might be worked inside or out, in groups or alone, and they can be very short and simple or more complex. Like most of the modern witchcraft we've looked at so far, there is no hard-and-fast way to do things.

Other Times for Witchcraft

Sabbats and full moon rituals aren't the only type of work that witches perform. There are many other reasons witches might feel the need to do something with gravity and significance, such as life transitions, daily events, or coven-specific ceremonies like dedications (for new students just starting on their path), initiations (to formally welcome those who are ready to make a commitment to the tradition or group), or elevations (to raise a practitioner to a higher degree in recognition of their learning and work within the tradition). Solitary practitioners, too, sometimes perform self-dedication or self-initiation rituals.

Witches also perform spells whenever necessary for worship, ancestor veneration, and healing. Yes, some witches perform (cast, if you like) spells. These aren't really any of the amazing supernatural feats you might see in movies and on TV—real life doesn't have a CGI budget, after all. But magic isn't always as formal as all that.

Witches who have theistic or animistic beliefs might perform ceremonies, devotionals, dedications, or other rites to celebrate and honour certain deities, spirits, or ancestors.

Solstices and equinoxes might form a part of a modern witch's work and celebrations; they might not. Likewise, rituals and workings for the dark, waning, or waxing moon. Some practitioners also plan their workings around certain planetary hours.

Witchy-Sounding Sayings You Might Hear or Read

When you join a new community or movement, you soon realise it has its own cultures, traditions, quirks, and even language. Witchcraft is no different. Some of the common phrases you might hear or read are:

"As Above, So Below"

This concept has its origins in Hermetic material and is sometimes referred to as the Hermetic Axiom. It's claimed to be the writing of legendary Hellenistic figure Hermes Trismegistus. In modern witchcraft and occultism, it's used as a way of expressing the correspondence between higher and lower levels of reality: macrocosm effects microcosm, and vice versa.

"Do as Ye Will"

In some modern witchcraft, this forms part of what's known as the Witches' Rede or the Witches' Creed: "An it harm none, do what ye will." These words, seen in the writing of many witches, are inspired by Aleister Crowley and Thelema, and they are used by some witches as a guide for "ethical" magic—magic that harms none.

"Magick"

An archaic spelling of *magic*, used in mediaeval and renaissance grimoires and history books. This spelling was later popularised by Aleister Crowley, who added the extra k to differentiate what he did from the illusions performed by stage magicians.[15] Today, the k is sometimes used, sometimes not.

"Merry Meet"

"Merry meet" is a shortened part of the phrase "Merry meet, merry part, and merry meet again," which is sometimes used as a closing for rituals, implying that the ritual has been a merry one and the participants are free to happily depart and will see each other again. Some claim the words were inspired by Shakespeare. They were popularised by early neopagan authors such as Starhawk. Some folks used to extend this as a general greeting to other Pagans or witches, especially online, but it's not so much a thing these days.

"Blessed Be"

This phrase is sometimes used in similar ways to "merry meet" or as part of specific rituals. Some witches even use it as an equivalent to the Christian

---

15. D'Este and Rankine, *Wicca Magical Beginnings*, 242–43.

"amen."[16] It appears in several historical texts and grimoires, including the King James Bible.[17] It's come to modern witchcraft via the writings of Gardner.

"So Mote It Be"

Often spoken at the end of a working or ritual to emphasise, reiterate, and finalise the work that's been done. It has its origins in Freemasonry and made its way into modern witchcraft via Crowley and Gardner.[18]

Modern Ethics and Building Awareness

I started here with a reassurance that there is no need to rush in and start labelling yourself as this or that as far as your practice is concerned. Your practice is your practice, and actually practising your witchcraft should always be more important to you than how you explain it to others.

When you do get around to thinking about naming what it is that you do, not all words are created equally. In recent decades especially, important conversations have been had and attitudes changed, and now that we know better, it's important that we do better.

Black Magic / White Magic

It is far too convenient to think that the idea of black magic being wicked and evil and white magic being healing and good doesn't have anything to with racism. The ideas are borne out of centuries of occult theories and practices being grounded solely in the writings of well-off white men. Recognising this is an important step in decolonising our practice as witches, and one that has taken much longer than it should have.

Instead of describing magic or practices as black or white, consider talking about healing/helpful magic, baneful or banishing magic, and so on.

There is always more being added to this discourse, and new witch or old, I encourage you to look into it. To learn more about how phrases like "black magic" came about, and the importance of ditching terms like this, read:

---

16. Drury, *The Watkins Dictionary of Magic*, 42.

17. Wigington, "Blessed Be."

18. Wigington, "History of the Wiccan Phrase 'So Mote It Be.'"

- "Black Magic, Black Skin: Decolonizing White Witchcraft" by Shannon Barber
- "Decolonising Witchcraft: Racism, Whitewashing, and Cultural Appropriation in Witchcraft and How to Decolonize Your Practice" by Willow
- "Is the Term Black Magic Racist?" by Brandi Williams

Complete citations for these works, including website URLs, can be found in the bibliography at the end of this book.

Celtic Witchcraft / Celtic Paganism

"Celtic" paganism comes to us from the neopagan boom of the 1970s–1990s, but its origins are older. Four of the sabbats—Imbolc, Samhain, Beltane, and Lughnasadh—are named after ancient Celtic (Irish, specifically) celebrations. Supposedly "Celtic" imagery and beliefs were prominent for decades in modern witchcraft and Paganism, and continue to be today.

Celts is a catch-all term for a collection of peoples descended from several different Indo-European cultures. Today, the modern Celtic nations include Ireland, the Isle of Man, Scotland, Wales, Cornwall, and Brittany—all specific and different cultures in their own right. By using a brush as broad as "Celtic" to talk about the beliefs and cultures of all of these, we risk dismissing, or even erasing, what are still living cultures. It would be like calling an Australian an "Oceanic witch" or some such and expecting their beliefs and practices to be identical to—or even blended in with—what someone in Papua New Guinea, Tonga, New Zealand, Indonesia, or the Philippines does and believes.

Second, Celtic heritage and beliefs have been considered fair game by witches and (neo)Pagans for some time, most likely because they're thought of as a conquered people.[19] In part, many Celtic peoples were conquered by the Romans, and later by the English. This is a narrative that is popular with (mostly white) people in countries such as the USA and Australia who have Celtic ancestry, as Margot Adler explained in *Drawing Down the Moon*:

> There is a non-exploitative European heritage, embodied…in "the old tribal/peasant heritage of Europe (still not absolutely

---

19. Gottlieb, "Cultural Appropriation in Contemporary Neopaganism and Witchcraft," 27.

corrupted, even today)," as well as in the philosophies of Rous-
seau, Voltaire, and others. Many Neo-Pagans are searching in
that "old tribal/peasant heritage" for their cultural roots...After
all, as Leo Martello has remarked on many occasions, "If you go
back far enough, all of your pre-Judeo-Christian and [Muslim]
ancestors were Pagans."[20]

By focussing on the colonisation and conquering of their Celtic ancestors,
white (neo)Pagans are able to have a victim narrative—much like the narrative of the "burning times"—that drives their beliefs and practice, and is often
reason to conveniently stop seeing themselves as being just another white person, an ancestor of colonisers.

It's not my intention here to gatekeep and drive people away from Celtic
Paganism. Far from it. What I'm suggesting is that, if the practices of a particular Celtic culture interest you, you look further than witchy books that paint
these intricate (often living!) cultures and practices with a broad, homogenising
brush. Even reconstructionist traditions will only ever give us a rough approximation of the spiritual/religious/ceremonial practices of ancient peoples. It's
important to remember that you are not exactly the same as them—and that's
okay.

Instead of using the word *Celtic*, see if you can narrow down where, specifically, the things that attract you come from. Look at mythology and history as
well as witchy texts. Better yet, look at the work that is being done by modern, native authors and academics when you can.

Witchcraft Traditions

Some witches work within one or more established traditions of witchcraft.
Some don't, instead following their own path. This list is not a menu you have
to choose from; rather, it's here to give you some idea of the many traditions
that are out there.

There are more traditions of witchcraft and Paganism than I could list
here—hundreds more! This is intended as a broad overview. Remember that
not all adherents to a tradition will agree on how exactly that tradition is practised, which can make definitions tricky sometimes.

20. Adler, *Drawing Down the Moon*, 380–81.

Faery Tradition: An initiatory tradition of witchcraft established in the United States by Victor and Cora Anderson and Gwydion Pendderwen. The tradition emphasises self-development and has a pragmatic approach to magic. The American author Starhawk is one of its best-known initiates and practitioners. Storm Faerywolf's book *Betwixt & Between* is a good introduction for contemporary practitioners.

Goddess Spirituality and Goddess-Centred Witchcraft: Borne out of radical changes during the 1960s and '70s, Goddess Spirituality is usually centred around the sacredness of the female form, and around aspects of women's lives that adherents feel have been traditionally neglected in Western society.

Norse Witchcraft, Heathen Witchcraft, and Seiðr: Heathenism, also known as Heathenry or Germanic Neopaganism, can refer to one or more of many contemporary Pagan traditions inspired by the historical religions, culture, and literature of pre-Christian Scandinavia. The earliest modern heathen traditions were devised in the 1960s and '70s. Some practitioners include witchcraft in their heathenry, or vice versa.

Seax-Wica: A contemporary witchcraft tradition founded by Raymond Buckland in the United States in the early 1970s. Seax-Wicca draws upon the traditions of the Saxons, early Germanic peoples. Unlike traditional Wicca, it has only one degree of initiation.[21]

Traditional Wicca: Traditional Wicca usually refers to traditions directly related to the one originating in the New Forest region of England and with traceable initiatory lineage back to it. Gardnerian Wicca and Alexandrian Wicca are two of the most well-known. In the USA, this is often referred to as British Traditional Wicca.

Traditional Witchcraft: A term used to refer to a variety of contemporary forms of witchcraft that do not have Wiccan-based craft roots, instead claiming older, more "traditional" roots. These traditions are often based on folklore and folk practices of specific areas.

---

21. Drury, *The Watkins Dictionary of Magic*, 256.

Witchcraft and DNA

In the formative days of modern witchcraft, many outlandish claims were made by folks seeking to make a name for themselves (as well as money). They said they had received super special and better-than-the-average witchy training through their mothers or grandmothers, who could of course trace their witch lineage back to the burning times or beyond. With the exceptions of specific cultural practices and folk magics, these stories were fabricated and were soon pointed out to be. But, time has marched on. There are now covens, working groups, and initiatory lines out there that have been practising for three, four, five, or more decades. Now it's becoming more plausible that if someone says their mother was a witch, they could very well be telling the truth.

It's also very cool that some folks are drawn to traditions of witchcraft that relate to their ancestral heritage. Knowing where your ancestors came from can give you some cool and romantic insights into the person that you are. But it stops there. Your DNA doesn't make you somehow closer to the "Ancient Mysteries" of any open practice.

The idea of ethnic "purity" or being more magically powerful because of your blood is fascism, and it's gross.

Not All Magic Is Witchcraft

Witch is a European word, and when it comes to folk magic, not all practitioners are comfortable with this label. Practitioners of the following traditions sometimes describe what they do as witchcraft; sometimes they don't. A good rule of thumb is to never label anybody anything unless they use a certain term to describe themselves first.

> **Brujeria:** Brujeria is a Spanish word that covers quite a few different folk magic practices and beliefs practised in Latin American and Afro-Caribbean cultures and influenced by indigenous religious practices, Catholicism, and European witchcraft.
>
> **Conjure:** Conjure, sometimes also known as Hoodoo or Rootwork, is a system of North American folk magic whose roots derive from Central and West African spiritual practices and has been influenced by

Christianity, Jewish mysticism, and some Native American practices. Conjure is not usually practised as a religion in its own right.

Santeria and Lucumi: Santeria is a religion that is now practised in many parts of the world but found especially in regions of the Carribbean such as Jamaica and Cuba, as well as Hispanic communities in some parts of the USA. It is a fusion of the worship of African deities—mostly from the Yoruba peoples of West Africa—and the veneration of Christian saints. Similarly, Lucumi—known as La Regla Lucumi in Cuba and Puerto Rico—also venerates Orishas, which are important spirits from the Yoruba religion. The word *Santeria* derives from a Spanish word meaning "saint." *Lucumi* was the colonial Spanish term for Yoruba people and their language, and this language is used in some rituals.

Vodou: Vodou is the Haitian manifestation of an African Traditional Religion. It's thought that the word is originally from the Dahomey people of West Africa and referred to deity or the sacred inner self.[22] While Vodou, Santeria, and Lucumi are among the most well-known African Traditional Religions, they are just a few examples from a long and nuanced list of practices and traditions.

Voodoo: The term and spelling used most commonly to refer to the New Orleans variation of an African Traditional Religion.

On Cultural Appropriation

Some of the cultures and belief systems mentioned here have been or are being pieced together by reconstructionists, including historians. Others have continued as a culture throughout history in some form or another.

It's important to be mindful of cultural appropriation. If you are part of a dominant, privileged culture, you do not always have the right to work with deities and systems that belong to cultures who have been (or who are currently being) oppressed, no matter how much these deities might resonate with you.

22. Dorsey, *Orishas, Goddesses, and Voodoo Queens*.

It's a good idea to be cautious and respectful when researching and enquiring about any closed tradition. If a tradition interests you and it is from a culture that is in some way marginalised, your best bet is to always get your information from practitioners within that tradition, and in a way that gives back more than what you're taking.

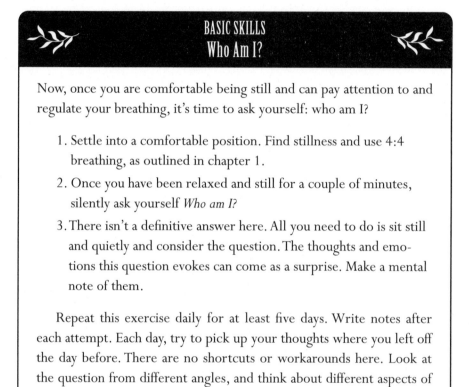

BASIC SKILLS
Who Am I?

Now, once you are comfortable being still and can pay attention to and regulate your breathing, it's time to ask yourself: who am I?

1. Settle into a comfortable position. Find stillness and use 4:4 breathing, as outlined in chapter 1.

2. Once you have been relaxed and still for a couple of minutes, silently ask yourself *Who am I?*

3. There isn't a definitive answer here. All you need to do is sit still and quietly and consider the question. The thoughts and emotions this question evokes can come as a surprise. Make a mental note of them.

Repeat this exercise daily for at least five days. Write notes after each attempt. Each day, try to pick up your thoughts where you left off the day before. There are no shortcuts or workarounds here. Look at the question from different angles, and think about different aspects of your life and your history.

))) ● JOURNAL PROMPTS ● (((

- Review the definitions and examples of operative versus ritual craft. Is the witchcraft you have done or seen so far more operative or more ritual? Why might that be?

- Look at the examples of different traditions and types of witchcraft and other magic. Challenge yourself to research the one you know the least about. Where did it originate? Did it have founders? Who are they? What are its core beliefs and rituals? Is it an open or closed tradition? What surprised you about this tradition? What did you already know?

Further Reading

The Dabbler's Guide to Witchcraft: Seeking an Intentional Magical Path by Fire Lyte

Weave the Liminal: Living Modern Traditional Witchcraft by Laura Tempest Zakroff

Wicca: A Comprehensive Guide to the Old Religion in the Modern World by Vivianne Crowley

"Cultural Appropriation in Contemporary Neopaganism and Witchcraft" by Kathryn Gottlieb

"An thread: if you want to know why some of us hated Harry Potter liberal centrism even before Rowling destroyed her own standing among the moderately progressive" by Hal Duncan

"White Light, Black Magic: Racism in Esoteric Thought" by Brandy Williams

PART II
The Hands

Sinking your hands into the soil. Feeling your way through. Learning by doing, doing by learning. Worthy experiments and important, valuable mess. Wiping off the grime and trying again. Feeling the fear but doing it anyway. This is the witchcraft of the hands.

CHAPTER 3
Energy

The thing I missed the most in 2020 was having experiences with other humans. Outside of the loved ones I missed, I yearned for music and dancing. I missed seeing bands. I missed going to gigs and standing and dancing and moving in close proximity to other humans as we shared an experience as strangers. And most of these experiences came down to a feeling, to the energy of the thing.

If you've felt the tension in the air when two people who openly dislike each other are present, you've felt and been in the presence of energy. Likewise, if you've had anticipation over a special event build for weeks or months, if you've felt absolutely awestruck experiencing a natural wonder or phenomenon up close, or if you and a date spent an entire dinner just knowing you would end up in bed together later that night, that's energy.

Think back to drama class or a live performance of some kind that you've been involved in. Many of the warm-up activities done in the performing arts are to get the performers' energy up. A show that is high energy will engage and enthral audiences, whereas a low-energy show will fall flat. These same ideas apply to public speaking, to parties, to creating art, and even to business meetings. The level of energy affects the outcome of these things, and with this in mind, we take steps to raise or lower the energy accordingly.

A director might take their cast through warm-up activities involving lots of physical movement and interaction to raise energy right before a show. A good school principal might take their teaching staff out to the pub after a particularly stressful school year so that they can blow off steam, releasing any pent-up tensions or negative energy so that everyone can "reset" over the holidays and come back refreshed in the new year. Even in these more mundane examples, humans are noticing and manipulating energy because they know that the level of energy affects the outcome.

The word energy comes to us from the Greek *energeia* ("activity, operation"), from *energos* ("active, working"), from *en* ("in") plus *ergon* ("work").[23] There are definitions of the words specific to certain energy, too, including the power that comes from sources such as heat or electricity. These definitions are all relevant to witches and practitioners of magic: we raise, direct, send, and use energy/power to make our work and our workings more effective. Doing this well is a step up to acting on our will—what we want or what we need to happen—rather than just wishing and hoping.

Grounding and Centring

Grounding and centring are often the two skills practitioners start to learn as they begin to work with energy in an intentional way. *Grounding* is the act of ridding oneself of extra energy when it is not needed. When we centre, we are stabilising and fixing ourselves firmly in the moment and in the world, often in preparation for (or to reset to a neutral state immediately after) magical, meditative, or ritual work.

Centring is an important step that's sometimes overlooked and often underestimated. Setting out calm and centred to perform our work as witches makes for a more solid foundation from which to build. Think about taking part in activities and tasks in the rest of your life: generally, things go much better for everyone involved when you're feeling your best rather than flighty, flakey, exhausted, or stressed out.

For some practitioners, centring oneself is as easy as taking a deep, steadying breath and spending a few beats in contemplative, solid silence. Some people visualise themselves becoming more "solid" in the landscape, maybe consciously bringing in any loose threads: wandering thoughts, worries, distractions, and so on. Others think of water flowing down into a still pool, swirling smoke slowly returning to a bottle, or a house slowly securing all its doors and windows.

23. *Online Etymology Dictionary*, s.v. "energy (*n*.)," accessed April 5, 2023, https://www.etymonline.com/word/Wicca.

Grounding, then, is the act of ridding ourselves of excess energy once we've finished using it. This helps us return to the "real" world after ritual and draws a line under the work performed. Generally, we ground after energy has been raised, directed, and sent. Raising energy often leaves us with "extra" energy that can cause practitioners to feel a bit wonky if it isn't dispersed.

EXERCISE
From the Ground on Down

Experiment with some of the centring techniques discussed in this chapter, or with others that you find online. Every witch is different, so different techniques will work for different people. When you've tried each one a few times, journal your findings.

Once you feel comfortable with centring, practise this simple way to ground yourself:

1. Breathe and centre yourself.

2. Focusing on your breath, visualise the energy you have raised dissipating. You might see it travelling down into the earth as roots or fading into the background like mist.

3. Finish the exercise by consciously focusing on breathing normally, and on concrete things you can see, hear, and touch in the room. Go quietly for the next hour or so: eat, relax, and don't do anything too strenuous.

Four Steps to Working with Energy

To effectively work with energy, you need to be able to sense, or be aware of, whether energy is present and where it is coming from. Then, you should be able to raise energy—to create or draw it from elsewhere so it can be used in rituals and workings. Once you have that energy, the next step is to manipulate it in some way, to move or change it to meet a specific need. Finally, you need to learn to work with and use the energy you have raised and controlled to bring about change.

Step One: Sensing Energy

Some witches refer to sensing energy as "becoming aware." This is a skill that manifests differently in different practitioners; how you experience energy is unique. Sometimes you can use one or more of the five senses to experience and describe energy. Sometimes it's a feeling or a sixth sense. It could be a prickly feeling at the back of your neck, a slight change in temperature, a feeling of excitement or elation, or even a more solid, heavy feeling in your working space. Different energies might feel different too; think about the aforementioned sexual tension versus what's passing between rowing coworkers versus the natural energy of an old-growth forest. Regardless of how you experience energy, it is a learned skill and one that takes time to master.

Step Two: Raising Energy

Once we are aware of energy, we should have a better idea of how to raise enough of it to achieve a goal, whether it is to simply align yourself during a difficult day by taking a few moments to yourself or as part of a more complicated ritual or working.

As practitioners of witchcraft, we raise and draw upon energy from a range of sources. Often a ritual, spell, or magical working draws on several sorts of energy at once. In her book *Magical Power for Beginners*, author and high priestess Deborah Lipp categorises energy in the following ways:

Deity: Gods and spirits

Stored or Accumulated Power: Items that have been ritually blessed, charged or consecrated

Supernatural Sources: The elements, ancestors, or other spirits or beings

Natural Sources: Natural places or objects, and the spirits/beings connected to them

The Self: The human body, either on your own or in a group

Words of Power: Chants, prayers, and true names[24]

---

24. Lipp, *Magical Power for Beginners*, 86.

Later in this chapter, we're going to focus on those last three: natural sources, the self, and words of power.

Step Three: Manipulating Energy

Manipulating energy is a tricky thing to master at first, and it cannot be done without first learning to sense and then raise energy. If you are new to witch-craft, you'll be laying a strong foundation for your practice if you practise sensing and raising energy for some time before going any further. This step and the next have been included to show you the process, but not necessarily to get you to do it any time soon. Work slowly and softly here, and your practice will be stronger in the long run.

Just as witches can consciously shape energy, they can have a subconscious effect on it too. The energy we raise as witches and practitioners of magic is neutral. It's then our job to work that energy to our desires. We flavour and imbue energy with our intentions, and once we're sure we've done that, we send it out into the world to make that change happen.

Once a practitioner can sense energy and raise it in a controlled way, the next step is to manipulate it, shaping it to power whatever it is you're trying to achieve. This is where we see the difference between just hoping something will happen and actually doing something, putting some oomph behind that desire.

In both a group and solitary context, this is usually done with visualisation, and the practitioners' ability to visualise will affect the efficacy. This is an ability that many newcomers are surprised is emphasised so much, but it really is crucial. If you can't see what it is you need to happen, you're going to have a lot of trouble sending energy toward it.

For example, a group of people working a healing would need to keep the intention of their working—in this case, for someone to be healthy—in mind as they raise energy. They might visualise the person looking and feeling healthier as well as all the things he'll do when he's feeling good again. To support this, they might have a photo of him nearby to look at as they work, or they may actually verbalise the intention, saying it aloud before they begin raising energy.

Step Four: Sending Energy

Using the energy we have raised and shaped, we can treat spells and rituals as procedurals or recipes for sending that energy to the right place to achieve our goals.

Whether it's a loose outline that we throw together in our heads on short notice or something much more formal and written down, when we plan or write a spell or a short working, we are charting a course for the energy we'll raise. Having a roadmap of where to send the energy, how it will get there, and what it will do when it reaches its target is just as important as raising the energy in the first place.

Raising Energy from the Self

Raising energy from your own being is the most commonly used means of raising energy—we can't help but put a little bit of ourselves into everything we create, after all. There are many different types and means of raising energy from the self, and some are done by achieving an altered state of consciousness. In her book *The Witch's Eight Paths of Power*, author and witch Sable Aradia writes:

> Much of the training in magick and Wiccan mysticism involves altering your consciousness from one state to another. There are two ways to do this. We can "go deeper" by relaxing and descending into deeper levels of meditation, or we can reach for higher states through stimulation. Different brain waves (measured in cycles per second, or hertz (Hz)), indicate different levels of consciousness, and the ability to change consciousness at will is the only real ability that is required for successful magick.[25]

There are many ways we can raise energy from ourselves and the people we are working with. If something gets you warm and/or raises your heart rate, you are probably raising energy. Here are a few examples:

---

25. Aradia, *The Witch's Eight Paths of Power*, 64.

The Body: Movement, dance, sex, clapping, snapping, singing, chanting, intoning, etc. This includes rhythmic activities such as drumming and repetitive activities like weaving, knotting cords, etc. Power raised from physical movement is sometimes used for issues involving stagnation, freedom or joy, personal fulfillment, etc.

The Mind: Visualisation, meditation, pathworking, trance, etc. These are all valuable skills overall and require regular practise.

EXERCISE
Sensing Energy

Experiment with multiple power-raising techniques explored in this chapter and focus on the "feel" of the energy. Energy raised in different ways is distinct. What changes do you notice?

Raising Energy from Natural Sources

It is also possible to raise energy from natural sources and places and the spirits/beings connected to them. These sources include, but certainly aren't limited to:

Physical Nature: Working outside in a natural area, like a forest or a beach, and drawing on the power of that place.

Nature, Nature Spirits, and Spirit of Place: Trees, mountains, rivers, rocks, etc., and/or nature spirits such as landwights, spirits, the fey, dryads, genii loci, etc.

Seasonal Cycles: The ebb and flow of the seasons; seasonal celebrations such as the Wheel of the Year.

Lunar Cycles: Working with the phases of the moon. Practising certain kinds of magic in correlation with different times of the lunar phases, such as:

Full Moon: Power, rebirth, worship (especially worship of the Goddess in traditional Wicca and some eclectic witchcraft).

Waning Moon (from full moon to new moon): Diminishment, endings, departure, reduction.

New Moon: Darkness, mystery/secrets, shadow work, divination.

Waxing Moon (from new moon to full moon): Growth, accomplishment, things coming to be and plans coming to fruition.

Solar Cycles: Solstices and equinoxes. Other special events like eclipses.

Magical Times: Astrological events, retrogrades, planetary hours, eclipses, etc.

Natural Substances: Plant matter such as herbs, leaves, wood, and flowers; stones and crystals; spring, ocean, or river water; or bones on your altar or included as part of the working.

The Elements: Either physical representations or elemental beings/forces.

EXERCISE
The Energy of Place

Visit a place that you love. Spend some time sitting in silence and notice the energy of this place. Use some of the vocabulary and discernment you've practised in this chapter to describe the energy of this place.

Chanting, Incantations, and Words of Power

The word *incantation* comes from the Latin *incantare*, which means "to bewitch, charm, cast a spell upon, chant magic over, sing spells."[26] In the context of witchcraft, an incantation is made up of words of power spoken—either read or recited—in a ritual or ceremony. Words can be used to raise energy in a number of ways and from a range of sources. Some of the most commonly used ways include verbalising your intention (either as a statement of intent at the start of a working or as a simple repetitive "call" as you raise energy), chanting or intoning, or words used to finish off, or "seal," a magical working.

In the context of magic and energy raising, chanting refers to the rhythmic repetition of sacred words, sounds, or phrases. This is usually done either in conjunction with meditation or movement, such as sacred dance, to raise power,

---

26. *Online Etymology Dictionary*, s.v. "incantation," accessed January 19, 2023, https://www.etymonline.com/word/incantation.

and sometimes to transport the practitioner(s) into an altered state of awareness. Saying or repeating rhymes especially creates rhythm, which can be used as a means of raising energy. They are also easy to remember and teach to a group.

Barbarous Words

These are words with unknown meaning used in magic. Many old spells consisting of barbarous words may be mangled or bastardised Old English, Latin, Egyptian, Hebrew, or another language that have been misunderstood and garbled somewhere along the way. Some barbarous words are completely made up, the intention being to pronounce or repeat meaningless words to achieve a magical effect.

Examples of barbarous words have made their way into modern witchcraft and eclectic paganism mostly via ceremonial magic. Here are some of the common ones you might have seen.

ABRACADABRA

This was used as a magical chant or incantation long before it was used by stage magicians and illusionists. On a Roman expedition to Britain in 208 CE, a physician named Quintus Serenus Sammonicus reportedly used this formula to cure ailments such as fevers and asthma. The word was written in rows in a triangular formation on an amulet, which was then worn by the patient for nine days before being thrown into a stream. It's thought the word might come from the name of the Gnostic deity, Abraxas.[27]

ABRAHADABRA

Considered the formula of the Great Work in the cosmology of Aleister Crowley, who considered it "the Word of the Aeon." Crowley believed that it would unite the microcosm and macrocosm, heralding the next stage of human evolution. It is related to—but not to be confused with—Abracadabra.[28]

EKO, EKO, AZARAK

These words are sometimes used as a chant, either on their own or as part of a longer piece. The phrase, thought to be part of an older, longer chant, can

27. Drury, The Watkins Dictionary of Magic, 1.
28. Drury, The Watkins Dictionary of Magic, 2.

be traced back to one of Crowley's disciples, J. F. C. Fuller, an occultist and senior British army officer who published it in a couple of different occult magazines in the 1920s.[29]

More Types of Energy

Here are some other types of energy you might read about.

Auras

In some occult and magical spaces, an *aura* is the psychic energy field that surrounds both animate and inanimate bodies. Those who claim to be able to see auras describe them as being dull or brightly coloured, and some use the auric colours to interpret the condition or state of the person or object.

Egregore

An *egregore*—sometimes spelled *egregor*, *eggregore*, or *egrigor*—is the residual and shared magical "atmosphere" of a working space. It's made up of the combined will and visualisation powers of the practitioners who regularly work or worship there. Egregore builds up over time, and the residual energetic power from past magical workings can be really beneficial as you set your sights on new ones.

But What Sort of Energy Works Best?

This depends largely on what you want to do with energy—the type of magic you want to do. There's a vitality, an innate *humanness*, that seems to go hand-in-hand with energy raised from the body. This—in my experience—makes this kind of energy good for workings centred around health and healing. Chanting and trancework are more outward facing and seem better suited to protection, or to shifting something—an attitude, resources, etc.—toward a goal. Keep in mind that these are broad examples. What works for you might be different, but you'll only learn by trying out multiple techniques.

Let's say a witch called Jocelyn wants to perform a simple working centred on healing. A friend of hers, Roland, has been sick on and off with chest infections for some time, and he has just been admitted to the hospital. She asks him if he'd be comfortable with her doing a magical working intended to

---

29. D'Este and Rankine, *Wicca Magical Beginnings*, 185–87.

aid his healing, and he says yes. As a precursor to any working, Jocelyn would need to make sure that she and anyone she intends to work with have some idea about energy and how to sense it. Once she is sure of this, she needs to decide what type of energy to use. Given that this is a healing spell, she might decide to write a chant for energy raising, with the intention of drumming to raise energy. She knows that something rhythmic is easy to learn and remember, and it's also easy to chant, so she might go with something like:

> *Winds gust and sails swell,*
> *Breathe easy, breathe well*

If she was working with others, they could even dance around in a circle as they chanted and repeated this, thus layering different methods of energy raising to shore up their chances at success.

BASIC SKILLS
Visualisation I

By now you should be able to find stillness and to breathe consciously, and you should have looked at yourself and what makes you *you*. In short, you should have some level of comfortability, or at least familiarity, with yourself and that fantastic and impossible construction of meat, bone, and lightning that is your body and mind.

Now we're going to make pictures with that brain-lightning. We're going to visualise. Again, you might feel like this is simple, but this is a skill that is key to many of the other concepts explored later in this book. Give it the time and attention it deserves.

You'll need an everyday object for this exercise, ideally something you can hold in your hands. The more everyday the object is, the better; bonus points if it's something you use regularly.

1. Hold the object in your hands. Look at it closely. See if you can commit every small detail—every angle, every part, every mark or imperfection—to memory.

2. Set the object aside and settle yourself into a comfortable, still position. Find stillness and use 4:4 breathing, as outlined in chapter 1.

3. Once you have been relaxed and still for a couple of minutes, start to picture the object in your mind. Try to "see" each detail you saw before. Imagine holding the object, moving your fingers over every surface. Try to "feel" each detail in your mind. This is visualising, and the "realer" you can see something in your mind, the better.

Repeat this exercise daily, for three to five days at least. Write notes after each attempt.

Visualising is a skill, and like all skills, it is something to be learned and practised. Some people will have more of a natural ability at first, but no matter where you start, this is something that should be worked on regularly in order to build and maintain good skills.

Modification: If you are still struggling with visualisation, try the suggestions in the appendix.

❭ ❭ ❭ ● JOURNAL PROMPTS ● ❬ ❬ ❬

• What makes you feel energised? What does "feeling energised" look and feel like to you? What drains your energy? How do you replenish it?

• Which energy-raising techniques discussed in this chapter appeal to you? Are there any you would you like to try? Which did you already know about? Which are you not so sure about?

Further Reading

Magical Power for Beginners: How to Raise & Send Energy for Spells That Work by Deborah Lipp

Elements of Ritual Magic by Marian Green

Transformative Witchcraft: The Greater Mysteries by Jason Mankey

"Energy in the Art of Magic" by Tom Swiss

CHAPTER 4
The Moon, the Sun, and the Planets

The positions of celestial bodies in the skies have made their mark on any number of belief systems, and the influence they have on the lives we live here on our little blue planet has fascinated spiritualists, seekers, saints, and even some sceptics for millennia. For centuries, the notion that stars and planets might affect our day-to-day has crept into the thinking and culture of people who wouldn't consider themselves a part of anything remotely occult or mysterious. For example, many healthcare workers could tell you whether the moon is full without so much as a glance at the sky. And, in modern witchcraft, we too look to the skies as they influence our practice, our worship, and our work.

The Moon

In Wicca and witchcraft, the moon plays a pivotal role in our practice, worship, and work. In Wicca and Wiccan-influenced eclectic witchcraft, there are usually thirteen full moon celebrations—sometimes called esbats "working" celebrations—in a year. But other moon phases can be utilised for specific reasons, too.

As the moon and the earth orbit the sun, the light from the sun illuminates half of the moon. The position of the earth creates a shadow, which—depending on the position—shows us more or less of the illuminated half. This is what causes us to see the moon in its different phases. And even though it has four distinctive phases throughout the month—every twenty-eight to twenty-nine-and-a-half days—the moon is always changing as it moves through these phases, and it will look slightly different each night.

As with almost everything discussed so far, there is no hard and fast way for how to time your workings, or how many times a month or year you should work with the moon. I would love to be outside on the exact night of every full moon, with my entire coven, a bonfire, and a bottle of wine to celebrate and worship the Wiccan Goddess and her consort and do our secret work. But this isn't something attainable for me or any of the others in my coven; we all work or study full-time and have families and other, more real-world commitments.

It can be tempting to go hammer and tongs at lunar work when it's all new and shiny and exciting—don't. Figure out what works for you with trial and error. What fits with your schedule, and what's sustainable as a part of—rather than apart from—the rest of your life?

Dark Moon / New Moon

This is the time of the month when the moon is between the earth and the sun. No direct sunlight illuminates it, though it does receive a small amount of light reflected back off the earth. This means that very little or even no moon is visible on this night. Many witches call the darkest night of the month the *dark moon*, with the *new moon* being the very slight sliver that appears the following evening. Others use the two terms interchangeably. There are some deities whose worship is aligned more with the dark moon than with the brighter times of the month.

The new moon is one of our moon's primary phases, in that it happens at an exact moment of the day or night and can be calculated to the minute, just like a solstice or equinox.

For some covens and practitioners, the dark or new moon is a time for more mysterious or more inward-looking practices focused on the self, for hidden work, and for divination. In Wicca, some covens hold special ceremonies at this time of the month. Others don't pay it much heed and save their magic-making for the full moon.

Waxing Crescent Moon

After the dark moon, the moon appears to grow again. For around a week after the night of the dark moon, the moon is in its waxing crescent phase. As a noun, *waxing* means "a gradual increase in magnitude or extent," and this crescent or sickle-shaped moon does appear a little plumper each night.[30]

Northern Hemisphere

During this time, as the moon grows stronger, so too do magical workings focussed on strength, growth, improvement, and gain. This is a time to focus on things coming into being and plans coming to fruition.

Southern Hemisphere

First Quarter

The moon is in its waxing crescent phase until it grows to 49.9 percent illuminated. Once it tips over to 50 percent illumination, it is in its first quarter, another primary phase: an exact, calculable moment in time halfway through the waxing phase. It is called the first quarter because at this point the moon has travelled a quarter of the way around the earth since the new moon.

Northern Hemisphere

On the night of the first quarter, the moon is angled 90 degrees away from the sun and appears half illuminated to us. Which half will depend on where in the world you are: in the Northern Hemisphere, it's the right half, while those of us in the Southern Hemisphere see the left half illuminated.

Southern Hemisphere

Magical workings at this time continue to focus on all things growing and improving. Between the waxing crescent and the first quarter, the focus might be on new plans and ideas that have been birthed and are coming into their prime. The nights after the first quarter work well as a time for kicking into action plans or undertakings that might be *almost* finished but need a little push.

---

30. Vocabulary.com, s.v. "waxing (*n.*)," accessed April 5, 2023, https://www.vocabulary .com/dictionary/witch.

Waxing Gibbous Moon

After the first quarter, the moon continues to wax but is no longer a crescent shape. Instead it is almost oblong shaped: *gibbous*,
a word that means bulging, rounded, convex. The moon is considered gibbous if it is between 50.1 percent and 99.9 percent
illuminated. The waxing gibbous phase lasts about a week, until
the moon becomes full.

*Northern
Hemisphere*

As the moon is continuing to grow, magical and devotional
workings still focus on gain, inspiration, strength, and abundance.

*Southern
Hemisphere*

Full Moon

The moon is full when it is angled 180 degrees away from the
sun and is as close as it can be to being fully illuminated from our
perspective. At the exact time of a full moon, the sun, Earth, and
the moon are aligned, but because the moon's orbit is not exactly

the same as Earth's orbit around the sun, they rarely form a perfect line. When
they do, the earth's shadow crosses the moon's face and causes a lunar eclipse.

For many witches, the full moon is a time for heightened energy and psychic awareness, and many choose to perform specific magical workings at
this time. For theistic practitioners, especially traditional Wiccans and others
whose practices involve a moon goddess and her consort, esbats are also a
time of celebration and feasting. The word *esbat* is thought to come from the
Old French *s'esbattre*, "to frolic and amuse oneself."[31]

As well as a time for Wiccan and Wiccan-inspired witches to celebrate, the
full moon is a time for workings that need the most power: consecrating and
charging objects, tapping into psychic abilities, transformative magic, workings for strength or wisdom, or any working that needs a super charge.

You may have heard of specific full moons having certain names. Many of
these—like "wolf moon" and "windy moon"—come to us from the witchy and
neopagan books of the 1980s and 1990s, and in many cases, they are clumsy
and appropriative interpretations of Native American or other First Nations
mythology.

31. Drury, *The Watkins Dictionary of Magic*, 94.

Waning Gibbous Moon

After the exact time of the full moon, its illuminated part begins to shrink (or wane), beginning the waning gibbous phase. This phase lasts from when the moon is 99.9 percent illuminated down to 50.1 percent illuminated, which takes a week or so.

Northern Hemisphere

Magic worked under the waning moon usually focuses on diminishment, or reducing things' power. This is a time when many practitioners do workings around binding difficult situations so that they can no longer cause harm or distress, or around reducing the problems in their lives.

Southern Hemisphere

Third / Last Quarter

Once the illuminated part of the moon has shrunk back down to 50 percent, it has moved another quarter of the way around the earth and is in its third quarter position. Now the half of the moon that wasn't illuminated at the first quarter is visible: the left-hand side in the Northern Hemisphere and the right-hand side in the Southern Hemisphere.

Northern Hemisphere

The third quarter moon rises in the middle of the night and is visible until it sets in the middle of the day. This is the opposite of the first quarter moon, which rises around midday and sets in the middle of the night. This final quarter is a time for magical "endings," resolutions, putting a stop to things, and so on.

Southern Hemisphere

Waning Crescent Moon

After the third quarter, the illuminated part of the moon continues to shrink back down to its crescent or sickle shape. This last phase is the final phase of the lunar month, beginning when the moon is at 49.9 percent illumination and ending at the new (dark) moon once illumination drops to 0.1 percent, when the moon has returned to its position between the earth and the sun.

Northern Hemisphere

This final waning phase is a time when many witches and magical practitioners focus on endings, aging, death, banishing, and release.

Southern Hemisphere

EXERCISE
The Charge of the Goddess

Witch and author Doreen Valiente's poem "The Charge of the Goddess" is considered an important piece of poetry to many Wiccans and Wiccan-inspired witches. Some even consider it liturgy.

Take a look at the most commonly known version, which can be found on the website of the Doreen Valiente Foundation. Write it out by hand if possible, and if you can, take it outside with you on the next full moon.

1. Stand or sit comfortably and gaze up at the full moon.
2. Breathe evenly and find stillness within yourself. Then read the Charge aloud. This might be harder than it sounds; you might feel silly or nervous. Do it anyway.
3. Once you've finished, sit or stand in quiet contemplation for a few moments.

Repeat this for at least three months—three full moon nights—in a row, and write notes about the experience each time you do it.

The Planets

The modern concept of planetary timing comes to us through the written traditions of the *grimoires* (magical "textbooks" from Europe and elsewhere), although the idea has evolved through many cultures and over thousands of years before becoming the system that many practitioners use today.

Today, magical practitioners operate mostly with the planets visible to the naked eye, from slowest to fastest moving: Saturn, Jupiter, Mars, the sun, Venus, Mercury, and the moon. This is the order that the planets follow in their rulership of the hours.

Monday is named after the moon, and it has been since the Romans coined the Latin name *dies lunae* ("day of the moon"). It's thought that this name built on even older, localised names that favoured the moon.[32]

Tuesday is associated with Mars. The name Tuesday is derived Old English *Tiwesdæg* and Middle English *Tewesday*, which both relate the day to Tiw or Tyr, a deity associated with combat and law in Germanic and Norse mythology.[33] In Roman mythology, Tyr was equated with the war god Mars.

Wednesday is associated with Mercury. In English the day is named after Wodan, one of many *heiti* (names) for the Norse and Germanic god Odin, who during the Roman era was interpreted as a Germanic form of Mercury, their god of messages and mercantilism.[34]

Thursday is associated with Jupiter. It is named after the Norse and Germanic thunder god, Thor, who was equated by the Romans to their own god of the sky and thunder, Jove, or Jupiter.[35]

Friday is associated with Venus. The English *Friday* is named after the Norse and Germanic goddess Frigg, who is most commonly linked to childbirth, marriage, and psychic power. During the Roman era, Frigg was associated with Venus, their goddess of love, sex, and fertility.[36]

Saturday is associated with Saturn, a complex deity within the Roman pantheon. He was and is associated with many things, including time, generations, and agriculture. Saturday is also associated with the planet Saturn.[37]

Sunday is associated with—you guessed it—the sun. This is a day of worship, rest, and strength in many cultures.[38]

32. Hocken, "Monday."

33. Hocken, "Tuesday."

34. Hocken, "Wednesday."

35. Hocken, "Thursday."

36. Hocken, "Friday."

37. Hocken, "Saturday."

38. Hocken, "Sunday."

PLANETARY DAY HOURS							
Hour	Sun	Mon	Tues	Wed	Thurs	Fri	Sat
1	☉	☽	♂	☿	♃	♀	♄
2	♀	♄	☉	☽	♂	☿	♃
3	☿	♃	♀	♄	☉	☽	♂
4	☽	♂	☿	♃	♀	♄	☉
5	♄	☉	☽	♂	☿	♃	♀
6	♃	♀	♄	☉	☽	♂	☿
7	♂	☿	♃	♀	♄	☉	☽
8	☉	☽	♂	☿	♃	♀	♄
9	♀	♄	☉	☽	♂	☿	♃
10	☿	♃	♀	♄	☉	☽	♂
11	☽	♂	☿	♃	♀	♄	☉
12	♄	☉	☽	♂	☿	♃	♀

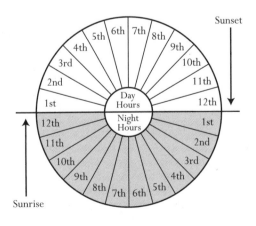

PLANETARY NIGHT HOURS							
Hour	Sun	Mon	Tues	Wed	Thurs	Fri	Sat
1	♃	♀	♄	☉	☽	♂	☿
2	♂	☿	♃	♀	♄	☉	☽
3	☉	☽	♂	☿	♃	♀	♄
4	♀	♄	☉	☽	♂	☿	♃
5	☿	♃	♀	♄	☉	☽	♂
6	☽	♂	☿	♃	♀	♄	☉
7	♄	☉	☽	♂	☿	♃	♀
8	♃	♀	♄	☉	☽	♂	☿
9	♂	☿	♃	♀	♄	☉	☽
10	☉	☽	♂	☿	♃	♀	♄
11	♀	♄	☉	☽	♂	☿	♃
12	☿	♃	♀	♄	☉	☽	♂

How Planetary Timings Are Used

Planetary days and hours are one method employed by some practitioners of magic to decide when is the optimal time to perform certain types of magic. Based on the Chaldean order, there are different associations with the days and hours of Saturn, Jupiter, Mars, the sun, Venus, Mercury, and the moon.

The Days and Hours of Saturn

Most well-known for its amazing rings, Saturn is the second-largest planet in our solar system, and the sixth closest to the sun. In ancient times, it was the most distant visible planet, the edge of the known universe. As such, the days and hours of Saturn are often associated with boundaries and endings. Death, dying, bereavement, and grief are all key themes of these days and hours when it comes to working magic.

In ancient Rome, it was the god Saturn who taught humans how to farm and grow food from seeds. For this reason, these days and hours are also associated with cycles, gardening, crops, and harvest; mentorship, succession, and planting seeds that will grow in the future.

The Days and Hours of Jupiter

Surrounded by approximately eighty moons, Jupiter is the largest of the planets and the fifth closest to the sun. In ancient Greece it was associated with Zeus. It was and is regarded as one of the most positive planets in terms of associations.[39] Jupiter is connected to religion, rulership, hierarchies, politics, priesthood, and so on. The days and hours of Jupiter also relate to the behaviour, ethics, and moral code of the individual, and to how they express themselves in wider society.

Jupiter absorbs heat from the sun as other planets do, but it radiates a lot more heat due to its size, which relates days and hours of Jupiter to expansion, growth, and improvement, as well as with physical health and well-being.

The Days and Hours of Mars

The red planet Mars was associated with various war or fire deities in a number of ancient cultures, though it was associated with agriculture and farming even earlier on.[40] Its two moons, Phobos and Deimos, are named for the sons of the Greek war deity Ares.

Unsurprisingly, the days and hours of Mars are considered appropriate for workings regarding war and courage in battle, victory over enemies, and so on. Just as the blacksmith's forge creates weapons of war, these times could also be utilised for "tempering" one's passions or anger into a constructive— or destructive—force.

39. Rankine and d'Este, *Practical Planetary Magick*, 33.
40. Rankine and d'Este, *Practical Planetary Magick*, 30.

The Days and Hours of the Sun

There are many sun deities and heliocentric belief systems throughout history, and it's easy to see why: the sun is literally the centre of our solar system, and its only star. At one hundred times wider than Earth and ten times wider than Jupiter, the sun would have been one of the first focusses of even the earliest and most primitive astronomy.[41]

The activity of the sun influences the nature of space throughout the entire solar system. Its light and heat are what give life to everything on our planet. Similarly, the days and hours of the sun in the Chaldean system are seen as prime time for workings related to wealth, power, dominance, success, gain, and advancement.

As humans, sometimes not getting enough sunlight can cause serious vitamin deficiencies or issues such as seasonal affective disorder. Sunny, bright weather is associated with happiness and lightheartedness, and so too are planetary days and hours of the sun associated with positivity, improved dispositions, hope, and friendship.

The Days and Hours of Venus

Venus is the planet nearest in size to Earth, and it's the second closest to the sun. Aside from the moon, it is the brightest object visible in the night sky. It is usually Venus people are referring to when they speak of the "morning star" or the "evening star," as it is so much more prominent than other stars at dawn and dusk.

Because of this planet's associations with the goddess Aphrodite by the ancient Greeks, it is in the days and hours of Venus that many practitioners perform workings geared toward love, sex, pleasure, and luxury. These times are also associated with platonic love, the forming of friendships and intimate bonds.

The Days and Hours of Mercury

The smallest planet and the one closest to the sun, the ancient Greeks associated Mercury with the gods Apollo in the morning and Hermes in the evening.

---

41. NASA, "Sun."

The Babylonians named it Nebu after their messenger god.[42] It's because of these associations that the days and hours of Mercury are considered a good time to perform workings centred around communication and messages, intelligence and knowledge, and books and reading. Commerce, success in business, and music are also associated with these times.

Because of Mercury's relationship with medicine and doctors, the days and hours of this little planet are also used often to perform works of health and healing. As a messenger, Mercury is fluid and adaptable, just like the quicksilver that bears its name. It can also be treacherous and slippery, and these hours are sometimes related to trickery, sleight of hand, and deception.

The Days and Hours of the Moon

The moon is another very visible object in our sky, and has been associated with magic and mystery for millennia.

When compared to Earth, our moon is much bigger than any other moons in comparison to their own planets. Its changing face was the basis of primitive calendar months. It influences the tides of our oceans, and as such it is connected to water, journeys, and navigation in the Chaldean order. And because our human bodies are made up of mostly water, so too are the hours and days of the moon associated with our behaviour, our dreams, and our mental health.

The cycles of the moon and its journey across our sky is far more obvious to the casual observer than the journeys of the distant planetary bodies. Its days and hours are associated with cycles, beginnings, endings, birth, death, and the dead.

Calculating Planetary Hours

The easiest way to calculate planetary hours is to use an app or website that lets you enter your location and gives you the planetary hours accordingly. If you want to try the calculation for yourself, it's relatively easy.

1. Find the time of the sunrise and the sunset. These are often listed on apps related to the weather or astronomy.

2. Add up the number of minutes in between.

42. Rankine and d'Este, *Practical Planetary Magick*, 21.

3. Divide this total by twelve. This will give you the number of minutes that constitute one planetary hour on that day.

Let's say one Wednesday in the summer, the sun rises at 5:58 a.m. and sets at 8:41 p.m. That's fourteen hours and forty-seven minutes of sunlight, or 887 minutes in total. Divided by twelve, that gives us 73.9 (we'll round it up to seventy-four) minutes per each "hour." To put it another way, this day is made up of twelve periods of seventy-four minutes each, with each period representing a different planetary hour. Because this is a Wednesday, it's a day ruled by Mercury. Today is a great day to perform workings around messages, communication, or business practices.

I can also look at specific planetary hours (see Figure 1), depending on what I intend to achieve with the working I am doing. For example, the hour of Venus is the seventh hour on Wednesdays. Knowing that this particular day has twelve "hours" of seventy-four minutes each, I can use that to count forward and work out when the seventh hour will be: the first six hours are a grand total of 444 minutes, which gets us to the start of the seventh hour. Four hundred forty-four minutes from sunrise at 5:58 a.m. takes us to roughly 12:30 p.m. as the beginning of Venus's seventy-four-minute hour.

Whether it's the phases of the moon, planetary timing, or just a bit of good old-fashioned star gazing, many witches work with one eye on the heavens. What we do may not be ancient, but a respect and acknowledgement of celestial bodies and their impact on our lives is certainly something that connects us to ages past.

EXERCISE
Getting Started with Planetary Magic

Use an app or do the math to determine the planetary hours for the remainder of the week. When would be the best time to perform magic for growth and abundance? For love? For banishing? Protection?

BASIC SKILLS
Visualisation II

Now that you've practised visualisation with something you can physically hold and see, it's time to work on visualising objects from "scratch." We'll start with two-dimensional shapes in simple colours.

The shapes I use here are the *tattvas*, symbols related to the elements that derive from Hindu philosophy. If these shapes and colours don't work for you, feel free to substitute your own. Keep shapes simple and geometric (circle, square, triangle, etc.) and all one colour for now.

1. Settle yourself into a comfortable, still position. Find stillness and use 4:4 breathing, as outlined in chapter 1.

2. Once you are relaxed and have found stillness, work on carefully visualising a two-dimensional (flat) blue circle. Concentrate until you can "see" the exact shade of blue, the size of the circle, its distance from you, etc.

3. Finish the visualisation once you feel you've satisfied the criteria above, or after a few minutes.

4. Repeat this process daily, remembering stillness and 4:4 breathing. Visualise a different shape each day: a blue circle, a red equilateral triangle, a silver crescent, or a yellow square. Do this until the shapes come fairly naturally to your mind's eye.

Remember, visualising is a skill to be learned and practised. Don't worry if this doesn't come easily straight away.

Modification: If you are still having trouble visualising, use the prompts in the appendix.

))) ● JOURNAL PROMPTS ● (((

- Look into the current moon phase where you are right now. If possible, go out and actually look at the moon too. Make a point of doing this for the next month, and make a quick note of your overall mood and energy levels that day. Do you notice any patterns?
- How might planetary hours and timings work for your magic? What are you keen to try? What are some obstacles or setbacks that may pop up when using planetary timings for specific goals?

Further Reading

Llewellyn's Complete Book of Ceremonial Magick edited by Lon Milo DuQuette and David Shoemaker

Practical Planetary Magick: Working the Magick of the Classical Planets in the Western Esoteric Tradition by David Rankine and Sorita d'Este

"The Charge of the Goddess: A History" by Jason Mankey

Online planetary hours calculator: www.planetaryhours.net

CHAPTER 5

The Wheel of the Year

The Wheel of the Year is used by most contemporary witches and Pagans as a calendar, to mark one year's worth of seasons and the continuing cycle of life, death, and rebirth—the seasonal cycles that are forever in motion at global, hemispherical, regional, local, and even cellular levels. This modern wheel is made up of eight sabbats, or holy days, including two solstices, two equinoxes, and four cross-quarter days. These typically include the winter solstice, Imbolc, the spring equinox, Beltane, the summer solstice, Lammas, the autumn equinox, and Samhain.

The Wheel comes to us from the work of Gerald Gardner, put together from a range of other sources. It was inspired and informed by earlier holidays and works that sometimes took a somewhat romantic view of agricultural life and the seasons. These early Wiccans and other occult trailblazers were not farmers, and it's important to keep this in mind when interpreting and celebrating these holidays. Following a Pagan or witch Wheel of the Year is less about recreating what ancient agricultural societies did before us and more about finding personal and spiritual meaning within the changes of the seasons—within us, around us, and in the universe as a whole.

The Names of the Sabbats

During the formative years of Wicca, the equinoxes and solstices, also known as the *solar festivals* or *lesser sabbats*, were usually celebrated on the nearest full moon date. This didn't change until the late '50s, and it wasn't until these sabbats were afforded the same importance and ceremony of the cross-quarter days that the Wheel of the Year as we know it came to be.

Gerald Gardner's earliest public material named the four cross-quarter days—Candlemas, May Eve, Lammas, and Halloween—after old Celtic (mostly English and Irish) seasonal celebrations. It is important to remember that there is little evidence of these festivals being practised in ancient times, and absolutely no record of any one area celebrating an eight-festival calendar cycle that resembles our own.

Throughout the 1960s and early 1970s, interest in "Celtic" language, culture, and mythology grew, and the names of the festivals evolved. By 1974, Gardnerian witch Raymond Buckland used the names Imbolc, Beltane, Lughnasadh, and Samhain to refer to the greater sabbats in his book *The Tree: The Complete Book of Saxon Witchcraft*. This was picked up and used by several authors, most notably Starhawk, who used most of them (except Imbolc, which she calls Brighid) in what became her most popular book, *The Spiral Dance*.

The solar festivals were simply called winter/summer solstice and spring/autumn equinox in the 1950s, and are still called that by many. These lesser sabbats were usually celebrated on the date of the nearest full moon until almost a decade later.

The two solstices were commonly referred to as Midsummer and Yule by the early 1970s.[43] These were the names that made sense to many witches: Yule (also called *jul*, *jol*, and *julmonat*) is a legitimately old winter holiday season in parts of Germany and Scandinavia, and there are records of different Midsummer rites and customs all over Europe for centuries. There were no ancient names for the equinoxes, because as far as we can tell, no specific celebrations were held at these times.[44]

Most North American witches and Pagans now refer to the equinoxes as Mabon and Ostara, names given to them by the American witch Aidan Kelly in 1974. Kelly wanted more poetic-sounding names than autumn/spring equinox, and names that matched the Celtic-sounding names of the other festivals. This is what caused him to give Midsummer the name Litha, while he was at it renaming the other two sabbats.[45] Kelly's names were printed in various Pagan

43. Mankey, *Witch's Wheel of the Year*, 32.
44. Mankey, *Witch's Wheel of the Year*, 32.
45. Kelly, "About Naming Ostara, Litha, and Mabon."

magazines, and like Gardner's revised greater sabbat names, they were what Starhawk printed in her most famous work, *The Spiral Dance*.

In Australia and elsewhere around the world, most people still use the terms spring/autumn equinox, although Mabon and Ostara are creeping into the vernacular as more newbies—who have often exclusively read American witchcraft texts—join the community.

Wheel of the Year

The Eight Sabbats

The eight-sabbat structure is a common way to celebrate the seasons throughout the year, but not all witches celebrate every sabbat, nor is there a "right" way to mark these occasions, if you choose to mark them at all.

I am going to stick mostly to explaining the Wheel of the Year as it is practised by many eclectic Wiccans and Wiccan-influenced practitioners: with the

Wiccan Goddess and her consort, the Horned God. This is one of the most well-known ways of looking at the Wheel, but, as it is with most of what you've read so far, it is not the only way.

Other common deities associated with the Wheel include Persephone, the goddess of spring and of the dead in the Greek pantheon, who descends to the underworld to reign as queen of the underworld for half of the year. Some modern Heathens and Norse-inspired witches apply the pagan Wheel of the Year—or parts of it—to known lore about Sunna, the personification of the sun. Many other practitioners relate the Wheel and the seasons to lore or knowledge about their own personal deities.

Winter Solstice

Dates: June 21 (approx.) in the Southern Hemisphere; December 21 (approx.) in the Northern Hemisphere

Also Known As: Yule

Key Themes: Rebirth of the sun, the turning tide, resolutions

Common Motifs: Evergreen boughs, snow, darkness and light, rebirth and transformation, holly trees, green and red

Activities: Mulling wine, bonfires, feasting, watching the sunrise, acts of charity and giving thanks (especially to loved ones), burning yule logs, making wreaths

This is the longest—and often the darkest—night of the year. After the autumn equinox, days get shorter and nights get longer, culminating in the winter solstice. After the solstice, light slowly begins to return, and daylit periods will get a little longer each day for the next six months.

The winter solstice has been marked with celebrations of some kind for centuries. In the Northern Hemisphere, many customs associated with it have been adopted into secular and Christian New Year and Christmas traditions. The ancient Romans held their midwinter festival of Saturnalia—in honour of Saturn, the god of agriculture—for the week surrounding the winter solstice. Scholars have asserted that it's likely that formal Christmas celebrations began around this time in order to Christianise this overtly Pagan holiday.[46]

---

46. Drury, *The Watkins Dictionary of Magic*, 255.

Many witches call the winter solstice Yule, which works well, as Yule (or *jol*, or *jul*, or *julmonat*) is a traditional holiday season in Germany and Scandinavia, where we find the origins of some of the most well-known midwinter customs. Modern witches often see this time of year as the rebirth of the sun. Modern Yule and midwinter festivals involve light and fire in many cases; there are lots of glowing candles, lanterns and bonfires to combat the long darkness.

In Wiccan-inspired witchcraft, this is often seen as the halfway point in the darkest period of the year: there is still a lot of dark to come, but the tides have turned and there's an end in sight. The Goddess is usually seen as being in her oldest stages of cronehood, or as the expectant mother about to give birth to the god, the solar child of promise.[47]

Imbolc

Dates: August 1 (approx.) in the Southern Hemisphere; February 1 (approx.) in the Northern Hemisphere

Also Known As: Candlemas (traditional Wicca), Imbolg, Brighid

Key Themes: First stirrings/quickening of the land, initiation, awakenings, sight

Common Motifs: Candles, light, newness, newborn babies, beginnings, inspiration, quickening, the first subtle signs of spring, milk, white and green

Activities: Lighting candles, replacing altar candles, cleaning/maintaining altar tools and supplies, performing divination, holding candle-lighting ceremonies

Relatively little is known from the ancient Irish festival of Imbolc, after which modern Pagan and witch celebrations are named. We do know that they took place in early February in Ireland, in areas where this date would have been the beginning of spring, and the goddess Brighid was connected in some way. Or *a* goddess Brighid—several Brighids were venerated throughout the British Isles, and it's unclear whether she was a universal deity or more localised to smaller areas. What we *can* be sure about is that the Brighid who was canonised by the Catholic church was not a real person. No historical records

---

47. Phillips and Phillips, *The Witches of Oz*, 72.

exist that point to a living Brighid, and the remaining myths about her are hig-gledy-piggledy and fragmented in places, presenting a Saint Brighid who, if she were a living person, would have had to have lived for centuries.[48]

Many of the symbols and customs that modern Pagans associate with Imbolc and the goddess Brighid—like Brighid's crosses, or building a bed for her in ritual—actually come from early Christian traditions and celebrations for Saint Brigid.[49] And while they sometimes share a similar date and the name was used by many witches in the 1950s and 1960s, Candlemas is actually a dif-ferent holiday altogether; it is a Catholic tradition that owes its origins, at least in part, to similar ceremonies held in ancient Greece.[50]

In areas where Imbolc occurs at the beginning of spring, rituals and altars feature the first flowers of the season. (Where I live, these are jonquils and snowdrops.) In some places, it is still quite cold and wintry by Imbolc, with no signs of spring at all. Modern Imbolc traditions in these areas sometimes include bringing fresh snow inside. Many also celebrate the return of the light, which is why candles feature so prominently in rituals for this season. Some witches like to use this time of year to do some spring cleaning: cleaning, repairing, or replacing working tools; replenishing altar supplies; cleaning and cleansing ritual spaces, etc.

In Wiccan-flavoured craft, Imbolc is usually that last step out of the dark half of the year. It's the final stretch before the equinox and the step into the light. The Goddess's power grows as her new child grows. She's now a goddess of inspiration, sometimes an initiatrix or muse, and the sunlight and the young god grow stronger every day.[51]

Spring Equinox

Dates: September 21 (approx.) in the Southern Hemisphere; March 21 (approx.) in the Northern Hemisphere

Also Known As: Vernal equinox, Ostara, Eostre

Key Themes: Balance, the dawn, birth, growth, strength

---

48. Mankey, *Witch's Wheel of the Year*, 108.
49. Mankey, *Witch's Wheel of the Year*, 108.
50. Mankey, *Witch's Wheel of the Year*, 109.
51. Phillips and Phillips, *The Witches of Oz*, 73.

Common Motifs: Flowers, eggs, baby animals, hares, rabbits, lambs, gardens, forests, youth

Activities: Spring cleaning, decorating eggs, holding egg hunts, building and lighting bonfires, gardening, arranging flowers

After Yule, the days begin to grow longer. By the spring equinox—a precise moment in time on a specific day when the sun is perfectly lined up with the earth's equator—day and night are more or less equal. Many witches and Pagans call the season around this day Ostara and celebrate balance, life, fertility, and springtime at this time.

In Paganism and witchcraft, the name Ostara was first used for the spring equinox by Aidan Kelly in 1974. Until a few decades ago, it was mostly used by American witches and authors, although as the community has globalised and more Pagans from further afield consume these authors' content, it has become more widely used. That said, many witches do still prefer to use pre-1970s names like the vernal equinox or spring equinox.

The name Ostara is derived from Eostre, the name of an old Germanic goddess reconstructed by Jacob Grimm (one half of the famous Brothers Grimm) in his book *Deutsche Mythologie* (*Teutonic Mythology*) in 1835. When Grimm was writing about Eostre, he was referencing a much earlier work by the Venerable Bede, an English Benedictine monk who lived from 672–735 CE and was considered by many to be the "father" of English history. In his work *De Temporum Ratione* (*The Reckoning of Time*), Bede wrote about the Germanic holiday season *Eosturmonath* ("Eastern month"), which he claimed was named after an ancient goddess named Eostre.[52]

But there's a problem here. This goddess—who Bede claimed was also known as Eastre, Eastro, and Ostra, depending on region and dialect—seems to have only been written about by Bede. No mention of her or her worship exists in any other written history or mythology, and as time goes on and more research is done, it's looking more and more like Bede might have made her up, embellishing on the name Eosturmonath. The closest researchers have come to evidence of a goddess Ostara/Eostre is mention of a proto-Germanic goddess called Austrō, a proto-Indo-European goddess of the dawn called Ausṓs, and the

---

52. Connor, *Ostara*, chap. 1.

Romano-Germanic Matronae called Austriahenae, but these are separate deities from completely different time periods.[53] If anything, these are namesakes that evolved into Eostre/Ostara, and even then, this is just a theory.

Many of the "ancient" symbols of Ostara/the equinox were not associated with the Goddess or celebration until the mid-1800s. Things like hares, eggs, and chicks were never mentioned by Bede or Grimm. The earliest mention was actually a fairly offhand comment made in 1874: "probably the hare was the sacred animal of Ostara."[54] As with the identity of the goddess Ostara, this one quote was picked up and used by several authors, who were cited by other authors, and so on and so on, until it appeared as "fact" in many of the pagan and witch books you might have on your shelf right now.

Regardless of where they came from or how ancient they're seen to be, modern symbols of Ostara and the spring equinox include painted or fresh eggs, fresh spring flowers, hares/rabbits, and baby animals. Some modern witches use this season for both magical and mundane spring cleaning; rites of abundance, fertility, and growth; returning to the outdoors after the winter cold; gardening; "small-c craft" such as egg painting, flower crown making, and flower pressing; and divination for the year ahead.

In Wiccan-inspired witchcraft, the spring equinox is the domain of the young dawn Goddess and the young God, sometimes seen as the youthful prince of the sun, as they grow and develop into a young woman and man.[55]

Beltane

> **Dates:** October 31 (approx.) in the Southern Hemisphere; May 1 (approx.) in the Northern Hemisphere
>
> **Also Known As:** May Day, Beltaine
>
> **Key Themes:** Pleasure, sacred marriage, sex, luck, fertility
>
> **Common Motifs:** Fire, bonfires, candles, torches, fun, love, sex, marriage, maypoles, morris dancing, flowers, flower crowns, music, red and white

---

53. Hutton, *The Stations of the Sun*, 180.

54. Connor, *Ostara*, chap. 1.

55. Phillips and Phillips, *The Witches of Oz*, 74.

Activities: Building and lighting bonfires, maypole dancing, playing music, games of skill, dancing, making flower crowns

Beltane was historically an Irish celebration/fire festival that later spread throughout the British Isles. It's likely that the name comes from the Irish word *bel*, meaning "bright" or fortunate.[56] Some have tried to attribute it to certain deities, but these links are tenuous at best; no historical evidence exists to support them. These ancient celebrations often involved big bonfires and using fire or smoke for protection. In some areas, farmers would pass their livestock through the smoke of the fires to protect them from evil.[57]

Beltane as we know it in modern witchcraft and Paganism is derived mostly from the English celebration May Day, a celebration from which we get traditions such as maypoles, may queens, Jack-in-the-Green, green men, etc. Traditional May Day celebrations involved fun, frivolity, and games to celebrate the start of the English summer. Blooming flowers were often used as seasonal decorations.

In modern Paganism, many consider Beltane to be a celebration of life and fertility. Celebrations sometimes include an enactment of the young Horned God courting the maiden Goddess, though the idea of a "chase" is slowly falling out of favour as the community and our values change. Maypoles, morris dancing, and bonfires are also a part of many rituals.

Wiccan-flavoured witchcraft often holds Beltane as sacred to the passionate, thriving earth Goddess and her consort, the Horned God of wild places. The holiday is sometimes celebrated as the lands and the people joining, just as the gods join in their sacred marriage, sexual union, or both.[58]

Summer Solstice

Dates: December 21 (approx.) in the Southern Hemisphere; June 21 (approx.) in the Northern Hemisphere

Also Known As: Litha, Midsummer

Key Themes: Life, strength, action, power

Common Motifs: Fire, the sun, sunflowers, sunsets, oak trees

56. Mankey, *Witch's Wheel of the Year*, 181.

57. Opie and Tatem, *A Dictionary of Superstitions*, 154–55.

58. Phillips and Phillips, *The Witches of Oz*, 74–75.

Activities: Building and lighting bonfires (if safe and legal!), singing, making wishes, watching the sun set, dressing up, trickery and telling jokes

Throughout the centuries, many records exist of people across Europe building huge bonfires to celebrate Midsummer or St. John's Eve, the night before the feast day of John the Baptist. Fires were lit not just to honour the sun on its strongest day, but in celebration of its magical powers—including the power to keep the "fair folk" at bay. The smoke from Midsummer fires was considered to have protective properties, and with this in mind, bonfires were built alongside crops and orchards. In some areas, these protective fires were separate from the "main" bonfires and contained animal bones.[59]

Midsummer has long been connected to the fey, partly because of William Shakespeare's play *A Midsummer Night's Dream*, one of the first works to present the fey as something other than malevolent and wicked, and certainly the most popular. Modern Pagan Midsummer celebrations sometimes include offerings and acknowledgements of the fey, oak/holly king rituals, bonfires (or, in Australia, representations of fire, as we have fire restrictions all summer), prayers and offerings to solar deities, solar wheels/discs, etc. Some also like to do divination for the year ahead on this auspicious date. Many witches view Beltane as the beginning of the summer season, the solstice as the middle, and Lammas as the first harvest and summer's end.

In Wiccan-inspired craft, the Goddess and God are often seen as ruling monarchs at the time of the summer solstice, though the virile sun king will start to slowly wane from now until he is sacrificed at Lammas.[60]

Lammas

Dates: February 1 (approx.) in the Southern Hemisphere; August 1 (approx.) in the Northern Hemisphere

Also Known As: Lughnasadh

Key Themes: Sacrifice, transformation, harvest (grain), reaping

Common Motifs: Bread, grain, the first harvest, abundance, creativity, passion, the arts

---

59. Mankey, *Witch's Wheel of the Year*.
60. Phillips and Phillips, *The Witches of Oz*, 75.

Activities: Baking bread, making corn dollies, produce swaps, creative performances and skill shares

Historically, the ancient Irish festival of Lughnasadh took place at sundown on July 31, with festivities running into the next day. Lammas was an Anglo-Saxon festival that took place at around the same time of year. These two names are sometimes used interchangeably for our modern pagan holiday, but the two original harvest festivals are totally different and not really connected.

Lammas later became a festival in the Catholic church, where it was sometimes called loaf-mass. It was a celebration of grain harvests and the loaves of bread that came from them. It was usually celebrated on the first of August, although some witches observe the second of August, which is the date given in Robert Graves' *The White Goddess*. Some witches observe the two holidays separately.[61] In many parts of Europe this was (and still is) the beginning of the cereal harvest, and modern celebrations often give a nod to this: grains and loaves feature prominently.

In modern Paganism, Lammas is still associated with bread and grain harvests. Some traditions include making corn dollies, which are generally seen as representing the Goddess in her role as the Earth Mother. Rituals around this time of year often honour the harvest in its many forms, and they are sometimes localised to specific harvests relevant to that area. In central Victoria, lavender harvest festivals are a common event at this time. Some groups and individuals celebrate their own harvests and incorporate the sharing, cooking, and eating of homegrown produce into Lammas rituals. Others celebrate metaphorical "harvests": schemes coming to fruition, the achievement of goals, important transitions, etc.

In Wiccan-flavoured witchcraft, Lammas is often when the god is sacrificed as the corn king.[62] Others have him die at the autumn equinox. The Goddess is seen as either a reaper or as a lover in mourning, or somewhere in between.

Autumn Equinox

Dates: March 21 (approx.) in the Southern Hemisphere; September 21 (approx.) in the Northern Hemisphere

---

61. Mankey, *Witch's Wheel of the Year*.
62. Phillips and Phillips, *The Witches of Oz*, 75–76.

Also Known As: Mabon

Key Themes: Balance, harvests (fruit and vegetable), abundance, taking stock

Common Motifs: Autumn leaves, root vegetables, the second harvest, the fading of the light, russet and brown

Activities: Produce swaps, markets, feasting, pickling and jam making, scrumping, gardening

There are no records of specific autumn equinox celebrations in ancient times, but there is evidence of harvest festivals held at this time of year in several different countries.

The name Mabon was coined by Aidan Kelly. It has been in use—mostly in North America—since the 1970s. The name comes from the Welsh mythological figure Mabon ap Modron, who appears in some Arthurian myths and in the Welsh collection of literature known as *The Mabinogion*.[63]

Many modern witches and Pagans treat the autumn equinox as a second harvest festival. As with Lammas, what constitutes a harvest is often localised or personalised and varies from area to area. In areas where there are no grain crops grown, witches might celebrate the local apple harvest, for example. In recent times, some witches have also done rituals and offerings dedicated to Persephone on this day. Many Americans treat the holiday as if it is synonymous with Thanksgiving.

At this equinox, we move back into the darker half of the year. Sabbats and their celebrations are more inward-facing work. In Wiccan-flavoured witchcraft and its more eclectic offshoots, the autumn equinox often sees the Goddess return to a darker form as she prepares to journey into the otherworld to be with her lover.[64]

Samhain

Dates: May 1 (approx.) in the Southern Hemisphere; October 31 (approx.) in the Northern Hemisphere

Also Known As: Hallows, All Hallows' Eve, Hallowmas, Halloween

---

63. Mankey, *Witch's Wheel of the Year*.

64. Phillips and Phillips, *The Witches of Oz*, 77–78.

Common Motifs: Ancestors and the dead, spirits, skulls, bones, darkness, the final harvest

Activities: Ancestor veneration, remembering those who have passed, death cafes, dumb suppers, neep or pumpkin carving

Samhain (pronounced "sow-in") was an ancient Irish-Celtic celebration, though records on just how it was celebrated are patchy: most "Halloween" traditions we associate with it do not date back to ancient paganism.

While modern pagandom largely considers this a season for the dead, there are no historical records to suggest that this was originally the case. Mythologically speaking, Samhain was a night of powerful magic and of the thinning of the veils between worlds. The connection of Samhain with spirits and the dead wasn't until Sir James Frazer released *The Golden Bough*, a wide-ranging, comparative study of mythology and religion, in the 1890s. Because Samhain occurred so close to All Souls' Day, Frazer wrote of the ancient festival being watched over by "the souls of the departed hovering unseen."[65] Some think of Samhain as the "Celtic New Year," but again, there is very little evidence that this was the case.

Many modern witches and Pagans use Samhain season as a time to remember the dead, especially those who have passed over the last twelve months. At the same time, Samhain is sometimes treated as the harvest celebration it was in days gone by: a time to bring in the last of the crops and hunker down as the days keep darkening and winter sets in. In recent decades, it has become tradition for some to do workings and rituals connected to the myth of Persephone and Demeter at Samhain.

In Wicca-inspired witchcraft, this is the time of the year that the Goddess in her darkest aspect travels to the otherworld to meet her lover, who rules there. It's their union that is often celebrated as the beginning of all creation.[66]

Holy Seasons, Not Holy Days

It's important to remember that sabbat days are to celebrate a seasonal time of the year that lasts for several weeks as it fades and overlaps with the next

65. Frazer, *The Golden Bough*, 633–34.
66. Phillips and Phillips, *The Witches of Oz*, 71.

season. As Wiccan author Julia Phillips points out, "The whole key to understanding the Wiccan philosophy can be found within the Wheel of the Year, as we learn how one phase of life proceeds from another."[67]

Author and artist Pauline Campanelli elaborates on this idea, pointing out that the sabbat days only mark the turning point (or thereabouts, depending where you live) in each sabbat season: Imbolc is when the light begins to return, Beltane celebrates the first inklings of summer, and so on.[68]

In this busy world, it can be easy to forget all about the Wheel of the Year most of the time, and the sabbats tend to creep up on us—or are sometimes forgotten entirely. One thing that can help reduce this is remembering that the year—the seasons—comes in tides. The sabbat days themselves are kind of like markers of those tides shifting. It's not a matter of a switch being flicked somewhere on a certain day and signalling that now—*only now*—it's Imbolc. The calendar of months and days as we know it is a relatively recent construct, and it's not like the seasons and tides of the year on our millennia-old planet are going to fit themselves into that.

As an example, it's late September in Australia as I write this. The spring equinox has passed, and many of us celebrated it as we do each year: as part of the Australian Wiccan Conference. In the weeks leading up to that, I've watched the wattle blooming fat and yellow all around where I live. The fruit trees bloomed long before the equinox, and this week beautiful white snowdrops have started to come out in my garden. The nights are still frosty and the days seem to alternate between gorgeous sun one day and heavy rain the next. This month and the next will be a series of beginnings and endings in the plants and flowers around me, depending on the weather and the rainfall. Spring, like the other seasons, is nuanced and complex, and there is not one specific day that is better than another for celebrating it.

To think about the year in this way, it can help to have a year-long planner with the seasons marked out. You can also use the Wheel to plan your witchy celebrations—whatever and whenever they may be—in a sustainable, manageable way that works for you.

---

67. Phillips and Phillips, *The Witches of Oz*, 68.

68. Campanelli, "The Wheel of the Year," 329–35.

EXERCISE
Your Wheel of the Year

Draw a Wheel of the Year for your part of the world. Write the sabbat dates appropriate to your hemisphere. Then, over the coming year, make a note of the seasons turning and what that looks like where you are. Are there any crops grown locally? When are they harvested? When does it start to get cold? Does it snow? When does that start? Write or draw the flowers or trees that bloom, bud, or drop their leaves. A good way to monitor all this is to set a reminder on one of your devices that goes off at the same time each week; this will remind you to jot down any changes you see. You'd be surprised at just how many subtle changes there are in nature when you really look.

Blank Wheel of the Year

BASIC SKILLS
Visualisation III

So far, you've worked on getting yourself still and relaxed and on visualising some basic shapes. Before we shift gears and bring these skills together in an upcoming chapter, let's add some detail to what you've worked on so far.

Remember, if these shapes and colours don't work for you, feel free to substitute your own simple shapes.

1. Settle yourself into a comfortable, still position. Find stillness and use 4:4 breathing, as outlined in chapter 1.

2. When you have been relaxed and found stillness, work on carefully visualising a blue circle, but work on making it three-dimensional: visualise a globe or orb rather than a flat disc.

3. Repeat this daily, visualising a different shape each time, this time in three dimensions: a blue circle (globe), a red equilateral triangle (pyramid or tetrahedron), a silver crescent, and a yellow square (cube).

4. If this comes easily to you, work on visualising the background against which these shapes sit. The blue circle might sit against a cloudy sky or a rising sun. The red triangle might sit in front of a bonfire or a table covered in lit candles. The silver crescent might sit in front of a raging sea or a serene lake. The yellow square might sit in a forest or moor. Use any of these examples or start creating some of your own—it's up to you. This is your mind's eye, after all.

5. Repeat these, remembering stillness and 4:4 breathing, until the shapes come fairly naturally to your mind's eye. Focus on one three-dimensional shape each day, then focus on giving them a solid background.

Modification: If you are still having trouble visualising, use the prompting questions in the appendix. Introduce them one at a time, in order, moving on to add the next when you are comfortable.

))) ● JOURNAL PROMPTS ● (((

- Where you live, what are signs that the season has changed? How do you know spring/summer/winter/autumn are on the way? Describe the changes in weather patterns, plant and animal life (this includes humans), daylight, etc.

- What's the upcoming sabbat where you are? Investigate some of the key themes and common motifs of this sabbat. See if you can relate them to yourself, your practice, your life, and the natural world around you. What rings true? What doesn't quite fit? Remember, the Wheel of the Year in its original form was devised for a very specific part of the world, and not everything will translate to where you are. With those things that don't quite work, are there any substitutions, localised to your area, that you could make?

Further Reading

A Year of Ritual: Sabbats & Esbats for Solitaries and Covens by Sandra Kynes

Witch's Wheel of the Year: Rituals for Circles, Solitaries & Covens by Jason Mankey

Year of the Witch: Connecting with Nature's Seasons through Intuitive Magick by Temperance Alden

"About Naming Ostara, Litha, and Mabon" by Aidan Kelly

"Witchcraft 101 – Sometimes You Have to Follow the Rules" by Bekah Evie Bel

CHAPTER 6
Deity and Spirit

Some witches work with deities, and some don't. Some witches revere and worship deities too, as well as working with them. As with any other religious belief, a witch's relationship to and attitude toward deity in general (and their deities specifically) is complex and deeply personal. If you are more interested in nontheistic practice, consider reading this chapter anyway to learn what others do.

Many practitioners of witchcraft and Paganism are drawn to gods, ancestors, or other spirits as part of their devotional or ritual work. If you're planning on honouring or working with any deity, it's important to understand all you can about the cultural, spiritual, and physical landscape that shaped them. These deities are just one piece of rich, complex cultures and traditions.

It's also important to be mindful of cultural appropriation. Remember: if you are part of a dominant, privileged culture, you do not always have the right to access cultures who have been (or who are currently being) oppressed.

Mythology and Folklore

Among the first books on mythology written for general public consumption were those by American banker Thomas Bulfinch in the 1850s and 1860s. Prior to this, works and collections of this nature were written for academics who could read and write Latin, German, or Greek. When you're reading about myths and mythical creatures, it's important to keep this in the back of your mind. Because much of what's available out there was translated during the Victorian era, many Victorian sensibilities have snuck in and flavoured what we consider to be the "true" form of some myths.

It's why myths—like the gods themselves—shouldn't necessarily be taken in isolation from their context and culture. If a myth, god, spirit, or mythical creature fascinates you, or if you're considering incorporating them into your practice, do a bit of research before you launch into anything. If you're not sure where to begin, even starting with Wikipedia will help deepen your understanding; look into the sources cited by the article to learn more. Jot down a few important points or get your nerd on and start a mini research journal. What was happening during the time these myths, beliefs, or stories originated? What was daily life like for the average person who lived during this time? What are the key changes that have occurred in this place/to these people between then and now?

Between the 1970s and 2000s, Neopagans had a pick-and-mix approach to deity. Most folks worked with deities from a range of pantheons without knowing much more than what those individual deities were "famous" for. Thankfully, this seems to finally be on the decline. People are starting—albeit slowly—to slow down and think. They no longer treat the gods as wish-granting genies or collectible statuettes.

Consider this quote from Saxon Pagan Alaric Albertsson in his book *To Walk a Pagan Path*:

> There are many Pagans today who take a more scattered, eclectic approach to connecting with Spirit, leaping from one pantheon to another, collecting "patron" deities as if they were Hummel figurines. Imagine yourself walking down a sidewalk in Manhattan, greeting everyone you pass. How deep is your relationship with these passers-by?…It can be difficult to develop truly meaningful relationships with a dozen gods and goddesses gathered from unrelated pantheons. I do not recommend this approach at all. If you want to become good friends with somebody, you spend a lot of time with that person. You meet his or her family and friends. Likewise, if you want a good relationship with a god or goddess, you should devote a lot of time to that deity.[69]

69. Albertsson, *To Walk a Pagan Path*, chap. 1.

Put simply, do the research, slow down, and take time to learn how to treat deity. And while there are no hard and fast rules with this whole witchcraft and Paganism thing, digging deep wherever and however you can manage will undoubtedly deepen your understanding and enrich your practice.

Some Helpful Terms for Discussing Gods and Practice

Talking about religion, gods, and belief can be tricky sometimes. There are terms used by theologians that are very Christocentric or otherwise problematic when discussing something as nuanced as pagan and witchcraft gods. Here are a few definitions to help you start thinking about gods and worship in a way that applies to witchcraft.

Altar: A surface or raised structure on which gifts or sacrifices to a god are made.

Deify: To elevate a person or creature to the status of a god. Example: *The ancient Egyptians deified their pharaohs.*

Deity: A supernatural being, like a god or goddess, that is worshipped by people who believe it controls or exerts force over some aspect of the world.

Devotional: An exercise, such as a ritual or prayer, expressing reverence for a deity. Example: *Some people perform daily devotionals.*

Libation: Pouring a liquid offering (especially wine) onto the ground or into an offering bowl as a religious or devotional act.

Pantheon: All the gods of a single belief system or tradition. Some pantheons common to modern witchcraft and Paganism are the Hellenic pantheon, the Kemetic pantheon, the Norse pantheon, the Roman pantheon, and the Irish pantheon. Remember to avoid saying Celtic pantheon—depending which "Celtic" country or region you're talking about, there are different pantheons and mythologies that are not always related.

Pathworking: Any visualised journey, usually undertaken in a meditative or altered state of consciousness. The term was originally used to describe the process of astrally or mentally projecting up and around the Tree of Life in order to meet entities, gain information, and ask favours of them.

Polytheism: Belief in multiple gods. Consider also *hard polytheism*, the belief that the gods are all individual deities, and *soft polytheism*, the belief that all gods are aspects of one god.[70]

Unverified Personal Gnosis (UPG): A term used in religious discussions to preface or qualify a particular statement on metaphysical reality. There is a more detailed look at UPG later in this chapter.

Learning about a Deity

Whether you are more comfortable approaching deity, ancestors, or local entities, the first and most essential step is to connect with spirit in some way. This usually involves learning about a deity or spirit that interests you. If you've been following along with the Basic Skills exercises in this book, you have some idea that being able to visualise will really help you in many areas of witchcraft, and this is one of them. Having a solid idea of the lore surrounding a deity will help you build a bigger "picture" of the type of entity they are in your mind's eye. This, in turn, will help you as you start to reach out and take the first steps to working with a deity.

EXERCISE
Myth Adventure

The purpose of this exercise is not to match you up with a deity and have you start worshipping them. Rather, it is to get you comfortable with interacting with and "getting to know" a figure that is human-created and known—and thus kept "alive"—by many humans.[71]

Choose a character from a story that you have read and know fairly well. It could be a myth, folktale, or any other work of fiction. What matters is that you know a lot about this character. Ideally, choose a character who hasn't been depicted in a movie or television show that retells the story, as this can really affect and influence your perception of them.

---

70. Beckett, *The Path of Paganism*.

71. This concept of belief feeding the existence of gods and spirits is looked at and prodded in *Small Gods*, a fantasy novel in Terry Pratchett's Discworld series.

1. Sit or lie comfortably in a quiet place free of distractions. Light a candle, burn incense, or put on quiet music if that helps you concentrate and go inward. Use the skills you have worked on so far to find stillness and regulate your breathing.

2. Visualise the character standing or sitting in front of you. Be as specific as you can as you visualise their appearance, their clothing, and so on.

3. When you're sure you have this as detailed as possible, silently ask this character about something from their story, then wait for their answer. The answer may not come the first time you try this.

As with everything else you've done so far in this book, this takes time and practise. At this point, a lot of this is you flexing your visualisation muscles, *but* try this out for at least five days. You might be surprised at some of the answers you get, and where they come from.

Making Contact with a Deity

Sometimes a god or spirit will call someone to them, but in most cases it's us that has to reach out first. Different ways people do this include setting up a household altar (if practical to do so), making offerings, or approaching the deity and speaking from the heart. If you choose the latter option, you're much better off using your own words rather than something out of a book.

A word of caution here: if you're think about using divination, such as a tarot spread, to "choose" which god or pantheon you should work with, think again. Tarot and other divination tools are one way to check in or confirm something with a deity, but please don't leave something as serious as working with deity up to a lucky dip. You might not be "meant" to work with any gods, or you might be meant to work with multiple. A tarot spread will not necessarily communicate this.

If you don't feel drawn to any particular deity, you don't feel drawn. Most practitioners experience deity very differently as their experiences and interests change. Some feel called to one deity, some to several. Others work a more nontheistic path. And then there are those that chop and change between the two.

Research

While nobody expects you to perform PhD levels of research into the background of a deity before you get started, I do recommend you look into them a little. An internet search is a simple first step. Wikipedia pages are hit-and-miss sometimes, as they can be edited by anyone, but their citations and further reading sections can take you down some delightful rabbit holes.

Look into the mythology of a culture that interests you. Again, the purpose here is not to partner you up with a deity and send you on your way. Read the stories, then look into what life was like for the people who told these stories. What influences were at play? What were people struggling with? What did they celebrate, and why? What about the land? What was that like, and how might that shape these stories?

Contemplation

Once you've researched a deity, you need to think about whether, knowing what you now know, you still want to build a relationship. If the answer is no, go back to the drawing board and look at other deities, myths, and stories that interest you.

If you still wish to attempt to make contact with the deity you have researched, it might be a good idea to meditate on it. Think on why you started this journey in the first place. Consider not only how a relationship with this deity might benefit you, but what it is that you can offer this deity.

Offerings and Opening Up

Offerings are gifts offered to deity as an act of devotion. These could be food, drink, a handmade item, jewellery, etc. Liquid offerings are sometimes poured straight onto the ground in outdoor contexts. If you're working indoors, consider having a libation bowl on your altar, which can be placed outside or poured onto the earth when you're done with it.

Some ideas for offerings to get you started:

Incense: Sticks or cones are fine, but a personal blend burned in a censer using charcoal discs is better. Read up on herbal/botanical associations for the deity or spirit to get some inspiration, and experiment until you get a scent you think will be pleasing.

Mead or Honey Wine: Favoured by many Northern European spirits and deities.

Olive Oil: Liked by some Southern European spirits and deities.[72]

Bread or Beer: A traditional offering for Egyptian deities.[73]

Something Crafted by You: Ideally made of natural materials.

Once you've made an offering, introduce yourself and ask for the deity's guidance and blessing. That's all you need to do at this time; it's not the time to make any specific requests just yet. If it's favours you're after, don't ask for them until much later, once you have established a mutual relationship. At this point, you are simply opening yourself to this deity, demonstrating your willingness to work with them and to accept any blessings.

Listening

Whatever your first step might be, the most important thing to do next is to listen. Try to be mindful of any pre-held ideas you might have about this deity. Signs or "messages" from gods and goddesses are rarely huge, audible statements. You might have a fleeting vision or daydream, recollect a memory, or something else entirely. Sometimes you will get a "knowing." It's very hard to put into words!

You might experience nothing at all, and that's okay. It's unlikely you will have a life-changing supernatural experience every time you reach out to gods and spirits. In giving an offering to the deity, you have made the first step and reached out to make a connection.

Keeping Your Feet on the Ground

By now you probably understand that an observer practising witchcraft doesn't look nearly as dramatic as it does in works of fiction. While a deity you're trying to contact won't arrive as a solid, breathing human and hang out with you on the couch, they will certainly make themselves known. How? That's hard to say. Different people experience these things in different ways.

---

72. Mierzwicki, *Hellenismos*, chap. 2.
73. Albertsson, *To Walk a Pagan Path*, chap. 1.

Be patient. All relationships take time. If you still feel no reciprocal connections after a reasonable period of time spent reaching out to deity—say, a month at least—it might be time to hit the books again. Try some more research and a slightly different approach, and if that doesn't work, it might be time to (politely!) move on to another god or goddess.

Altars and Sacred Space

Having a place where you can tend and maintain your connection with deity is a good idea once an initial connection has been made. This will look different depending on your space and your circumstances, but ideally there should be somewhere in your house (or nearby) that is sacred and set aside for the worship of your gods. It could be as simple as some empty space on a shelf or a shoebox you can pack away when you're done, as detailed as a fully equipped temple room with all the bells and whistles, or anything in between.

Some more points on altars to get you started:

- Although many people include traditional tools on the altar, you can use whatever fits your budget, needs, and circumstances.
- Ancestral altars might include photographs of ancestors as well as symbolic representations of more distant ancestors. Remember that your "ancestors" are not always related to you by blood.
- Hellenic (Greek) altars and some others will often involve a flame, but please don't leave candles unattended![74]
- Be sure your altar contains everything you need for a ritual before you begin a ceremony.

Making Time for Sacred Work

When you have an altar or sacred space set up, it is important to work with it and your god(s) consistently. Yes, life happens—but life happens consistently too. It's important to build a regular practice that works with your life rather than a practice that is squeezed in when you have the time. Consistency is key, and the key to keeping your practice consistent is having something manageable.

---

74. Mierzwicki, *Hellenismos*.

Rather than planning for a thirty-minute meditation followed by a devotional every day, maybe try for fifteen to twenty minutes a week to begin with. Choose a day and a time when you will spend at least fifteen minutes at your altar, giving offerings to gods/spirits and listening to what your gods may have to say. The day and time should fit your lifestyle. Try it for a month, then make small, slow adjustments as needed. You might never get to a point in your life where you have the time and space to work every day. Don't worry about what you "should" be doing and, instead, build a practice that's yours.

UPG: Unverified Personal Gnosis

UPG is the term we use for information and knowledge that comes to individuals through means that can't be objectively confirmed. This includes things you learn in dreams, in trance/journeying, or through divination. It isn't the same as making something up or thinking something is true. It's something you believe is true because you trust the source, even though you can't "prove" it's true to yourself, much less to someone else. If multiple people get the same message, it becomes *SPG*, Shared Personal Gnosis, which is sometimes called *Community Gnosis*.[75]

UPG is important for you and your relationship with the gods and spirits, but don't rely on it too heavily. UPG should not be taken as the gospel truth or used to influence others in any way. It's becoming good etiquette in Pagan and witchy circles to explicitly declare UPGs when talking about them, especially if they are not consistent with documented evidence about a deity.

Building Your Practice

Once you have been working with deity or spirit for an extended period of time, you might also consider:

- Working up to daily offerings, prayers, or other devotional acts.
- Observing more formal offerings or rites once a month or so.
- Researching and observing holy days or other important dates connected to your deity, including but not limited to the Wheel of the Year.
- Seeking out groups or individuals who also work with this deity.[76]

75. Beckett, "UPG."

76. There are some great tips on how to go about this in Alaric Albertsson's *To Walk a Pagan Path* and John Beckett's *The Path of Paganism*.

Raising Energy from Deities or Spirits

I shared some ways to raise energy in chapter 3. Another way of energy raising that's used by theistic practitioners (practitioners who worship, work with, or have devoted themselves to a god or gods) is to seek energy from those deities for magical and ritual work. If you are exclusively an atheistic or animistic practitioner, this may not be an appropriate method of power raising for you.

Energy from deity is sometimes drawn on for acts of mercy, or for help with issues or goals in which the deity may be invested. Drawing energy from deity is different than prayer, which is usually done solely for devotion and without too much focus on technique. In magical workings, the practitioner has (some) say in the direction of the outcome, whereas in prayer the outcome is often left up to the god(s) in question.

As with all other ways of approaching deity, when you're petitioning one to lend their power to your ritual/working, it's important to be respectful. Consider the deity's will and autonomy in the specific matter as well as that of your fellow practitioners, and your own.

Evoking versus Invoking

In prayer, a practitioner is "talking" directly to deity, with the assumption that the deity is listening. When that practitioner asks for that deity to be present with them, or to give them a "sign," what they are doing is getting closer to invocation and evocation, which both involve raising and sending energy.

Evoking is summoning a deity to be present in your ritual/working to lend their power or to preside over celebrations or important work. *Invoking* is summoning a deity into your own body, someone else's body, or an object of worship like an idol. Invoking a deity into a person is sometimes called *channelling*, *summoning*, *possession*, *drawing down*, or *aspecting*. This is generally much more advanced, complicated, and risky than evoking.

As with most energy-raising techniques, invoking/evoking is very much a two-way street as far as energy is involved. The practitioner(s) form a connection when "contact" with the deity occurs, and by inviting them and their power into your space, an energy exchange is occurring.

Both invoking and evoking can take some work to master, and even the most adept practitioner won't succeed perfectly every time they try. Deborah

Lipp outlines some of the key components of an effective invocation and evocation in her book *Magical Power for Beginners*:[77]

1. **Invitation or Summons:** Specifically call to the deity or ask them to be present.

2. **Specificity in Words and Atmosphere:** Use titles you know. Research the deity and be specific about the qualities/version of the deity you are calling. Nonverbal "calls" should also be specific: from your research, you should get some idea of the atmosphere you need to set with specific offerings, symbols, incense, colours, music, etc.

3. **Descriptiveness:** Be detailed about appearance or qualities of a deity. This will not only make them more receptive to you, but will help kick your human brain into ritual mode, making you more receptive too. Words have power.

4. **Praise:** Be respectful and reverent at all times.

5. **Need or Reason:** Remember to say why you are summoning a deity. This might be as simple as "so that we may honour you."

6. **Greeting and/or Thanks:** Always assume success at the end of an invocation or evocation call. Welcome the deity and/or thank them for their presence.

Keeping all this in mind, I wrote the below words for the Norse trickster god, Loki, to be used in a *blot*, a type of Heathen ritual:

> *Hail Loki, flame-haired fire keeper! Join us on this night.*
> *Bring your cunning and wit, and help us see truth.*
> *Scar lip, roaring god, we call you with love, that you may*
> *bring us levity and courage on this night.*
> *Hail Loki!*

77. Lipp, *Magical Power for Beginners*, 90–94.

**EXERCISE
Invocation/Evocation**

Use the steps in this chapter to write an invocation/evocation to a deity you have researched. Try it with the deity once you have made contact and have established a relationship of some kind.

❭ ❭ ❭ ● JOURNAL PROMPTS ● ❬ ❬ ❬

- What does the word *dedication* mean to you? What does it mean to be dedicated to something? What are you dedicated to? A cause? A person or people? Maybe an organisation? Is dedication permanent? Have you been dedicated to something in the past, then had that dedication end or change? What did that look like?

- Why do you think some witches dedicate themselves to a deity or deities? What do you think would be the advantages in terms of personal practice? The challenges? Why does dedication to a deity even matter? *Does* it matter?

Further Reading

The Horned God of the Witches by Jason Mankey

Queen of All Witcheries: A Biography of the Goddess by Jack Chanek

To Walk a Pagan Path: Practical Spirituality for Every Day by Alaric Albertsson

Weave the Liminal: Living Modern Traditional Witchcraft by Laura Tempest Zakroff (especially chapter 5)

Wicca: A Comprehensive Guide to the Old Religion in the Modern World by Vivianne Crowley (especially chapters 8–10)

"How Do I Get in Touch or Communicate with a God or Daimon?" by River Enodian

"What Is Theology?" by Yvonne Aburrow

"Why Worship" by Thorn Mooney

CHAPTER 7
The Elements

If you've been reading about or practising modern witchcraft for any amount of time, you will have come across the elements of earth, air, fire, water, and—sometimes, depending on your tradition—spirit. You might acknowledge them as you cast a circle or prepare sacred space, both of which I will discuss in chapter 9. You may also decide to include representations of the elements on your altar.

Why Four Elements?

The idea of four (sometimes five) elements being the essential "building blocks" for all things in the natural world was a widely held belief in many ancient cultures; there were similar lists of elements in ancient Babylonia, Greece, Persia, Japan, and India, to name a few. The ancient Chinese system Wu Xing—a shortened form of *wǔ zhǒng liúxíng zhī qì* ("the five types of chi, or energy force, dominating at different times")—had wood listed as a fifth element.[78]

For centuries these concepts were considered mostly in philosophical terms. In addition to being used to explain or analyse naturally occurring things, the elements were used to explain cosmological and mythological events. It wasn't until the rise of science and scientific study that this theory began to be studied more closely, and many more elements were verified and classified along the way.

78. Zai, *Taoism and Science*, 133.

But what does any of this have to do with witchcraft, and how did the elements get into our rituals and Books of Shadows and onto our altars? The answer lies partly in European grimoires and grimoire traditions.

Alchemy and the Four Elements

Alchemy is a school of thought and a proto-scientific tradition that was practised across Europe, Asia, and Africa for centuries. Its practitioners sought to condense, purify, transform, and perfect certain materials. Some practitioners saw alchemy as fundamentally spiritual and philosophical; one of the primary sources for alchemical theory was work attributed to the ancient Greek figure Hermes Trismegistus. Many are also sacred texts of Hermeticism: an esoteric tradition that influenced some ceremonial magic orders, fraternal orders such as Rosicrucianism and Freemasonry, traditional Wicca, and, in turn, some of the eclectic witchcrafts and paganisms that are practised today.

AIR   FIRE

WATER   EARTH

Element symbols

Alchemists distinguished between the four elements based on their "qualities": the hot, the cold, the moist/fluid, and the dry. Each element was identified with a different combination of two qualities. As opposites, hot/cold and fluid/dry could not be coupled together. The four combinations of qualities that are possible were applied to the four elements: water with cold and fluid, earth with cold and dry, air with hot and fluid, and fire with hot and dry. In each element, one quality dominates the other: dryness in earth, coldness in water, fluidity in air, and heat in fire.[79]

In their notes and writing, many alchemists used symbols to represent different elements, ingredients, and processes. This was less about being mysterious and confounding outsiders than some people think—in most cases, it was merely a form of shorthand.[80]

The Four Elements

The four elements are considered among the easiest things to work magic with because of their immediate and concrete presence in the world. We can see and feel and experience very literal representations of them all around us: the wind between our fingers as we drive with the windows down on a sunny day; the cosy, flickering flame of a candle; the choppy waves of the ocean or the glass-flat surface of a lake on a warm, still night; or the tender but vibrant green of a new shoot growing from a seed.

Air

Air is all around us and keeps us alive with every breath we take. It is an element of the dawn, the east, and of the intellect. The element of air encourages us to step back and see the bigger picture, as a bird circling overhead might. In taking in a wider view of a situation, you are improving your relationship with this element and seeing yourself as a small moving part in something much bigger.

BEGINNINGS

Air often brings about beginnings, like the fresh breezes that signal spring is on the way. We often take a deep, sharp breath of air before we embark on a new journey.

79. Holmyard, *Alchemy*, 27–28.
80. Holmyard, *Alchemy*, 247.

FREEDOM AND LOGIC

Air can represent freedom, like that of a bird that glides on the air currents. By disentangling ourselves from bias and viewing the "big picture," we can exercise discernment, logic, and analytical skills. We can approach an issue with the wisdom of experience.

INSPIRATION

The meaning of the word *inspiration* in its literal sense means to breathe in. Someone who is inspired has ideas moving around in their mind, and movement is a physical quality of air. The power of wind can be anything from a light breeze to a howling, dangerous windstorm.

KNOWLEDGE, INTELLECT, THE POWER OF THOUGHT

With knowledge comes communication, and with communication, we can share that knowledge, often by speaking words or sending messages, by singing or by making music—all of which travel through air to be received and interpreted. Knowledge is also required to develop skills, and to learn.

EXERCISE
The Element of Air

Spend some time thinking and reflecting upon your relationship with the element of air within yourself, in your interactions with others, and in the world around you.

Are you able to step back and look at the big picture of a situation without bias? When was a time that you did that successfully?

What does freedom mean to you? What are you free to do? In what areas of your life are you not free?

When did you last watch a sunrise? What was that like? What memories do you have of sunrises?

Look into the elevation of the land around you. You can do this with a quick internet search. What's the highest natural point that is nearby? Go there when you can, then reflect on this element again. What do you notice?

Fire

The element of fire is sometimes associated with the direction of south and the noonday sun. Fire is especially unique in that it is the only one of the four elements that can be created: it can come from lighting a match, rubbing some sticks together, or even flicking a switch on a heater or furnace. So too is it the only element that can be destroyed by the other three: you can pour water over a blaze, heap earth over a campfire, or blow out a candle.

Within us, the element of fire is our energy and our enthusiasm and determination, often symbolised by an athame or ritual knife. To have a good relationship with this element is to really understand your wants, and to know what you need to do to obtain them.

CREATION, CHANGE, AND ENERGY

Fire is sometimes called the living element, probably because of its ever-changing, spontaneous nature: flames can dance and flicker, rage up or die. Fire can be both creative and destructive, as we are all too aware in the physical world. In this same way, it represents our will and our passions: If controlled, they can be creative and constructive, and we devise and do all kinds of wonderful things. But if we let our passion and will get out of control, they can cause total devastation and destruction.

ILLUMINATION AND SEEING

With the light of fire, we can see our paths more clearly, which can keep us from getting stuck or losing our way on journeys of transformation and change. Willpower keeps us walking these paths without giving up.

TRANSFORMATION

Even though it is not obviously present in the physical world, fire causes some of the most noticeable and drastic changes. The fire of the furnace changes or destroys things beyond recognition. The blacksmith's forge is key in shaping what seemed unbendable into something malleable, ready to be transformed into something new.

EXERCISE
The Element of Fire

Consider your relationship with the element of fire within yourself, in your interactions with others, and in the world around you.

When was the last time you really yearned for something? For someone? What did you do about these feelings? Did you act on them?

Can you think of a time when your heightened emotions caused damage of some kind? Have you worked on yourself since then? How?

Apart from the obvious answers of providing enough light and heat to sustain life, how does the sun influence the land around you? Is your area prone to drought? To bushfire? Do you have heat waves? How does the way the sun impacts the land and its creatures relate to the element of fire and its correspondences?

Water

Water is where life on this planet began, and it sustains life. It is sometimes associated with the direction of west and with dusk and endings. In the physical world, it exists in solid, liquid, and gaseous forms and has the ability to change between these states. It is all around us in nature, and it makes up most of our physical body.

Your relationship with water as an element has to do with your emotions, your feelings, your reactions, your dreams, and your psychic ability.

EBBING AND FLOWING

The seas on this planet move in tides, and so do our own lives. As humans, we need to dare to control our emotions and not let them dictate our lives (or the lives of those around us) like a flood or a tidal wave. We also need to challenge ourselves and push boundaries in our learning.

DEATH, JOURNEYS, AND REBIRTH

Sometimes water can represent dying. It may initiate the journey out of the physical world and into the unknown.

ENERGY

Water can represent feelings of serenity, as in the still surface of a large body of water. It can also represent love and sexual energy, which are as varied and as unpredictable as an ocean on any given day.

TRANSPORT, TRAVEL, AND DREAMS

Just like air, water can transport things and bring mysteries from far away. The sense of taste is associated with water, as it helps us know what we want. Water is also associated with dreams, messages transported to us from our unconscious mind.

EXERCISE
The Element of Water

Takes some time to think about your relationship with the element of water within yourself, in your interactions with others, and in the world around you.

How well do you regulate your emotions? What do you do to handle stress? What does your body need when it is tired? Energised? Worried? Grieving? In love?

Do you consider yourself "psychic" in any way? Why or why not? How do you know if someone is psychic, anyway?

How far away is the nearest large and publicly accessible body of water from you? Spend some time visualising its every detail before your next visit.

Earth

It is from earth that we get the solidity and "realness" of our physical world. This element is sometimes associated with the direction of north and with midnight and stillness. As the most solid of the elements, earth is associated with qualities such as resilience, patience, and tolerance. It's also associated with sensuality and the pleasures of physical activity.

As a magical practitioner, the element of earth relates to your physical body. Having a good relationship with earth means knowing your body—its needs and its limitations—and treating it as sacred.

Nurturing, Life-Giving

It is from earth that we get the food that sustains us and the materials that build shelter. Creatures eat, work, make love, and give birth—all while the earth remains constant and steadfast in its support.

Fruitfulness

The bounties and boons brought in at harvest—both physical harvests of fruit, grain, or other produce and the less-tangible harvests of creative endeavours—are attributed to the fertility of the earth.

Silence and Stillness

The element of earth has an enduring stillness and calm, which is what some practitioners are seeking to emulate when they meditate. Because earth is so quiet and still, it is seen as being nonjudgmental in nature.

Stubbornness and Distance

In many ways earth is the least malleable of the elements, and the qualities of stubbornness, immovability, and even stagnation are related to this element.

EXERCISE
The Element of Earth

Think on your relationship with the element of earth within yourself, in your interactions with others, and in the world around you.

When is your physical body at its best? What can it do well?

What is your favourite natural place? What makes it so special? Try to use some of the vocabulary and skills you've learned so far to describe its energy.

Using the internet, explore how the land you live on was first formed. How old is the ground you are living on? How has it changed over time? How might it change in the future?

Working with the Elements

Working effective magic with the elements has a lot to do with how well you understand them, both in the physical world and within yourself, and how those things work together.

The elements are all around us in the natural world: the earth gives form to the land and everything on it, we breathe air and it blows as wind, the light and warmth from fire sustains life, water falls as rain and flows into our rivers and oceans, and so on. Meditating or even just spending time in different natural places helps strengthen your relationship with different elements and your understanding of their qualities.

The Elements in a Magic Circle

The elements are usually used as part of the casting of a circle. In Wicca, sacred space is purified by blessing and consecrating salt (earth) and water on the altar and then sprinkling it around the space. Many Wiccans also include other techniques for purifying the space, borrowed from other traditions: censing the space with purifying incense or censing sticks, shaking a rattle, or beating a drum.[81]

Many traditions have representations of the elements on their altar and/or mention them in the circle cast itself. Fire might be represented by the literal flame of a candle, water by a vessel of water, earth by salt or dirt, and air by incense smoke.

Once a Wiccan magic circle has been cast, many practitioners will then "call the quarters," inviting the elemental powers of the four cardinal directions, sometimes called the guardians, the watchtowers, the quarters, the elements, and so on. These are spirits or entities that are invited to the circle—or to stand watch just outside the circle—to witness and guard the circle's boundary, and to lend their power to the circle as it contains the energy raised within the ritual.

When we invoke elemental guardians, we are calling on the elemental energies of the four elements and inviting each one, along with their energy and qualities, to join us in circle. These beings are not always associated with the elements directly. For example, sometimes the four winds are called upon at the four directions.[82]

81. D'Este and Rankine, *Circle of Fire*, 67.
82. D'Este and Rankine, *Circle of Fire*, 74.

It's useful to visualise elemental guardians while performing invocations in order to build on the strength of your call. When the rite is over and you're closing the circle, it's important to say farewell to the elemental guardians, often going in the reverse order that you invoked them, as if retracing your steps. As you speak, see the elemental guardian leaving and returning to their realm, taking any energy or qualities that they brought when summoned.

Elemental Pentagrams

The elements can be attributed to the points of the pentagram. Starting with spirit at the top, move clockwise to water, fire, earth, and air. Some practitioners use the pentagram points when invoking and dismissing the elemental guardians, treating them as energetic placeholders or "keys" to attract certain elemental energy.

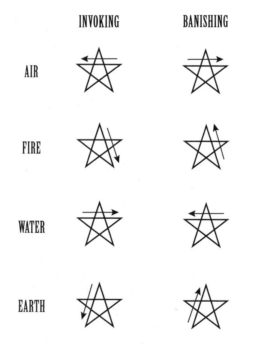

Elemental Invoking and Banishing Pentagrams

When they're drawn, often during the casting of a circle or the setting up of ritual space, they are called *invoking pentagrams*. *Banishing pentagrams* are used to help close a circle or bring down ritual space.

EXERCISE
Elemental Pentagrams

Learn and practise the elemental pentagrams. Using your finger, draw them in the air in front of you. They should be quite large—your arm should be fully extended as you reach each point of the pentacle.

Use what you've learned about energy sensing to examine the energy and feelings you experience—if any—when you perform these gestures.

))) ● JOURNAL PROMPTS ● (((

• What do you consider the benefits of working with the elements in witchcraft?

• What would you say are the main correspondences for each element? Think about colours, herbs, scents, and other motifs.

Further Reading

Air Magic by Astrea Taylor

Earth Magic by Dodie Graham McKay

Fire Magic by Josephine Winter

The Four Elements of the Wise by Ivo Dominguez Jr.

Water Magic by Lilith Dorsey

"My Quest to Find the Elemental Guardians of the Watchtowers" by Heron Michelle

"Seekers and Guides: An Elemental Journey" by Sable Aradia

PART III
The Heart

Dancing to the beat of your most secret drum. Listening to your guts, your blood, and your bones. Bending, breaking, bonding. Getting personal with magic bigger than people. Living as a lover of life. This is the witchcraft of the heart.

CHAPTER 8
Tools, Props, and Accoutrements

Different witches use different tools for different purposes, but it's important to remember that not all witches use tools. Some traditions of witchcraft are more specific about their use than others, and practitioners have their own preferences too.

While many of the tools explored in this chapter can be purchased, keep in mind that being a witch doesn't necessarily mean going out and spending lots of money on shiny things. Nor is there a requirement that a witch own or use any tools whatsoever—focus on the work, and don't get too caught up in the accessories and "stuff" side of things.

The Altar

Tool? Prop? Ritual furniture? Regardless, altars are important for many witches and magical practitioners. I discussed a devotional or deity altar in chapter 6, but altar can also be any elevated place or structure at which religious or magical rites are performed.

Altars have been used in traditional forms of religion and in the practice of ceremonial magic for a long time. Most cultures that have or had some form of religious or ceremonial practice throughout history had altars. In short, it is a ceremonial workspace or workbench, and these would have been a practical necessity for anyone doing work with any kinds of tools, props, or offerings.

In traditional Wicca and many forms of witchcraft, the altar is often where the working tools of the witch and any images/likenesses of deities are displayed and readily accessible.

Your altar could be as elaborate as a purpose-built cabinet with everything that opens and shuts, as simple as a few inches of spare space on a shelf, or anything in between. Play around and find what works for you.

The Athame, Dagger, and Sword

Ritual knives like daggers and athames might look scary, but they're not generally used for cutting (or stabbing!) anything physical. Instead, daggers and athames are usually used for enforcing the will of the wielder in ritual, including directing energy and marking out the borders of the magic circle or other sacred space.

The word *athame* (and no, I am not going to wade into the long-standing debate over how it should be pronounced) is a relatively new one, first used in 1949 to describe a knife—usually double-edged with a crossguard, handle, and pommel—used for magical purposes.[83]

If you're buying an athame, keep in mind that it's considered good practice not to haggle over the price of working tools. If you know metalworkers or blacksmiths, you could have a go at forging your own; you could even carve one from a wood that is significant to you or your tradition.

Some folks like to consecrate their athames before use. There is no set way to do this. You might try leaving it out in a safe place where it can sit in the moonlight, or you could drive it gently into the earth.[84]

In ritual, swords are used for similar purposes to the athame, depending on the flavour of witchcraft or magic being practised. Many modern eclectic witches don't tend to bother with one or make do with a handmade staff instead. Some traditions of witchcraft consider the sword to be the symbol of the High Priest, able to be worn by the High Priestess if he is absent.[85]

Always check out local laws about owning and possessing edged weapons before you try to procure one, and avoid carrying athames or other blades

83. Mankey, *The Witch's Athame*.

84. There are some great athame consecrations out there. I like the ones in *The Witch's Athame* by Jason Mankey.

85. Tuan, "The Working Tools of the Witch," 42–44.

in public or using them in rituals held in public places. Even this far into the twenty-first century, non-Pagan folks aren't always accepting or accommodating—not to mention that the sight of anyone wielding a blade in public can be cause for alarm. In many places, local laws have hefty fines if you're caught with a weapon, ceremonial or otherwise.

The Censer

A censer is a container in which incense is burnt for religious or ritual occasions. Smoke from the censer, thurible, or incense burner is used to purify practitioners and the space they work in. It is also used to represent the element of air on altars and in some rituals.

There are many kinds of burner available, but most are ornate metal or fireproof containers designed to hold charcoal discs and burning incense. Some hang from chains, much like the thuribles you may have seen in Catholic churches. Others are freestanding.

The Cords

Many witches and covens have a set of ritual cords, used in cord magic (spells that bind negative influences with knots or braids, for example) initiations and other workings. Cords are often made of silk and are traditionally nine feet long. They have different symbolic applications depending on their colours. For example, a witch might be given a specific-coloured cord when they are first initiated or attain a specific degree. Certain colours of cords may be worn around the waist for different occasions. For example, a yellow or orange cord might be worn for solstices and equinoxes, a green cord for Beltane, and a brown cord for Lammas.

Cords are available from most fabric shops in a variety of colours, materials, and thicknesses. They're also relatively easy to make yourself, either with a purpose-made cord winding tool or with a friend who has strong fingers and a lot of patience.

The Chalice

Often associated with the element of water, emotion, and healing, ritual cups or chalices are a cup used in honouring and toasting deities and in some coven-based ceremonies. They are also sometimes used in spellwork. In ritual, they hold liquid—like water or wine—that is offered and drunk in the name of the gods. Some practitioners have two cups on their altar: a cup of water to represent its elemental form and used to consecrate the circle, and a cup of wine/drink for offerings, blessings, and libations.

Holy cups and chalices have featured in myth and legend for centuries. In some traditional witchcraft rituals, the cup and athame are sometimes used to symbolise the coming together of male and female energy. As a holder of life force, they often represent reproduction or female sexuality.

Cups can be made of any food-safe material. Ceramic, glass, wood, brass, and stainless steel are all popular choices. Additionally, most people prefer to use a stemmed cup.

The Pentacle

A pentacle is a flat disc with a pentagram (a five-pointed star) carved into it. Pentacles have their origins in ceremonial magic and are usually made of some kind of metal or wood. As they are commonly associated with the element of earth, some people opt for pentacles made of clay, stone, beeswax, or even a slice of geode. You can buy or make wooden pentacles that have been created with a woodburning tool. Some traditions stipulate what material should be used or other symbols that should be included along with the star.

In rituals and spellwork, the pentacle is often associated with consecration and/or is the centrepiece of the altar. Items are sometimes placed on the pentacle to energetically charge or bless them. If you are making your own pentacle, remember it needs to be large enough for you to set things on; it should be no smaller than a saucer for this reason.

The Wand

Wands have been associated with magic and ceremony since ancient times. Some practitioners prefer to associate the wand with the element of air and the creative abilities of the human mind. Others associate them with the element of fire because of the relationship between fire and wood, or to the fragments we know about tree worship in ancient Europe.

While the dagger commands, the wand creates. This is often why it is a wand and not a blade that is used to consecrate a new working tool, and it's also why a blade rather than a wand would be used for banishing. Wands are also sometimes used to evoke gods and goddesses, bestow blessings, charge objects, and so on. They are also the key tool featured in sabbat rituals in certain traditions of witchcraft.

There are many different types of wands, and some witches have more than one for this reason: plain wooden wands, phallic wands, staves, walking sticks, solar wands, lunar wands, seasonal wands, and more.

Wands are one of the easiest of the working tools to create yourself. Many traditional instructions for wand-making give the old measurement of one cubit: the length from the fingertips to the elbow. The wood from a hazel or other nut-bearing tree is often suggested as suitable material.[86]

Again, there are no rules about which wood you must choose. Research different types of wood and their magical associations first, but if there is a specific tree that is special to you, go for it. Some people like to ask a tree for permission before they cut or break any branches. This can look however you like: you might sit with the tree for a while to get a feel for it and the place it grows.

Once you've cut wood from a tree, strip the bark from it, oil it with linseed or olive oil, and leave it for a few days before you try to shape it further or carve any symbols or details into it. In the last few decades, it's become more and more trendy to have crystals and other bits and pieces glued onto one's wand. This is completely optional; your wand(s) can be as simple or as intricate as you'd like.

Other Tools You Might Come Across

So far, I've listed some of the most commonly used tools in witchcraft, but there are plenty of other props and accoutrements that some folks like to use. Remember that there is no expectation that you use any of these.

Altar Cloths

Decorative or functional cloths that cover the altar. Some folks like to use coloured cloths at different times of year or for ritual purposes. Most of my altar cloths are interesting tablecloths I've found in secondhand shops.

86. Rankine and d'Este, *Practical Elemental Magick*, 89.

Bell

Some witches have a bell amongst their working tools. This is usually a small handbell made of brass or silver. Depending on the tradition of witchcraft being practised, bells can be used for opening/closing rituals, for clearing energy, in healing rites, or for rituals concerning certain deities.

Boline

Some witches keep a knife, separate to their athame, that is used for mundane cutting in ritual: chopping up herbs, cutting cords, taking cuttings from plants, etc. Some witchcraft texts and traditions refer to this as a *boline* or *bolline*.

These knives sometimes have a white handle and/or a curved blade. White is thought to reflect energy, while the black handle of an athame is thought to absorb it. It's unclear when the name "boline" was first used to describe these knives, but we know it comes to us from early grimoires. In his *Book of Ceremonial Magic*, published in 1911, Arthur Edward Waite references a number of early works on magic that mention the "bolline" or sickle.[87]

Broom

The broom or besom is a near universal symbol of the witch in literature, art, and popular culture. Brooms are very easy to make, and they range in complexity from simple branches to bespoke works of art and everything in between. Ritually, brooms are used in some ceremonies such as handfastings (weddings) and for "sweeping" the ritual space of unwanted or negative energies.

Cauldron

Like the broom, the cauldron is a universal witch symbol. The cauldron is usually a metal pot with a handle, although the word is also sometimes used to describe clay or stone pots used in ritual. Cauldrons can be used for scrying, to heat magical brews, or even to make food or tea. For some, the cauldron even doubles as a fireproof container for candles or other sacred flames.

Some traditions and practitioners consider the cauldron a symbol of the Goddess and of feminine energy. Others relate it to inspiration, creativity,

87. Waite, *The Book of Ceremonial Magic*, chap. 2.

power, and rebirth, as in the stories of the Welsh goddess Cerridwen. It's generally associated with the element of water.[88]

Sistrum

A sistrum is a metal or wooden rattle used in ritual. In ancient Egypt, worshippers of Isis used metal sistra as part of their devotional practice. Similar instruments were also used by the Aztecs and the Romans.[89] There are contemporary practitioners who incorporate the use of sistra in their work, especially some (but not all) folks who work with or venerate Kemetic—ancient Egyptian—deities and spirits.

Stang

A stang is a forked staff made of ash or another wood. In some traditions, stangs are used to represent the Horned God in his various forms. The prongs of a stang are sometimes tipped with iron. Stangs can be decorated seasonally, depending on the celebration or time of year.

Witchy Supplies

If you practise witchcraft regularly, you'll soon realise that there are some "consumables" that you need to keep stock of. In addition to your usual ritual work, as you go deeper down the witchcraft rabbit hole, you'll find it helps to check in on these from time to time. There's nothing worse than setting up for that all-important witchy thing and realising you're out of one of the essentials.

Candles

Candles feature in the ceremonies of religions across the world, including most Pagan and witchcraft traditions. We use candles on our altars to signify fire, the sun, or deity; to mark the quarters; in remembrance; and in magical workings.

88. Drury, *The Watkins Dictionary of Magic*, 52.
89. Drury, *The Watkins Dictionary of Magic*, 263.

Charcoal Discs

Charcoal discs are needed if you plan to burn loose incense in a censer. You can buy these from new age stores, tobacconists, and some Middle Eastern grocery stores (as they are also used in hookah pipes). Always burn charcoal discs in a heatproof container, maybe with some sand, gravel, or scrunched tinfoil at the bottom to increase airflow. To light a disc, hold it in a flame with a pair of tongs or tweezers and wait until you see sparks travelling across the surface. Once it's lit and in place, you can sprinkle a pinch of loose incense on top to burn it.

Incense

Loose/raw incense smells nicer and is often less padded with toxic chemicals than stick or cone incense. Plus, if you use loose incense, you can experiment and make your own blends to burn on a censer, all fancy-like.

Jars

Witches hoard jars. Hang on to lidded food jars when you're done with them and use them to store your witchy goodies, if you have the space. My favourites are salsa jars because they're squat and roomy and hard to knock over.

Ritual Clothing

What you wear when you're doing magic could be an elaborate costume complete with funny hat. It could be a plain black robe. It could even be nothing at all. Comfort and practicality are key, as well as purpose. You will find that some occasions might call for a slight change of wardrobe.

Jewellery

In many traditions, it is customary for priestesses to wear a necklace of some kind in ritual. In traditional Wicca, this is sometimes a necklace of amber and jet beads. Other common choices include necklaces with pentacles, moons, symbols of specific deities, or even just a necklace that is special to the wearer in some way. Some witches wear ritual bracelets, circlets, crowns, or other headwear as well. And in some traditions, witches wear a garter on their leg as a symbol of rank and for ritual purposes.

Robes

Some witches work in everyday clothing that is comfortable. Some work in robes. These are usually black, but different groups and individuals have their own preferences. If you're buying or making a robe, go for natural fibres where you can. Synthetic materials are often more flammable and pose a risk around candles and fire. So too do long, dangly sleeves.

Witches who often work outdoors may have thinner linen robes for summer and thicker wool robes and/or a cloak for colder months. Ritual gumboots are not unheard of, either.

If you're into sewing, there are robe patterns in many witchy books, but some of the best are sold commercially as patterns for costumes for biblical plays: McCall's 5568 or Simplicity 8275, to name a few.

Skyclad

Some practitioners work *skyclad*, or practise ritual nudity, at times. This is a legitimate practice with real significance, but it's only practised in certain situations. Nobody can insist you go skyclad if you don't feel comfortable, and working skyclad is not an invitation for sexual activity of any kind. It is also illegal to work skyclad with those who are under the age of eighteen.

You Are Such a Tool

Don't take this the wrong way, but you really are a tool. Your physical body is the most constant thing you are bringing into ritual. It is the most important magical tool you possess, and it probably deserves more credit than it gets for your magical experiences thus far.

I meant it when I said that witchcraft isn't about stuff. Tools, incense, and costumes are all well and good, but they should be the window dressing to your skills, not a distraction from them. A clever witch should, in a pinch, be able to make do with just themselves.

EXERCISE
Your Tools

Challenge yourself to procure one of the tools mentioned in this chapter without having to buy it new. (Note: this is not permission to shoplift!) This could be as simple as making a pentacle from wax or painting one on a plate. You could go to a secondhand shop and look for a cheap but pretty bowl for libations. If crafts other than witchcraft are your thing, you could even have a go at something more elaborate, like carving a wand or making your own robe.

))) ● JOURNAL PROMPTS ● (((

• Which of the tools mentioned in this chapter can you see yourself using the most? Which have you already had experience with? Were there any you hadn't thought of before?

• Think about your ideal witchcraft. What would you wear at your ideal ritual? Why?

• What would be the benefits and drawbacks of going skyclad?

Further Reading

Elements of Ritual Magic by Marian Green (especially chapter 4)

Witchcraft on a Shoestring: Practicing the Craft without Breaking Your Budget by Deborah Blake

The Witch's Wand: The Craft, Lore & Magick of Wands & Staffs by Alferian Gwydion MacLir

"I Don't Care Where You Get Your Tools: You Do You, Boo" by Patti Wigington

CHAPTER 9
The Magic Circle

In myth and story the world over, circles are a symbol of totality and wholeness. While not all witches use them, in Western magic—including many traditions of witchcraft—magic circles are an important part of ritual, magical, and ceremonial workings.

In ceremonial magic, a magic circle is often a physical circle, inscribed on the floor of a temple for magical ceremonial purposes. Practitioners perform various rituals to "activate" the circle, or render it sacred. This is where modern witchcraft gets most of what we do with regards to magic circles, with maybe a sprinkle of pop culture influence on the side.

In modern witchcraft, a magic circle might be represented by a physical circle drawn or marked out on the ground, or it might not. Magic circles that are visualised can be just as strong as those that are drawn. Circles are often set up at the beginning of a working, and usually (but not always) closed or dismissed when the work is done. They serve a number of purposes, which we'll look at throughout this chapter.

What Are Magic Circles Used For?

While circles aren't always required or necessary for every ritual, witches, occultists, and other magic practitioners use circles for a number of reasons.

When cast, the space within a magic circle is considered to be a time outside of time, a place outside of regular places. When we cast a circle, we are delineating a special space to work or worship. Work done within a magic circle is considered more powerful, and generally more effective, because the parameters of the space are set by the practitioners: they create and manage the space and consciously set it aside from the everyday world. Circles are also thought to make interactions with entities such as deity, ancestors, and spirits easier.

Circles also act as a container for the energy that the practitioner raises. Power raised in a properly cast circle remains there until the practitioners use it in some way, such as putting into a specific spell/working, sending it to a person, or sending it into an object. Circles also help amplify energy (some practitioners like to visualise the circle doubling in on itself and growing), which gives workings and rituals more oomph.

A circle is a space created intentionally separate from the world around you, made up of the building blocks of that world. It is sacred space, both for ourselves and for our work. Whatever else might be going on in our lives or in our physical vicinity, this space is sacred, it is special, and it is ours to be shared only with the people and entities we choose.

Practise circle casting for a while and you will notice that your mind tends to kick into "ritual mode" once that space is set up. A circle reminds us of the work at hand, and it helps us focus on that work.

The magic circle can be seen as a symbol for one or several things, such as:

- A place between worlds, where we can work ritual closer to our gods.
- Continuity; cycles; birth, life, death, and rebirth; an entire day, an entire season, the movement of the seasons; the Wheel of the Year.
- Celestial bodies, especially the moon or sun.
- Creation and fertility.
- Unity, both of a group/coven working together and of that group's relationship with the gods.
- Flawlessness and perfection, as it has no beginning and no end, with no corners or shadowy spots that energy can build up or get stuck.

Magic circles protect the occupants from unwelcome entities and energies, just as they do in ceremonial magic. The ceremonial magic systems from which Wicca is descended often involved protecting the practitioners from harmful entities while they worked. One remnant from these older systems is that in Wiccan-based witchcraft, everyone and everything that comes into your circle—deities, elementals, spirits, ancestors, guardians, etc.—can only do so if they're invited in.

Getting Ready to Cast a Circle

Casting a circle might be the first magical act you attempt. There are many different ways to go about this. Simpler ways might only take a minute or two; some traditional ceremonial circles take longer. As a beginner, experiment with multiple circle casts that interest you and record the results in your Book of Shadows or magical journal. I recommend starting with the simple circle presented in this chapter. Do not try to simplify or condense circle casts until you know them and their significance by heart. Reading back over notes you take will help you determine what works best for you.

During a circle cast, acknowledgement is usually made to the four cardinal directions, also called the quarters. Each direction has an element associated with it, so one way to do this is by having a symbol or physical representation of the element for your circle. (Refer back to chapter 7 for more information about the elements.) Another way to call the quarters is by inviting and welcoming specific protective beings, spirits, or forces: archangels, lords/ladies, elemental forces, ancestors, etc. (These beings will then need to be thanked and farewelled as part of closing the circle later on.) Sacred objects may be set out, candles may be lit, or god names may be used to assist in the completion of the circle. This will protect the circle from harm and lend power to workings.

When you stand in a well-cast circle, you will feel noticeably different than how you felt, standing in the same place, before it was cast. Many people feel sensations in circle: you might feel a tingle of excitement, be more relaxed and at ease, or feel slightly warmer. Or you might just come to a knowing that what you are doing is important or special.

Visualisation is what differentiates casting a circle from standing around and making weird gestures. Don't get me wrong—circle casting can involve both of these things. But it is the intention and energy we put into it that makes circle casting work, and for that, we must be able to visualise. If you've had a go at some of the exercises in this book, you should be in good stead to have a go at setting up your own sacred circle.

Deosil and Widdershins

In modern witchcraft books, *deosil* and *widdershins* are terms for moving clockwise or counterclockwise as you cast and work in your circle. *Deosil* is an interpretation of similarly spelled words in Gaelic, meaning "toward the south" or "toward the right." It's also related to *deas*, which means "right" or right-hand."[90] *Widdershins* is a Scottish word that first appeared in written text around 1500, meaning "contrary to the course of the sun or a clock." At the time, it was considered an unlucky direction. It's thought to come from the Middle Low German *weddersinnes*, "against the way," from *widersinnen*, "to go against."[91]

Some witchy and magical books hold that deosil is the act of moving in the same direction as the sun and that widdershins is the opposite way of the sun. This thinking works okay if you're in the Northern Hemisphere. Here in the Southern Hemisphere, the sun appears to—*appears to*—move the other way. Look toward the sun at noon in Melbourne and it will seem to move to your left, while in London at noon it will seem to move to your right. Both directions are west, though.

When deosil is reduced to "the direction of the sun," it's really only applicable to witches in the Northern Hemisphere. As a Southern Hemisphere person who is fed up with having to "translate" Northern Hemisphere–specific language in my witch books, I'm going to use the terms *clockwise* and *counterclockwise* to save confusion.

Whether you cast your circle moving clockwise or counterclockwise is up to you. Many Northern Hemisphere practitioners prefer to do so clockwise, but like everything else here, there is no hard-and-fast rule. Some Southern Hemisphere practitioners cast counterclockwise—the way the sun is perceived to move—and some don't. What's important is that you find a way that works for you, figure out *why* it works for you, and use it consistently.

90. *Online Etymology Dictionary*, s.v. "deasil (*adj.*)," updated July 4, 2018, https://www.etymonline.com/word/deasil.

91. *Online Etymology Dictionary*, s.v. "widdershins (*adv.*)," updated April 2, 2014, https://www.etymonline.com/word/widdershins.

Working with the Elements

Calling on or having representations of the elements—earth, air, fire, and water—gives your circle balance and power. As I discussed in chapter 7, the four elements are considered the building blocks of everything else in the universe, magically speaking.

There are many ways to associate elements with the cardinal points. Try a few and journal about your findings. Here are two popular ways to associate elements with the cardinal points.

CASTING CLOCKWISE

> East: Air
>
> South: Fire
>
> West: Water
>
> North: Earth

CASTING COUNTERCLOCKWISE

> East: Air
>
> North: Fire
>
> West: Water
>
> South: Earth

Quarter Calls, Chants, and Rhymes

Quarter calls are usually voiced aloud, whether you are calling to the elements or the cardinal directions or both. Many of them rhyme, as they are easier to remember and flow well when spoken, but this isn't mandatory. Get accustomed to using and writing different types of calls.

Here is a sample circle call to the four elements, written for a full moon ritual during the middle of winter. It includes a circle cast, a statement of intention, quarter calls, and an invitation to the Lady of Night and the Lord of Winter. I will talk more about some of these pieces in the next chapter.

1. Walk the perimeter of the space you wish to use, or spin slowly while pointing out the perimeter, imagining the circle being drawn around you in silver light. Say:

I cast this circle that it be a place between the worlds, where only love may enter and leave. In this space, I work, my will undisturbed. In this space, I sit in the presence of the Gods and my true will. So mote it be.

2. Once you have cast a circle or delineated your sacred space in some way, walk its perimeter with your athame, wand, or finger, saying:

   The night is dark, the world it stills,
   The land at rest under frost-covered hills
   Waiting for spring, I turn within,
   To inner realms, 'tis time to begin.
   I create sacred space with this circle of light in the darkness.

3. Walk to the edge of the circle in each direction, respectively, as you speak the following:

   Hail, spirits of east, of frosty air and shrouds of fog. Your blanket of white brings a quiet stillness to the world. Be with me on this night.

   Hail, spirits of north, of fire warm and inviting. Keep alive the spark of life that sleeps within. Be with me on this night.

   Hail, spirits of west, of cold, clear water. You have brought life and new ideas as you returned to our rivers and lakes. Be with me on this night.

   Hail, spirits of south, of earth wrapped in slumber. Below winter's chill you rest and wait for the time of awakening. Be with me on this night.

4. If you have a candle for the Lord of Winter, light it now. Say:

   Hail, Lord of Winter, harsh, challenging, and hidden. Your storms and frosts bring both beauty and challenges. Be with me on this night.

5. If you have a candle for the Lady of Night, light it now. Say:

   Hail, Lady of Night, of the star-speckled heavens and crisp, cold darkness. Your light is ever changing but always with me. Be with me on this night.

Notice that this circle casting began in the east. Many witches start there, but not all do. A circle is a sacred space of your own creation, and as such, you can cast it in whatever way—and beginning at whichever point—you'd like. East is seen as a direction of beginnings, of sunrises, of air, good tidings and fresh starts, which makes it a logical place to begin creating your space. Try it and see if it works for you.

Once the circle is cast, you are ready to get on with the main part of your ritual or working. In the example ritual, this circle is cast and all deities/spirits have been welcomed, so the practitioner(s) would go on to perform a ritual to celebrate the midwinter solstice.

Closing the Circle

When you're done with your spellwork, rituals, or celebrations that needed to be done in a magical circle, it's important to close the circle. Closing a circle brings a finality to the work you've been doing and draws a line under it, so to speak. It's also important to disperse any extra energy and dismiss or farewell any spirits/deities that you welcomed at the beginning.

The closing for the provided ritual goes as follows:

1. Stand in front of the altar when addressing the Lord and Lady. For the cardinal directions, walk to the edge of the circle in each direction as you dismiss them. Extinguish the Goddess candle on your altar, if you have one. Say:

    Lady of Night, of energy that moves us with the tides of the moon, thank you for your presence. Hail and farewell.

2. Extinguish the God candle on your altar, if you have one. Say:

    Lord of Winter, of frost and winter winds, thank you for your presence. Hail and farewell.

3. For the cardinal directions, say:

    Spirits of the east, of air that catches our breath in wintry wisps, thank you for your presence on this night. Hail and farewell.

    Spirits of the north, of fire that keeps the icy chill from our bones, thank you for your presence on this night. Hail and farewell.

    Spirits of the west, of icy waters and frost that sparkles like crystal, thank you for your presence on this night. Hail and farewell.

    Spirits of the south, of earth that sleeps until spring calls, thank you for your presence on this night. Hail and farewell.

4. When you are ready, take a deep breath, then let it out. With the tool you used to cast your circle, open it now. Say:

This circle of light in the darkness is open,
But it remains unbroken.
In light, and in darkness, blessed be.

Having this final statement helps to let participants know that the ritual is over, and it sets one final intention of fellowship among each other, encouraging everyone to depart in peace. Saying something like this also helps you visualise the circle finishing, fading, but never breaking.

When closing a circle, some practitioners move in the opposite direction that they cast it, farewelling the quarters in the reverse order to "unwind" the energy. Others move in the same direction and farewell quarters in the order they were welcomed. This is purely a personal preference. I've seen both ways work well.

Using Tools to Cast a Circle

Many witches use tools and other accessories to cast their circle, but these are not mandatory. Here are some common tools used for circle casting, their uses, and some possible alternatives.

Athame/Wand: Some practitioners use an athame or a wand to draw or "cut" the boundary of the circle in the air as they cast. You can also do this with your finger.

Candles: Used to represent/honour deity, or to represent the element of fire. To represent fire without a candle, you could use red/orange/yellow leaves, fabric, or stones, or even charred wood.

Censer: Used to represent the element of air, a censer is an incense burner that is sometimes walked around the circle's boundary or used to cleanse the entire space. You could also do this with a bundle of dried herbs as a censing/smoking stick, a burning stick of incense in a holder, etc. I've also seen this done with a handheld pinwheel/windmill, or a blue or white ribbon on a stick.

Working Indoors

When working indoors, one of the main things to consider is space. Unless you have access to a large, empty room or hall, there will be some things you just can't do indoors—especially if you have more than a few people participating in your circle.

Another consideration is time. Unless you have a dedicated room for ritual, chances are you will need to do a bit of furniture Tetris and vacuuming/sweeping to get ready. This means allowing a bit of extra time before you begin (or before other ritualists arrive, if working in a group).

One of the benefits of working indoors is a safe, familiar space, and this can be a plus if you are new or not sure about practising outside. You also have more control over the temperature and (I hope) biting insects!

Things to Remember When Working in a Circle

Whether you're working in a circle of your own making or joining a ritual run by somebody else, there are a few basic courtesies to keep in mind.

Concentrate and Behave with Reverence and Respect

This doesn't just apply to how you treat yourself and any other humans in your circle. The elements, spirits, and beings you are inviting to your circle are a part of a balanced universe. They are always present. It is *you* who is awakening to their presence, not the other way around.

Remember that you are working in sacred space. While that doesn't necessarily mean you need to be solemn and sombre throughout every ritual, it is important to be present, to be open, and to respect your sacred surroundings. Keep mundane issues out of circle as much as possible and concentrate on the task at hand. If you find yourself getting distracted or losing focus during a working, spend some time re-examining your intentions for that working. Only you are in charge of what you do in circle, and only you will know and be able to address the reasons for it.

Pay Attention to the Direction of Energy

Energy moves either clockwise or counterclockwise in most circles. Unless you're told otherwise, try to walk in the same direction if you move around in the circle once it's cast. People have their reasons for casting either clockwise or counterclockwise, and they're are all okay. What's important is that you move in the same direction consistently.

"Cut" a Doorway

If you're working alone and need to step out of the circle for any reason, it's considered good practice to use your athame or finger to "cut" a doorway in the circle for you to leave and re-enter through. If you're in a group ritual and you aren't sure about the etiquette for that particular circle, discretely ask one of your ritual facilitators to do this for you.

Take Clear Steps to Return to Normal

Once your work is done, always make sure you clean up, clear energy, and return a room or working space to its everyday setting. This will help you clearly delineate the beginning and end of sacred space and time for your working. If you work outdoors, you should restore a space to how you found it, as much as possible.

A Basic Circle Cast

This circle cast requires some visualisation. Use what you've learned from the exercises in this book so far to help you. In this example, you will be moving clockwise during the ritual, but that can easily be adapted to moving counterclockwise if you prefer.

You will need a small white, red, or orange candle (to represent fire), a stick of incense you like (to represent air), a small dish of salt (to represent earth), a small bowl of water (to represent…well, you know). You'll also need matches or a lighter to light your candle and incense as well as holders or fireproof dishes for each. Work on an altar if you have one, or clear a tabletop and put down a cloth to protect it from spills. You'll need to be in a space big enough that you can walk around in, and you'll need enough time to do this without interruption—say, thirty minutes minimum.

1. Make sure the space is clear and free of interruptions, and have a good idea of where your circle should be. It should be big enough to comfortably contain you and your tools, with enough room to walk around. Set up your altar either at the east quarter or in the centre

of the circle, making sure the candle and incense are lit and will stay lit for the duration of the working.

2. Stand or sit at the altar. Ready yourself by taking a few deep breaths. Relax your shoulders and try to quieten the "background fuzz" of the everyday. Some folks like to meditate for a few minutes at this point. Find stillness within yourself, as you did in the early exercises in this book.

3. When you feel ready, stand up and begin to walk clockwise around the boundary of the circle, starting and ending in the east. In this first rotation, you are marking out the physical space of the circle with your footsteps, and in doing so you are drawing a definite line between here (the sacred space) and there (the rest of the world). As you do this, visualise your footprints creating deep impressions in the ground or floor, leaving a light-soaked path around the edge of the circle.

4. At the altar, take up the dish of salt and face east. Hold the dish out, presenting it to the east, then place it on the altar. Touch the salt with the tip of your finger and visualise the same light that soaked your footprints filling the bowl and coating its contents. Say:

I bless you, salt of earth. May you be pure.

5. Take a few good pinches of salt and add them to the dish of water. Stir it with your finger and say:

I exorcise you, water. May you be rid of any impurities that linger.

6. Take up the bowl of salted water and walk the circle clockwise again, sprinkling water around the edge of the circle as you go. In this second rotation, you are using the combined powers of earth and water to start building up your circle. As you do this, visualise the droplets of water expanding to fill up the deep footprints you visualised on the first rotation. In your mind's eye, see the water completely fill and then overflow from the tracks you made until there is a shallow, unbroken "moat" of water around the entire circle's edge.

7. Take up the censer or whatever holds your incense. Say:

I bless you, smoke of air. May you clear the way and purify this land.

8. With the incense, walk another lap of the circle, wafting the smoke around the perimeter. This is where those swinging censers on little chains come in handy. In this third rotation, you are adding the power of air to the construction of your circle. As you do this, visualise the incense smoke forming a translucent, then more solid, wall growing out of the water you visualised. Imagine the walls curving up as well as down beneath the earth until you and your ritual space are enveloped in a large sphere.

9. Now take up the candle. Say:

I honour you, flame of fire. May you light the way and bear witness to my work.

10. With the candle held before you like a lantern, walk one final round of the circle. This fourth rotation is completing the construction of your circle with the element of fire. As you do this, visualise the warmth and light from the candle flame illuminating and sealing the walls you built with the incense.

11. Now it's time to set up the quarters of your circle. You do this by standing at the edge of the circle at each of the cardinal direction points. Face outward, toward the east. Raise your arms in greeting, if it feels right. Say:

Element of air, please attend our rite and lend us your power. Hail and welcome.

It might help to visualise things you associate with each element: naturally occurring things such as forest, the wind, volcanoes, and rivers; correspondences; colours; sounds; or even the elements themselves.

12. Move clockwise to repeat step 11 at the south (element of fire), west (element of water), and north (element of earth).

13. Once you've welcomed the element of earth, your circle is cast, and you can move on to any spell or celebration that you have planned: a healing spell, a Beltane celebration, a rite to honour a deity, a self-dedication, an initiation of a new coven member, or whatever you'd like.

Bringing Down the Circle

Do this once you have finished your main working or ritual. This is much quicker than casting the circle. For many practitioners, this is the only time you would move counterclockwise in a circle.

1. Start at the west quarter. Raise your arms in farewell, if it feels right. Say:

   Element of water, thank you for attending, and for lending us your power.
   Hail and farewell.

2. Moving counterclockwise, repeat this step for the south (element of fire), east (element of air), and finally north (element of earth).

3. Once you have farewelled the element of earth, the circle has been brought down. Say:

   The circle is open, but unbroken.
   Blessed Be.

EXERCISE
A Circle of Candlelight

You will need a candle for this exercise. It should be sitting steadily at eye height, not far from where you choose to sit. When lit, the candle's flame needs to burn steadily. Use a clear, draught-proof candleholder if you need to.

1. Sit comfortably in a darkened room. Light a candle and sit quietly until you find stillness. Keep your breathing relaxed—use 4:4 breathing if you want to.

2. Focus on the candle's flame. Half-close your eyes to squint at it and notice the flickers of colour around the middle of the flame. Adjust your gaze and notice the golden glow around the flame itself.

3. Now close your eyes and start to visualise that glow slowly spreading, with you at the centre. See it grow sideways, upward,

and downward until you are sitting within a sphere of white-gold light. Focus on stillness and on feelings of stability and warmth.

4. Practise this a few times until you can easily conjure the image of sitting within this sphere of light in your mind. This is one of the key visualisations you'll need when it comes to casting and maintaining a magic circle of your own.

))) ● JOURNAL PROMPTS ● (((

- What makes something sacred? Is there a difference between sacredness and holiness? What is it?
- What physical spaces or objects do you consider sacred in your life?
- Why is sacred space important? *Is* it important?
- What does a magic circle feel like to you? If you haven't been inside one, what do you think a magic circle would feel like?

Further Reading

A Witch Alone: Thirteen Moons to Master Natural Magic by Marian Green

Everyday Witchcraft: Making Time for Spirit in a Too-Busy World by Deborah Blake

Wicca: A Comprehensive Guide to the Old Religion in the Modern World by Vivianne Crowley (especially chapter 4)

"Casting a Circle – Creating Sacred Space" by Gwion Raven

"Circle Casting Basics: All You Need to Know about Magick Circles" by Michelle Gruben

"S1 Ep16: How to Cast a Witchcraft Circle" on the *Seeking Witchcraft* podcast

CHAPTER 10
Magic, Spellcraft, and Ritual Work

Spells come in many different shapes and sizes. Magic can be in the form of more "traditional" spells with multiple components and a list of instructions, or they can be as simple as a few words or gestures. This chapter brings together previous concepts to explore and explain the basic components related to magic, spells and spellcraft, and ritual.

Modern definitions of magic usually refer to unlikely events or phenomena that seem to have a supernatural force behind them. But the etymology of the word gives us some more clues about the history of magic itself, and why it forms a part of our religious and spiritual practices.

The English words magic, mage, and magician come from the Latin magus, through the Greek μάγος, which is from the Old Persian maguš. The Old Persian magu- also referred to members of a certain priesthood and is derived from the Proto-Indo-European *magh ("be able").[92]

So which definition describes the magic we do as witches: the old or the new? Usually, it's both. As witches, we actively and intentionally practise magic as an art to bring about change, and its use often forms a part (but not all) of our spiritual or religious practice.

---

92. Phillips and Phillips, *The Witches of Oz*, 43.

Above all, magic is experiential. You could read this and a thousand other books in a thousand different languages, but until you actually get out there and do the thing for yourself, you won't have a good idea of what it is you're reading about. The magic is in the doing.

Spells

We've looked at raising energy in different ways so far, such as via magical timing, elemental correspondences, and the tools that can be used to perform magic. A spell brings many of these things together in a kind of recipe or roadmap for performing a specific magical act or achieving a certain goal. Before we go on, there are a few important things to know about spells.

- **Not all witches perform spells.** They don't form a part of everyone's practice, and that's okay. Your practice is your business, and no one else can decide how much witchcraft is "enough" to make you an authentic practitioner.

- **As you get better at magic, you're less inclined to use it.** When performed properly, spells take a lot of energy. Experienced practitioners will often go out of the way to tick all the "mundane" boxes before resorting to a spell, if at all. It's a lot easier to tell someone how you feel rather than to cast an effective spell. It's easier still to keep silent and watch and wait a while before deciding a course of action with a clear head.

- **Spells don't have to be complicated to be effective.** This isn't to say we should shy away from complex workings, but not all spells require dozens of ingredients and days of preparation. Less is often more.

- **Being successful in magic requires practise, just like any other skill.** Different witches will have different interests and talents in specific magical areas, but generally, these things need to be worked at.

Considerations

Before you begin researching your spell or putting together the ingredients, you need to consider the target and your intended goal as well as yourself and your own circumstances, abilities, and limitations.

Here are some questions to ask yourself before you begin preparing for a magical working:

- What, exactly, do you want to achieve? Be as explicit and as exact as you can here. Write your goal down. Set it aside and come back to it after a day or so. Are there any improvements you can make to it? Any changes?

- What will it be like when the goal is achieved? What will be different? What will have changed for the better? For the worse? Who will be affected? In what way? How will you know you've succeeded?

- Which energy-raising techniques should you use? Different techniques work better for different circumstances, as discussed in chapter 3.

- What ingredients are appropriate? What do you have on hand? Do you need to make substitutions?

- Who or what is the target of this spell? Very specific targets that are local or known to you are easier to perform magic on/for, as they are easier for you to visualise. For example, it's easier to visualise one of your friends than to visualise "a man."

- Where is the target? Be as exact as possible.

- How can you connect to the target? Do you have a picture of them to help focus your efforts? Or do you have something else related to them?

- When is the best time to perform this working? Think about planetary hours and moon phases, but keep your own life and schedule in mind too.

Answer these questions honestly, and think about your responses before you continue with the spell. The more honest and forthcoming you can be with yourself at this first stage, the greater your chances of success later on.

Spell Preparation

Performing a spell actually begins hours or even days before you cast a circle or set up your sacred space. As you plan a working and start getting together the ingredients or tools needed, you'll likely start thinking about and focussing on the working—it's only natural. These preparatory behaviours begin to focus your intention and even direct energy toward the goal.

It's not time to start writing or planning a spell in any great detail until you're really satisfied with the goal you formulated in the previous section. Wording is important, and you need to make sure yours is as specific as possible. "I want to be rich!" is not a very specific goal, for example; "I need to cover my bills and live comfortably, with enough food" is better. Try to leave very little room for ambiguity or misinterpretation.

You also should aim to be as clear as possible about who or what the target of your spell is. This will help you decide which type of power you will need to raise. Make sure you understand and differentiate between what is your goal and what is your target. For example, if your friend has an infection in his eye, your working might target the infection, but your goal is good health, not the other way around.

Once you have these two things clear, it's time to properly set your intention. To do this, focus your mind firmly on what you want to achieve. You might visualise this in meditation or just as you go about your life in the days leading up to when you plan to cast your spell. (I do this best when I'm doing the dishes or pegging out the washing.) If you're having trouble really seeing in your mind's eye what life will be like when your goal is achieved, try revisiting some of the questions in the previous section. By visualising our desired outcome, we as practitioners are fully committing to the spell's goal and our ability to achieve it.

Once the who/what, why, where, and how are sorted out, you should start researching, gathering, and thinking about spell ingredients. Depending on the spell, types of things you might gather could be:

1. **Magical Tools:** For example, an athame, wand, pentacle, cord, etc.
2. **Object Links:** Photos or likenesses; directly connected objects, such as nail or hair clippings of a targeted person; or indirectly connected objects, like soil from the path of a targeted person,

something that is theirs, or something that was given by them. These all lend power to a spell and help direct your energy. These are also known as *sympathetic links*.

3. **Corresponding Ingredients:** Herbs, incense, stones, coloured candles, altar cloths, wood, elemental correspondences, runes, tarot cards, iconography, astrological symbols, etc. that correspond to the goal of the spell.

4. **Magical Consumables:** Candles, matches, lighters, incense, charcoal blocks, etc.

Following the advice in this chapter should give you enough of a foundation to begin building your spell. You might write it out as a structured working or just jot down a rough outline or bullet points to work through. Play around and find what works for you.

Spell Casting

When it comes to actually casting the spell, many follow a structure that often looks something like this:

1. **Gather ingredients/tools.** If you've gone through the previous section carefully, these should be ready to go.

2. **Prepare yourself. Centre. Focus on intention.** Use the information in chapter 3 to centre yourself. Remember, when you focus your intention, you are committing wholly to the process of casting this spell, and you're setting your resolve toward getting it done—and done well.

3. **Set up sacred space.** You will read all about how do to this in chapter 9.

4. **Explicitly state your goal.** Say your goal aloud at the very beginning of your spell. It should be explicit and clear, leaving very little room for misinterpretation or ambiguity.

5. **Visualise the target and raise energy.** Exactly how you raise power will be dictated by what you want to achieve. For example, a healing spell might use lots of "human" body-related energy like

dancing, singing, or clapping. It's worth taking another look at chapter 3 if you need ideas here.

6. **Send the energy to the target.** Just as with the last step, the way you send the energy you have raised will depend on the kind of working you're doing. Do you need to send energy all at once, or gradually over a few days? What "flavour" energy are you sending, and will it be noticed by others and cause upset or unrest?

7. **Finish the spell.** Declare success, ground and centre, and close down the sacred space you set up when you began.[93]

The End Is Important

A working isn't over when the energy is sent. There are a few final things to be done to ensure yours and your target's well-being, and to give you the best chance of success.

1. **Always declare success.** This is the final seal on the energy and focus you have put into this working. Phrases like "so mote it be" and "it is done" are sometimes used here.

2. **Ground and centre.** Always ground any excess power raised and bring yourself back to the "real" world by centring. Sometimes this is done with cakes and ale.

3. **Close down sacred space.** Always remember to close any sacred space you created (for example, by circle casting).

Once you're done with a spell, try to put it to the back of your mind, and avoid discussing it too much (if at all) with others, at least until you know your spell has worked. Ridding yourself of excess energy includes ridding yourself of conversations or overly obsessive thoughts about what you used that energy for.[94]

---

93. Adapted from Lipp, *Magical Power for Beginners*, 195–227.
94. Adapted from Lipp, 195–227.

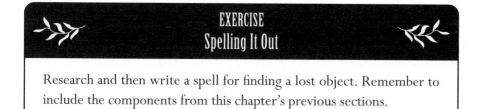

EXERCISE
Spelling It Out

Research and then write a spell for finding a lost object. Remember to include the components from this chapter's previous sections.

Ritual

Rituals are different from spellwork, as the magic being performed is often in devotion and celebration of deity, spirit, or the practitioner(s) themselves. *Ritual* is a word used for a ceremony or action that is performed in a customary way. For many witches and Pagans, rituals make up a part of our practice, both devotional and otherwise.

To understand the different reasons witches or other magical practitioners conduct rituals, we need only to look back at ritual and operative witchcraft. *Ritual witchcraft* is witchcraft that is done for or in aid of deity, spirits, the earth, etc., while *operative witchcraft* is witchcraft that sets out to alter the world in some way, such as through spells, charms, or divination.

The Elements of Ritual

The key components of most rituals fit under one of the following five headings. Complete rituals will usually have one or more examples of each of the following elements.[95] I've included multiple examples for each, but not every ritual will have every single thing listed—that would make for a very long ritual!

CLEANSING / PURIFICATION

This part of ritual consists of preparing the space and the individual witch for ritual.

Cleansing/purifying the space is done to remove any unwanted energies from where your ritual will take place. This is sometimes done with smoke (from incense or bundled herbs) or with salted water. Using both incense and salted water is called *censing and asperging*. Other popular methods include

---

95. These five headings/elements have been adapted from Mankey, *Witch's Wheel of the Year*, 13.

using a ritual broom (sometimes called a *besom*) or sound such as drumming/
chanting/music.

Many of these techniques are also used by some witches to purify themselves. Some witches like to take a bath or shower before ritual or engage in
ritual handwashing.

INVITATIONS

This part of ritual includes inviting deities, spirits, ancestors, powers, and ritualists to attend the rite. Often, several parts of the ritual fit under this heading. It might look like:

A Statement of Intent: A few sentences often spoken aloud at the
beginning of the ritual to explain the purpose and/or observance of
the ritual. For example, "Today we are here to celebrate the summer
solstice, to honour the shortest night of the year and to celebrate the
light as it begins to wane. Today, the lord of the sun is at his strongest,
but even as he begins to fade in the coming months, we take heart
knowing he will be reborn again as our sacred Wheel turns."

Casting a Circle: Many witches use magic circles when they do rituals
or magic. They are usually cast at the beginning of a rite and brought
down at the end.

Calling the Quarters: Often done as part of casting a circle, many
witches invoke elemental energies, creatures, or entities at each of the
cardinal directions to represent the four elements of earth, air, fire,
and water. There are many different ways to do this, and not everyone
associates the same element with the same direction in their workings.
Some people call these *watchtowers* or *guardians* rather than *quarters*.

Inviting Ancestors: While it's not appropriate for every occasion, it's
commonplace for witches to invite ancestors, mighty dead, spirits, etc.
to preside over some rites.

Calls to Deity: Verbalised calls for deities to be part of a ritual. This can
be done either by specifically naming them or by calling to "greater"
concepts such as Lady/Mother or Lord/Horned One. These invitations can be short or more complex. Whether or not the deity attends
is up to them.

Main Working

The working is the main part of the ritual—it's the reason you are doing it. Workings can be acts of either operative or ritual witchcraft. Again, a ritual may include one of the following examples listed, or it may have several. It might look like:

Devotional Work: Prayers, offerings, praise, etc. to deity or spirit.

Divination: When done in the context of a ritual or at an auspicious time, divinatory readings can be more powerful. Some groups do divinatory readings at seasonal festivals to see what's in store for the next season/year.

Group-Specific Work: In the context of a coven, there may be initiations or elevations to perform, or teaching of a practical skill that needs to be done in a ritual setting.

Invocations or Evocations: When a deity or aspects of a deity are invited to be present at the ritual.

Magical Acts: Spells, charms, healing, candle magic, etc.

Raising Energy to Direct toward Magical Goals: This can be done in a number of ways, including dancing, drumming, or singing.

Sacred Drama: This is like a play, where participants act out a story or facet of the gods or season that is relevant to the ritual. This is usually done in large group rituals.

Seasonal Observances: This includes any work done to celebrate seasonal festivals/the Wheel of the Year.

Grounding

Grounding refers to the act of getting rid of excess energy raised after a magical working is done. It is not done in every ritual. There are many different ways to ground energy. One of the simplest involves putting your bare hands or feet on the earth and visualising the energy flowing down into the ground.

Some witches eat food or drink wine (or both) that has been ritually consecrated in circle. One way that cakes and ale are consecrated involves a chalice (cup) and athame (knife). This is known as *cakes and ale* or *cakes and wine* in Wiccan-inspired craft. Cakes and ale is both as a sacrament to the gods and a means of grounding. Common cakes and ale foodstuffs are wine and bread, but really it could be anything that works for you/the group you are working with. It's common during cakes and ale for witches to make toasts or libations to the gods.

Dismissals

This is the final part of a ritual before returning to the mundane world. It might look like:

Honouring, Thanking, and Farewelling Any Spirits, Powers, Entities, or Deities Called at the Beginning of the Ritual: This includes any quarters called.

Closing the Circle: Removing the boundary and protection of the magic circle and letting the space settle back into the normal world.

A Closing Statement: This might echo or round off what you set out to do in the opening statement. This is also a chance to wish ritualists well as they return to everyday life.

EXERCISE
Spelling It Out Again

Research and then write a ritual to bring health and prosperity to attendees of a sabbat of your choice. Remember to include the components from this chapter's previous sections.

Simple and Effective Magic

Candle magic is one of the simplest and most effective ways to perform magic. There are loads of different ways to perform candle magic. Read through my suggestions and then read up on some alternatives, experiment, and use what works for you.

1. **Set your intention.** Think carefully about who this magic is for, who it will affect, and what the ideal outcome will look like. Always get someone's consent before performing magic for them. I like to

spend a good couple of days mulling all this over, visualising, considering, and daydreaming. This seems to work best when my mind is half-focussed on something mundane, like doing dishes or sorting laundry.

2. **Gather the components for your working.** Coloured candles have different correspondences. A white or black candle will do in most cases, if coloured candles aren't available. Gather any herbs and oils and other ritual bits and pieces you might need for casting a circle, if you plan on using one.

3. **Set the scene.** Make sure it is safe to burn candles where you will be working. If you're working indoors, tidy up the room and remove as much clutter as possible. Many people find it beneficial to give the floors and surfaces of a room a good clean before they begin a magical working. Make sure the space is quiet and that electronic devices are off, away, or placed on silent.

Ensure you have a space to work. An altar is ideal, but you could use any clear surface, like a coffee table, as long as you're okay with accidents happening, such as wax dribbling . Put down a non-treasured cloth if you're really worried.

1. **Prepare yourself.** Different traditions give different instructions for readying oneself for ritual. A simple and generally agreed upon method is just to make sure you are rested, clean, and fed. Bathe or take a shower. Put on clean clothes or ritual garb (or go skyclad, if that's what you're more comfortable in). Make sure you have eaten. You will concentrate much better if your basic needs are met.

2. **Begin.** Many folks like to burn incense or light a "working" candle to get into a ritual mindset at this point. You might like to do the same. Quite a lot of the candle magic workings printed in modern witchy books require incense to be burned alongside your working, so if this is something you plan on doing semi-regularly, it might be worth investing in a censer or thurible. Censers allow you to burn raw incense blends on charcoal disks, which is just lovely—once

you get the hang of this, you won't want to go back to premade sticks and cones!

If you're so inclined, cast a circle or set up your sacred space in a way that works for you. Centre yourself with a few deep breaths while you remember the actions and intentions you thought about and visualised in step one. When you're ready, verbalise this intention. Speaking words out loud gives them power.

3. **Dress your candle.** This involves anointing it in oil, rubbing the oil onto the wax from the candle's centre to its ends. Concentrate hard on the issue or intention of this working as you do so. Oil is flammable, so don't use too much.

   After dressing a candle, some practitioners like to roll it on the altar while focusing on the intention of the ritual. For workings to bring energy to you or the subject of the working, roll the candle toward yourself. If you are performing this working to banish or disperse something, roll it away from you.

4. **Inscribe your candle.** This could involve carving a certain sigil, rune, or even your subject's name onto the candle. In doing this, you are charging the candle with your intention. For workings that involve burning the candle a little each day/night, some folks like to put notches down the candle to indicate how much should be burned at a time.

5. **Light the candle.** Omit this step if you are preparing the candle for somebody else. If you plan to burn the candle yourself, place it in a firesafe container and light it.

6. **Finish.** Thank any deities or spirits you need to and make offerings. Close down your sacred space and ground yourself.

   Many workings require you to leave the lit candle burning until there is nothing left. Leave the candle burning if it is safe to do so. If not, blow or snuff it out.

Candle Colour Correspondences

In candle magic, coloured candles can be used to achieve different goals. If you can't get your hands on a specific colour, go for a standard white, black, or cream candle instead.

Black: Time, age, knowledge

Blue: Inspiration, wisdom, devotion

Brown: Extraordinary favours, an end to sorrow

Gold: Wealth, abundance, finances

Green: Harmony, fertility, abundance

Orange: Health, ambitions, legal matters

Pink: Love, romantic affection

Purple: Psychic or spiritual workings

Red: Strength, energy, courage, sex and sexuality

Silver: Intuition and divination

White: Spirituality, peace, purification

Yellow: Intellect, memory, the mind

))) ● JOURNAL PROMPTS ● (((

- What's your experience with magic and spells? What has been effective for you in the past?
- Now that you've learned more about how to perform it, how would you define "magic" in your own words?
- How can you ensure your magic is as ethical as possible?
- What everyday or "mundane" criteria would you have to meet before you attempted a spell for a new job? A spell for love? A money spell?

Further Reading

Circle, Coven & Grove: A Year of Magickal Practice by Deborah Blake

Magical Power for Beginners: How to Raise & Send Energy for Spells That Work by Deborah Lipp

Wicca: A Comprehensive Guide to the Old Religion in the Modern World by Vivianne
    Crowley (especially chapter 5)

"Eight Essential Elements of Good Pagan Ritual" by John Beckett

"Ritual Crafting: Creating Rituals That Work (Part 1)" by Katrina Rasbold

"Three Elements Required for a Successful Ritual" by Todd Brison

CHAPTER 11
Divination

Divination, or the ability to glimpse the future by esoteric means, is considered by many an important skill in a witch's repertoire. But approaching divination as a new practitioner can be daunting. It's certainly not expected that you master all of the forms of divination outlined in this chapter. Rather, it is intended as an introduction to the categories and purposes of divination within eclectic practice, including some less-common forms of divination.

The word *divination* is related to words like *divine* and *divinity*, which are both associated with gods and godliness. Today, the practice has fewer devotional connotations, and the focus is on the reader and their skill rather than their ability to provide a conduit. There is also a focus on symbolism and archetypes, as well as the interpretation of both.

We use divination to get a glimpse of things not easily seen—to gain insights that are outside of our immediate, conscious awareness. This is why many practitioners perform divinatory acts before enacting spells or magical workings. Divination is a good way to look at possible outcomes, and while it should never be the hinging factor in your decision-making, it can certainly help.

In his book *The Origin of Consciousness in the Breakdown of the Bicameral Mind*, American psychologist Julian Jaynes divided divinatory practices into four categories: omens, augury, spontaneous divination, and sortilege.[96]

---

96. Jaynes, *The Origin of Consciousness in the Breakdown of the Bicameral Mind*, 236–50.

Omens

Omens are unusual or important events. This is possibly the most misunderstood form of divination. The zillions of people who post in witchy social media groups asking what it "means" to see a certain type of bird in your backyard are a good example of this misunderstanding.

The emphasis here should be on *unusual or important*. Many cultures have their own omens. Some obvious examples are a black cat crossing your path, a double rainbow, a broken mirror, and so on.

As a witch, the most meaningful forms of omens will be deeply personal and framed in the context of your magical practice. In short, an omen is an omen if you've asked for or are expecting an omen. You will also begin to notice certain things that stand out to you as you build and maintain a regular practice. This is where your magical journal comes in handy. Record these instances, and use your records to build up and understand your personal omen "vocabulary."

Augury

The verb *augur* means to portend or foreshadow. It comes to us from ancient Rome, where an augur or augury was a magician-priest who interpreted the flight of birds as a means of predicting future events. Signs on the augur's east side were generally seen as favourable; signs in the west were thought to be unfavourable.[97]

Augury under Jaynes's definition includes any divinatory activity involving the ranking of probabilities and interpreting the results. This is a conscious act and does not happen spontaneously, unlike omens, which can happen to you without your deciding to sit down and look for them.[98]

One example of augury is scrying. Scrying is divination in which the practitioner gazes at a surface—usually a shiny surface—to induce a trance state in which scenes, people, words, or images appear. The stereotypical fortune teller with a crystal ball is probably the most common image of scrying. Other forms include the use of mirrors; polished metal, coal, or bone; or containers of liquid.

---

97. Drury, *The Watkins Dictionary of Magic*, 29.

98. Jaynes, *The Origin of Consciousness in the Breakdown of the Bicameral Mind*, 236–50.

Other examples of augury include:

Alomancy: Salt divination. The diviner sprinkles salt and interprets the future by analysing the patterns formed. It's possible that this is where the superstition about spilled salt being unlucky comes from.

Astragalomancy: This is a category of divination that uses items such as bones, stones, or small pieces of wood marked with letters or symbols. In these forms of divination, the reader usually asks a question and interprets symbols depending on how the objects lie. The use of dice for divination is a form of astragalomancy.

Astromancy: Any ancient system of divination by the stars.

Austromancy: Divination conducted by interpreting the wind.

Catoptromancy: Mirror divination. The ancient Greeks would place mirrors underwater or hold them under running water, like a fountain, and interpret the reflections made.[99]

Crystallomancy: Divination performed by looking into a crystal ball or the mirrorlike surface of a pool/bowl of water.

Dactylomancy: A means of divining the future by looking at rings, often wedding rings. Generally, a ring is held on a string and allowed to swing unassisted against the side of a glass, indicating yes or no to questions asked. Sometimes, a ring is suspended over a round table or board inscribed with the letters of the alphabet and used as a type of pendulum.

Gyromancy: Divination enacted by the diviner walking around in a circle until they collapse. The position of the reader in relation to the circle is interpreted to predict the outcome of future events. Do not attempt this while drunk.

Hippomancy: Interpreting the gait of horses—especially white horses—as a form of divination. This was allegedly practised by some Celtic tribes.[100]

---

99. Drury, *The Watkins Dictionary of Magic*, 52.

100. Drury, *The Watkins Dictionary of Magic*, 136.

Hydromancy: A form of divination that involves studying and interpreting the patterns and colour of flowing water. This is sometimes done by examining ripples from stones dropped into a river or stream.

Ichthyomancy: Inspecting and interpreting the entrails of a fish.

Lecanomancy: A form of divination in which the reader drops a stone or similar object into a bowl of water. The image of the object in the rippling water and the sound it makes dropping to the bottom are both interpreted. Another method of lecanomancy is to drop oil onto the surface of a bowl of water and study the shapes that form.

Lithomancy: This is a means of divination using precious stones. One method is to take the stones (each of which has a planetary or symbolic significance) and scatter them on a dark surface. The stone that reflects the most light is the main omen to take notice of.

Ornithomancy: A form of divination that interprets the songs or flight patterns of birds.

Rhabdomancy: This refers to any divination done with a wooden rod. This includes dowsing, in which practitioners use a hazel rod to find untapped water sources in dry areas. It also includes interpreting the flight of arrows.

Tasseomancy: Divination performed using tea leaves. I will look at this in more detail in chapter 13.

Spontaneous Divination

This category includes the interpretation of whatever is in front of you. Some examples are reading auras, psychometry, psychic intuition, and bibliomancy. Dreams, also, were considered portentous by many ancient cultures. This perspective was investigated and reformulated by the psychologist Carl Jung, who held that dreams often reveal spiritual archetypes from the collective unconscious.[101]

---

101. Drury, *The Watkins Dictionary of Magic*, 218.

Sortilege: The Tarot

Sortilege is the most common and popular category of divination in modern times. It includes any system involving the casting of lots, or taking a "lucky dip," to interpret a random selection of one or more pieces of a larger set.

Tarot is easily the most popular form of sortilege used today. Some of the oldest tarot decks were decks of playing cards. Decks have been created and used specifically for divinatory purposes for centuries. The history and mythology surrounding the tarot is fascinating. This section is a tarot overview, but I do encourage you to keep learning about the tarot if it appeals to you.

Choosing a Deck

Many tarot decks are based on the structure of the Rider-Waite-Smith deck. That is, they have seventy-eight cards, including twenty-two major arcana cards, with the rest of the cards divided into four suits of fourteen cards.

There are thousands—maybe hundreds of thousands—of different tarot decks out there. But how many decks does a reader really need? This is a contentious question amongst many. Humans are, by and large, pack rats—we're drawn to shiny, pretty things, and we love to collect them. That being said, it's important that, as a new reader, you don't fall into the trap of buying more and more decks when what you *really* need to do is focus on learning how to read the deck(s) that you have. Don't get me wrong, I own a few different decks. But in reality, I regularly read only a couple of decks, one of which is a first edition of *Mythic Tarot*. It's really banged up; I've had it since the early 2000s. I keep it wrapped in an old stripey sleeve, which was the style at the time, and it's stored in a tin that originally held caramels.

If you like collecting tarot decks and you have the money to do so, then go for it! But owning a zillion decks will not make you a better reader. Neither will posting artsy pictures or videos of your decks on social media. The only thing that will make you a better reader is…reading. So get to it. Work with the cards, take your time deciphering their meanings, and do lots and lots of readings—both for inane questions and curiosities, and for the big things too.

Interpreting the Minor Arcana

The thought of memorising the meanings to seventy-eight cards is pretty daunting. I think this is why new readers tend to gravitate toward learning the meanings of the twenty-two major arcana first. But, if anything, the major arcana is more complex. A much more manageable method for learning the tarot is to look at the four suits of the court cards, then at their numbers, *then* at the major arcana.

THE FOUR SUITS OF THE MINOR ARCANA

Cups: Cups cards generally refer to topics like emotions, love, intuition, dreams or the subconscious, the otherworld, and the underworld. They are associated with the element of water.

Pentacles: The suit of pentacles usually deals with the physical body, health, fertility, sustenance, prosperity, steadfastness, material gain, and career. They are associated with the element of earth.

Swords: Cards from the suit of swords generally deal with intellect, logic, knowledge/learning, planning, problem-solving, messages, and communication. They are associated with the element of air.

Wands: Wands cards usually deal with topics such as healing, creativity, destruction, the hearth and home, passion, movement/action, and energy. They are associated with the element of fire.

NUMBERS IN THE MINOR ARCANA

Once you have a good understanding of what the different suits in the minor arcana are associated with, it's only a matter of looking at the numbers. When you combine the meaning of a card's suit and number, that card becomes a lot easier to interpret.

One/Ace: Beginnings, creative power, initiative and leadership, single-mindedness. This is the number from which all other numbers arise.

Two: Duality, duplication, reflection, receptiveness, alternation, antagonism. Polar opposites: positive and negative; good and evil. Because duality never resolves, this number can also represent creativity unfulfilled.

Three: Growth, expansion, ambition, development. Two coming together to make three. The threefold nature of humanity: mind, body, and spirit.

Four: Order, logic, classification, measurement—think the four perfect sides of a square. Hard work and rest after a job well done, practicality, memory. Four is the material, physical universe that rises when the trinity of three becomes four.

Five: Many forces operating at once, and not always in unison. Change, uncertainty, versatility. Some occultists also associate five with human aspiration, relating the five-pointed star or pentagram to the head, arms, and legs of a human.

Six: Balance, harmony, equilibrium, beauty, love, loyalty. Six is sometimes represented by a six-sided cube, which is a symbol of symmetry and solidness. This number is also associated with marriage and parenthood.

Seven: Perfection, security, completeness, safety, victory, rest after a job well done. Seven also represents wisdom: there are seven colours in the rainbow and seven notes on the musical scale.

Eight: Health, balance, justice, progress, individual thought. Eight is often associated with rational intellect, strength of character, and individuality of purpose.

Nine: Completion, attainment, fulfilment. Spiritually speaking, nine is also the number of initiations.

Ten: The end of a cycle and the return to the beginning. Perfection through completion.

Court Cards in the Minor Arcana

After the ace through ten come the page, knight, queen, and king. These are known as the court cards, and they are representative of the different qualities of fire, water, air, and earth. The king represents the air element through all four suits, the queen represents aspects of water, the knight represents fire aspects, and the page represents aspects of earth. Taking into account the elements represented by the four suits, you get something like this:

Page of Cups (Earth of Water): Self-reflection, meditation, inner work.

Page of Pentacles (Earth of Earth): Study, hard work, learning new skills (especially vocational skills).

Page of Swords (Earth of Air): Communication, vigilance, learning something new, critical examination of a problem.

Page of Wands (Earth of Fire): Inspiration, working hard at a creative project, family intelligence or gifts.

Knight of Cups (Fire of Water): Romance, poetry, invitations and incitement.

Knight of Pentacles (Fire of Earth): Real world, "mundane" responsibilities. A prompt to keep passions in check and take note of the current situation before making any rash decisions.

Knight of Swords (Fire of Air): Defence and destruction. A messenger in motion. The consequences of actions.

Knight of Wands (Fire of Fire): Ambition, confidence, making headway in a passion project.

Queen of Cups (Water of Water): Wisdom, success. A prompt to explore one's emotions and spiritual side more deeply.

Queen of Pentacles (Water of Earth): Opulence and riches, but used generously for healing and for charity.

Queen of Swords (Water of Air): The ending of a relationship, often of a romantic nature. Independence and solitude.

Queen of Wands (Water of Fire): Success or good news relating to a passion project. Emotional upheaval.

King of Cups (Air of Water): Philanthropy, emotional intelligence, the arts and sciences.

King of Pentacles (Air of Earth): Aptitude for money and business, self-reliance, financial stability.

King of Swords (Air of Air): Authority, law, mastery of a topic studied.

King of Wands (Air of Fire): Honesty, tolerance, socialising. The completion of a passion project.

EXERCISE
Learning the Minor Arcana

Use a pack of plain playing cards to practise reading and interpreting the cards of the minor arcana. This will encourage you to focus on the cards' numerical and elemental associations. Try reading hearts as cups, spades as swords, diamonds as pentacles, and clubs as wands. It may seem like a drag, but in time, this will really hone your skills as a reader.

EXERCISE
The Minor Arcana and the Elements

Look back over any notes you have about the elements. What other qualities could you attribute to the minor arcana cards, based on elemental associations? Use the number and suit associations to create a table of interpretations for the cards ace through ten in each suit.

Interpreting the Major Arcana

Here is one way of looking at the minor arcana versus the major arcana: in readings, minor arcana cards generally represent day-to-day occurrences, lesser influences, and happenings in the "real" world, whereas major arcana cards often represent more complex concepts, influences, lessons, and occurrences.

The meanings shared in this section are an overview. Each card in the major arcana has dozens of meanings, symbols, and archetypes. I encourage you to look into other interpretations of the major arcana, if that's something that interests you.

(0) **The Fool:** The supreme card. Someone who knows nothing, who is setting out. A leap of faith; a lack of discipline; a need for guidance. Sometimes a prompt to look before you leap.

(I) **The Magician:** Magical energy, apprenticeship, and inspiration. Will and willpower. The connection between the mundane and magical worlds. The steps required to see something through to completion. Counterpart of the High Priestess.

(II) The High Priestess: The potential to manifest and realise different forms. Transcendence, intuition, the supernatural, self-awareness. Secrets, oaths, and mysteries. Introspection and going inward.

(III) The Empress: Creativity, abundance, the harvest. Projects, both passion projects and artistic projects. Happiness and pleasure. Nurturing the self and others.

(IV) The Emperor: Responsibilities, leadership, logistics. Careful planning and preparation for a stable and well-organised future. Ambition and authority. The opposite of the destructive qualities symbolised by the Chariot.

(V) The Hierophant: Mercy and divine, priest-like authority. Spiritual initiations and teachings, higher/further education, faith. Wisdom and forgiveness. A need to reflect on higher purpose and personal growth.

(VI) The Lovers: Union, love, relationships. Attraction, harmony. The coming together of polarities, the transcendence of duality. Sometimes the need to choose between two very different options.

(VII) The Chariot: Movement, travel. The need to regain control, or the need for revenge. Destructive energy. War and battles. The chaos here is in contrast to the calm and organised nature of the Emperor.

(VIII) Strength: The victory of the higher aspects of the soul over the lower, animalistic soul. Patience, empowerment, fortitude. Bravery in the face of peril or adversity. Spiritual strength and consolidation in preparation for the Hermit's dark night of the soul.

(IX) The Hermit: Quietness, inner work, solitude or introversion. Stillness, wisdom, and inner power. The lonely, inward-looking work of the mystic and occultist.

(X) Wheel of Fortune: Unseen forces at work. Changes; moving onward and upward. Mastery of opposite polarities within the psyche. Faith in destiny and luck.

(XI) Justice: Examining past wrongdoings. Balance, justice, impartiality in assessing one's spiritual well-being and direction. Seeing clearly. Inner strength. Truth, honesty, unbiased diplomacy.

(XII) The Hanged Man: Reflection, sacrifice, compromise, initiation. Changes, death, loss, self-improvement. Eschewing mundane distractions to focus on the spiritual.

(XIII) Death: Profound change, transition, metamorphosis. An ending; a metaphorical death. Leaving something behind in order to attain spiritual illumination.

(XIV) Temperance: Action, balance, and symmetry. A prompt to pause and focus on healing and stillness. Patience and love. Individuation; harmony and wholeness with the inner self.

(XV) The Devil: Oppression, loss of control, addiction, indulgence. Sometimes a sign that the querant has less control over things than they think. Anger, especially poorly managed anger. The need to transcend an animalistic nature.

(XVI) The Tower: Total destruction; massive transition and challenging change. A symbolic warning against pride during the mystic journey. The need to balance personality and ambition, to work with humility. A warning not to get too big for your boots.

(XVII) The Star: Balance, insight, and guidance. Inspiration, hope, psychic power, the cosmos, the otherworld. The first glimmer of hope or a small sign of better times to come. Sometimes signifies a divine presence or influence.

(XVIII) The Moon: Biological and spiritual evolution. Sexuality, fertility, dreams, the subconscious. Danger, secrets, or obstacles ahead. Hidden influences at work—something is not as it seems.

(XIX) The Sun: Childlike wonder and play; innocence. Spiritual immaturity. Successful ventures: the beginning of understanding. Optimism, positivity, joy, and good fortune.

(XX) Judgement: Ascension, revolution, fulfilling a mission. Rebirth and renewal. Examining the past before embracing a new life or way of being. A decision to be made.

(XXI) The World: A completed cycle. The descent into the "underworld" of the unconscious psyche. Initiation, attainment, completion, satisfaction, wholeness, enlightenment.

How to Perform a Tarot Reading

There is no right or wrong way to read tarot cards. With that being said, here are a few options to explore.

PAST, PRESENT, FUTURE

Pull three cards and interpret them left to right, one representing the past, one the present, and one the future.

SINGLE CARD PULL

Draw a single card to get a general idea of things as they stand. This is a good method to include in a full moon ritual, once you have cast a circle and raised energy.

CLOCK / CROSS SPREAD

Draw five cards. Place the first card down. Place the second card to its left, the third card to its right, one above it, and one below. The middle card represents the situation as it stands. The card to the left of this indicates the past, or what led up to the situation as it is. The card at the bottom represents unseen or as-yet-unacknowledged influences on the current situation. The card above the middle card represents possible outcomes or influences that may come into play. The card to the right of the middle card represents the outcome of the situation if it is allowed to continue without action or intervention.

Sortilege: Norse and Germanic Runes

Early Roman accounts of Germanic tribes describe them as using systems of "taking lots" of marked tiles, stones, or wooden discs for the purposes of divination. This idea was built upon much later by occultists in the 1700s and 1800s, and later again by Norse and Germanic Neopagans in Europe and the United States during the 1970s and '80s, when the first modern systems of divinatory runes were produced and sold on a commercial basis.[102]

Today, sets of runes are made on wooden discs, stones, pieces of bone or antler, ceramic or plastic tiles, and more. The most commonly available sets of Norse and Germanic runes include the following alphabets.

---

102. Paxson, *Taking Up the Runes.*

The Elder Futhark

Consisting of twenty-four letters, the Elder Futhark is the Germanic alphabet of runes used in pagan northern Europe between the fifth and eighth centuries CE. The use of these runes continued until at least 1000 CE.[103] Several Anglo-Saxon variants had more letters added. Modern Heathens, pagans, and occultists started using these as an organised divinatory system in the early 1980s.

Fehu ("Cattle"): Also sometimes spelled Feoh, this rune letter is considered sacred to Freyr, the Norse god of fertility and the harvest. It is associated with energy, wealth, gold, and success. Alphabetical equivalent: F (as in *fox*).

Uruz ("The Aurochs"): This rune letter is also sometimes called Ur. It is associated with good fortune, strength vitality, and a successful career. Alphabetical equivalent: U (pronounced like the *o* in *who*).

Thurisaz ("Thorn"): Sometimes simply called Thorn, this rune letter is the rune of the will, and it is associated with the sky god Thor and his hammer. It usually stands for force, will, protection, and the ability to make good decisions in the face of an enemy or a troubling situation. Alphabetical equivalent: Th (as in *the*).

Ansuz ("Ash Tree"): Also sometimes called Os, which means "god" or "deity" in Old English, this runic letter is specifically linked to the god Odin. It is associated with sacred power, wisdom and good counsel, inspiration, good communication, and inheritance. Alphabetical equivalent: Aa (pronounced like the *a* in *far*).

Raidho ("The Wheel"): This rune letter is also sometimes called Rad. It is associated with riding, travel, and—specifically—heading in the "right direction." Because of this, Rad is also sometimes connected with reason, progress, and rationality. Alphabetical equivalent: R (as in *red*).

Kenaz ("The Torch"): Sometimes called Cen, this torch is often interpreted as the light of inspiration and initiation. It can also refer to guidance, illumination, creativity, and self-knowledge. Alphabetical equivalent: K (as in *work*).

103. Drury, *The Watkins Dictionary of Magic*, 109–10.

Gebo ("Gift"): Also known as Gyfu or Gifu, this rune letter often represents a literal gift or the giving of gifts. In pre-Christian northern Europe, gift giving was associated with high social status, and generosity and hospitality were considered virtues. In a ritual setting, offering a "gift" to the gods often meant a sacrifice of some kind.[104] Alphabetical equivalent: G (as in *give*).

Wunjo ("The Wind-Vane"): Sometimes called Wyn, this is considered the rune of joy, happiness, and glory. It represents the absence of hardship, sorrow, and tragedy, and it reminds us to recognise and value precious moments. Alphabetical equivalent: W (as in *wind*).

Hagalaz ("Hailstone"): This rune letter is also sometimes called Hagel or Haeg. It is the rune of frost, ice, and winter. Many occultists associate it with the element of air for this reason. It can represent unexpected and unwelcome surprises, like adverse occurrences that happen without warning. It symbolises the stress that is often associated with sudden change, and when it appears in a reading, it is often a prod to reconsider our priorities in times of crisis or adversity. Alphabetical equivalent: H (as in *hail*).

Naudhiz ("Need"): Also sometimes called Nyd, this is the rune of necessity. It encourages us to make the best out of a situation in difficult circumstances. Alphabetical equivalent: N (as in *need*).

Isa ("Ice"): Sometimes spelled Is, this is another rune of ice, but this time it refers to ice on the ground. Isa represents ice that is cold and slippery and slows progress. It prompts us to be still, concentrate, and summon our inner resolve so that we might focus on what's to come on the road ahead. Alphabetical equivalent: Ee (pronounced like the *ea* in *east*).

Jera ("Year/Season"): This rune letter is also known as Ger. It is the rune of growth, fertility, and regeneration, particularly the time of harvest. It represents positive results and reward, especially when working in harmony with nature. Alphabetical equivalent: Y (as in *year*).

---

104. Drury, *The Watkins Dictionary of Magic*, 122.

Eihwaz ("Yew Tree"): With alternate spellings like Eiwaz and Eihwas, this rune represents the yew, a tree with remarkable longevity and poisonous bark, leaves, roots, fruit, and resin. The rune is often associated with death, longevity, and rebirth. Alphabetical equivalent: Eo (pronounced a bit like the *er* in *her*).

Perdhro ("The Dice Cup"): Also known as Perthro and Peorth, this rune letter is associated with change, coincidence, and fate. It is also connected to the idea of receiving unexpected help from external—often unknown—sources. This rune is a reminder that there are always mysterious external forces at play in our lives, and it's a prompt not to depend too much on external appearances. Alphabetical equivalent: P (as in *pin*).

Elhaz ("The Elk"): Sometimes known as Eolh, this rune is one of protection and guardian spirits, used to ward off magical attack. It is a stern reminder of the dangers that are possible with any quest or journey as well as the negative forces that can potentially divert us from our goals. Elhaz is considered sacred to the guardian deity Heimdall and is associated with the sacred elk.[105] Alphabetical equivalent: Zz (as in *buzz*).

Sowulo ("The Sun"): Also known as Sigil, this is a rune of the sun. It is associated with light, health, and vitality. It also represents the force of light overcoming darkness and chaos, and by extension, it can symbolise the higher self. Alphabetical equivalent: S (as in *sun*).

Teiwaz ("Tyr"): This rune letter is also known as Tyr or Tir. It is the rune of victory, courage, and self-sacrifice. In Norse mythology, the god Tyr (also known as Tir or Tiwaz) is the god of war, and this rune is shaped as his spearhead.[106] This rune represents honour, strength, and the power to achieve great things for yourself and those around you. Alphabetical equivalent: T (as in *Tuesday*).

Berkana ("Birch Tree"): Sometimes called Berkano or Beorc, this is the rune of birth, rebirth, rites of passage, and healing. It's associated with birch trees, which were an important part of some northern European

105. Drury, *The Watkins Dictionary of Magic*, 92.
106. Drury, *The Watkins Dictionary of Magic*, 292.

pre-Christian pagan rituals: some acts of flagellation used bundles of birch twigs.[107] Possibly for this reason, this rune is also associated with acts of atonement. Alphabetical equivalent: B (as in *birch*).

Ehwaz ("The Horse"): Also known as Eh, Ehwis, and Ehwaz, this is a rune of self-control, trust, and partnership. It can also represent strong friendships and working relationships. Alphabetical equivalent: E (as in *every*).

Mannaz ("The Person"): Mannaz is also known as Man or Manu. It can relate to a person specifically or to humans in general. It is associated with kinship and family ties, and it reminds us of our potential and awareness as individuals. Alphabetical equivalent: M (as in *mill*).

Laguz ("Water"): Laguz or Lagu can sometimes refer to a lake or other body of water, and as such, many occultists closely associate this rune with the element of water, specifically with water as essential to life. Lakes and oceans can be fraught with danger, and so this rune can also be associated with rising to face life's challenges, or with the transition from life to death. Alphabetical equivalent: L (as in *lake*).

Inguz ("The People/The Firebrand"): Also known as Ing, this rune refers to people and community. The deity Ing was the male consort of the northern European fertility goddess and earth mother Nerthus, who travelled the land in a wagon dispensing peace, prosperity, and happiness.[108] This rune is associated with collecting resources, conserving or storing energy, and more generally with harmony, balance, and completion. Alphabetical equivalent: Ng (as in *long*).

Othala ("Land/Farm/Farmhouse"): This rune is sometimes also called Odal. It refers to ancestors, specifically ancestral property or inheritance. In magic, it is used to call on ancestral powers to guard family land or fortunes and to enhance personal power. Alphabetical equivalent: O (as in *hot*).

Dagaz ("Day"): Dagaz or Daeg is the rune of the dawn, when dark and light are momentarily equal. It can represent balance, equivalence, and duality. It can also symbolise the coming together of two extremes

107. Drury, *The Watkins Dictionary of Magic*, 39.

108. Drury, *The Watkins Dictionary of Magic*, 147.

to bring about creativity, growth, or exploration. Alphabetical equivalent: D (as in *day*).

The Anglo-Saxon Futhorc

This alphabet includes the runes of the Elder Futhark, plus four Frisian runes and one additional rune, to make a total of twenty-nine letters in all.[109] The additions are:

- Ac ᚪ ("The Oak")
- Aesc ᚫ ("The Ash") / Os ("Mouth" or "Speech")
- Yr ᛦ ("The Yew" / "Yew Bow")
- Ear ᛠ ("Soil" / "The Earth Grave")
- Ior ᛡ ("The Water Beast")

These letters were added to earlier Germanic alphabets as language changed throughout Frisia, an area of northwestern Europe that includes parts of modern-day Germany and the Netherlands.

The Gothic Runes

The Goths were early Germanic people who would go on to split into two specific branches, the Ostrogoths and the Visigoths. There were among the first peoples of Northern Europe to use the runes, especially in religious dedications of jewellery and other items.[110] Their runic alphabet is very similar to the Elder Futhark, but with slightly different emphasis. In the fourth century, the bishop Ulfila used the gothic runes as the basis for his new alphabet, which he used to translate Christian scriptures into the Gothic language.[111]

The Northumbrian Futhark

This alphabet builds on the Anglo-Saxon Futhorc by adding four more figures, making thirty-three in total. They are:

109. Pennick, *The Complete Illustrated Guide to Runes*, 62.

110. Pennick, *The Complete Illustrated Guide to Runes*, 72.

111. Pennick, *The Complete Illustrated Guide to Runes*.

- Cweorth ᛢ ("Sacred Fire")
- Calc ᛣ ("Offering Cup")
- Stan ᛥ ("Stone")
- Gar ᚸ ("The Spear")

These new figures first appeared in the Anglian kingdom of Northumbria, which spanned parts of northern England and southern Scotland. In this area, there was linguistic and cultural influence from some Celtic tribes, from Frisia, and from Scandinavia at this time.

The Younger Futhark

Associated with stone inscriptions found in Norway, Sweden, and Denmark, the Younger Futhark alphabet has only sixteen letters, as opposed to the twenty-four in the Elder Futhark. It, too, has been used as a formal divinatory system since the late 1900s.

How to Perform a Rune Reading

Like all divinatory systems, your ability to read runes hinges more on how much you do it rather than how many books you read. There are many different ways to use runes for divinatory purposes. I've included a few simple ones here, but I encourage you to look into more methods, and maybe even devise some of your own.

Taking an Omen

This is usually done as part of a seasonal celebration or at another auspicious time. The reader draws one or two runes from a full pouch of runes and interprets them as signs for the coming year or season. It can also be done as a quick, one-rune answer to a pressing question.

Past, Present, Future

As discussed in the section on tarot cards, you can draw three runes and lay them in a row. The rune on the left represents what has passed and is now finished. The one in the middle represents forces that are currently at play, and the one on the right represents what has not yet come to be. This reading works well as a quick looky-loo when you want to know about a general situation but have no specific questions.

GRID OF NINE

This layout is written about by Nigel Pennick and others, and it is based on the idea of a magic square of Saturn, sometimes used in ceremonial magic.[112] To perform this reading, think of a question you want answered. Then draw nine runes from a pouch, placing them in the order shown:

4: Hidden influences on the outcome of the question	9: Best outcome to the question	2: Attitude to the outcome of the question
3: Hidden influences on the present	5: The present state of things	7: Attitude to the present
8: Hidden influences on the past	1: Effects of the past	6: Attitude to the past

The runes' position on the grid indicate whether they apply to the past, the present, or the future outcome. Some people find it easier to focus during these readings if they have a physical grid to place the runes on. To do this, just sketch a three-by-three grid on a piece of paper before drawing runes. I've even seen this done outdoors, with the grid scratched directly into the earth.

Sortilege: Ogham

Ogham is sometimes referred to as an "alphabet of the trees." It is an Irish-Celtic divinatory system featuring twenty-five characters associated with trees and plants. The original ogham alphabet consisted of twenty letters; five more were added later. It was used for stone inscriptions in parts of ancient Ireland, Scotland, Wales, the Isle of Man, and elsewhere, often for things like place markers and signposts. The ogham was a practical system of writing; the characters consist of vertical and oblique strokes of varying lengths, which made it relatively easy to carve into memorial stones and other monuments.

112. See Pennick, *The Complete Illustrated Guide to Runes*, 190–91.

Sets of ogham are usually a series of sticks or wooden rods with the characters carved or marked into one end. Many practitioners perform readings similar to "drawing lots," pulling one or more rods at random while the marked ends are covered, then interpreting the resulting message(s).

There is no historical evidence of ogham being used in a divinatory sense. This came much later, with the rise of Neopaganism in the late twentieth century.

Beith (Birch): Good fortune, new beginnings, transition and change. Preparing for new work ahead. Removing that which does not serve us in order to make way for the new. Alphabetical equivalent: B.

Luis (Rowan): Practicality, common sense, healing. Innovation; overcoming difficult times and problems with creative solutions. Inspiration, protection, courage, and insight during unprecedented or surreal times. Alphabetical equivalent: L.

Fearn (Alder): Support, protection, boundaries, courage/bravery. Strong foundations, creativity, poetry, music, art. Alphabetical equivalent: F.

Saille (Willow): The moon, dreams, the otherworld, intuition, empathy, knowledge, emotions, relationships. Alphabetical equivalent: S.

Nuin (Ash): Determination and steadfastness; working hard to achieve a goal; working alongside others; strength, connection, and creativity. Alphabetical equivalent: N.

Huath (Hawthorn): Challenges/tests, difficulty and discord, sacrifice, hard work and transformation. Alphabetical equivalent: H.

Duir (Oak): Strength, shelter, safety, confidence, stability, self-reflection. Alphabetical equivalent: D.

Tinne (Holly): Family, the home and hearth, ancestors, energy, balance, hope, light, fire. Alphabetical equivalent: T.

Coll (Hazel): Messages, communication, knowledge/wisdom, learning, academia, secrets, hidden influences, creativity. Alphabetical equivalent: C.

Quert (Apple): Kindness, love, generosity, joy, birth/rebirth, taking calculated risks. Alphabetical equivalent: Q.

Muinn (Vine): Plans, goals, and schemes; peace in the home and family; inner work; the harvest. Alphabetical equivalent: M.

Gort (Ivy): Transformation and growth, transition, personal and spiritual development. Alphabetical equivalent: G.

Ngetal (Reed): Resourcefulness, lateral thinking/thinking outside the box, flexibility in the face of changed plans. Healing, communication, adaptability. Alphabetical equivalent: Ng (as in *ring*).

Straif (Blackthorn): Challenges, facing fears, maturity, authority, spiritual growth, initiation, magical/otherworldly power. Alphabetical equivalent: St (as in *stick*).

 Ruis (Elder): Sacrifice, the animalistic side of consciousness, reflection, self-awareness, transition. Alphabetical equivalent: R.

Ailm (Silver Fir): Contemplation, peace, strength through adversity, healing, regeneration, renewal. Alphabetical equivalent: A.

Ohn (Furze): Hope, new ideas, inspiration, prosperity, fertility. Alphabetical equivalent: O.

 Ur (Heather): Time spent with loved ones, passion, generosity, prosperity, good fortune. Alphabetical equivalent: U.

Edhadh (White Poplar): Prosperity, success, communication, movement, humility in success. Alphabetical equivalent: E.

Ido (Yew): Monumental change, death and rebirth, perseverance, endings, closings. Alphabetical equivalent: I.

Eabhadh (Aspen or White Poplar): Journeys, pathways, gateways, transitions, rites of passage. Alphabetical equivalent: Ea (as in *each*).

Oir (Spindle): Creativity and the arts, inspiration, abundance, passion projects. Alphabetical equivalent: Oi (as in *voice*).

Uilleland (Honeysuckle): Manifestation, release, resistance, revolution, change, magical workings. Alphabetical equivalent: Ui (as in *juice*).

ᚼ **Iphin (Pine):** Psychic power, cycles, seeing clearly, ancestral and divine forces at work. Alphabetical equivalent: Io (as in *scion*).

ᚻ **Emancoll (Beech):** Healing, purification, cleansing, light, clarity, journeys, health. Alphabetical equivalent: Ae (as in *hale*).

An additional character called "grove" is sometimes added, representing a collection of trees and the totality of knowledge and knowing.[113]

The Witches' Runes: Stones O'Leary

Consisting of ten marked stones, this divinatory system first appears in the writings of psychic and occultist Dolores Ashcroft-Nowicki, who wrote about a system of fortune telling using "gypsy" stones, the Stones O'Leary, in 1977.[114] They have since appeared in the published work and private materials of authors and witches such as Patricia Crowther, Simon Goodman, Marian Green, and others.

The stones' imagery—an eye, birds in flight, two crossed spears, the sun, the moon, a star, three rings, a sickle, water, and grain—is simple enough that readings are fairly easy to perform, but their meanings are layered and complex, especially in certain combinations.

Readings are performed by placing the eye stone faceup and holding the other nine stones in both hands. The reader then blows on the stones and casts/drops them onto and around the eye stone. Any stones that lie facedown are discarded, and the remaining stones are interpreted in a spiral pattern, reading outward from the eye stone.

The Eye: Represents the querant, the signifier. Placed faceup at the start of a reading. Australian witch Simon Goodman proposed that it was related in some way to the god Odin.[115]

The Birds: Messages, unexpected news, communication, children, journeys, travel. Adjacent to the moon stone, the birds can sometimes signal a sudden and serious illness.

---

113. Drury, *The Watkins Dictionary of Magic*, 217.

114. Ashcroft-Nowicki, "The Gypsy Runes."

115. Simon Goodman, private documents, 1987.

The Crossed Spears: Conflict, discord, unrest, clashing energies. Heated parting words. Alongside the sickle, this is a serious argument or falling out.

The Moon: Clouded vision, something hidden or not yet come into awareness, dreams, the otherworld, intuition. Dolores Ashcroft-Nowicki related this stone to feminine energy, and to the querant's personality.[116]

The Rings: A bonding or partnership, a link between two situations or people, binding. Patricia Crowther surmised that the combination of the rings and the waves pointed to a romance that would take the querant abroad.[117]

The Sickle: Death, monumental change, an abrupt and drastic ending. When present near the waves, it often points to a physical parting, likely someone moving away.

The Star: Ambition, ideals, energy, inspiration, hope, seeing clearly. When the sun and the star land near each other, they represent the querant's hopes and dreams, but these hopes and dreams will go unfulfilled if the moon is present without the sun.

The Sun: Strength, growth, positive aspects, energy, fruitfulness. Patricia Crowther claimed that having the sun as the "leading" stone in a reading (i.e., the stone closest to the eye) signified a successful year ahead.[118] When the sun appears near the wheat, it usually signals the birth of something new.

The Water/The Waves: High emotions, fluid situations, the underworld. Alongside the moon, this stone sometimes points to an accident or illness. The waves with the star is often the birth of a child in the querant's family.

The Wheat/The Ripe Grain: Harvest, profit, the reward of hard work (especially physical work), endings, climaxes. Simon Goodman wrote that the combination of the wheat and the rings often speaks to a busi-

---

116. Ashcroft-Nowicki, "The Gypsy Runes."

117. Crowther, *Lid Off the Cauldron*.

118. Crowther, *Lid Off the Cauldron*.

ness partnership.[119] If the rings and the wheat are present in a reading with three or more other stones (other than the main eye stone), this is often a sign that the entire reading is for the querant's family rather than just the querant.

EXERCISE
Your Own Set of Runes

There are lots of beautiful sets of runes available these days, but it can be another experience entirely to make your own. Collect or acquire some small, smooth stones and create your own set of Elder Futhark or other runes. If you've got the skills and resources, you could even do this on discs of wood sliced from a dried, seasoned branch.

EXERCISE
A Toast for the Dark Moon

If you are interested in divination, the dark moon is the perfect time to give it a try. This is a short, sweet working you could try before divining with your preferred system. I recommend you try performing the toast on its own for a few months before asking for assistance and performing a reading.

You will need:

- A quiet space free of distractions, ideally where you can see the moon/sky
- A candle and matches or a lighter
- Your preferred divination tool (tarot, runes, scrying mirror, etc.)
- A bottle of wine (or pomegranate/fruit juice if you don't drink alcohol)
- A cup, glass, or goblet

---

119. Simon Goodman, private documents, 1987.

1. Take time to gather your things and get comfortable. Sit in such a way that your body language is open. Light the candle and take some deep breaths to calm and centre yourself.

2. Visualise (or look at) the dark moon: a tiny, sometimes imperceptible sliver of something that was full and brimming with light only two weeks ago. What bathed the lands in silvery wonder now sits sullen and dark while the stars twinkle, and the nighttime lands below are murky and hidden.

3. Pour a cup of wine and raise it to the sky in a toast. Say:

   Darkest mother, lady of night
   Mysterious queen of hidden waters
   May my vision be true
   The future's face half-hidden
   I ask but a glimpse
   All in your praise

4. Take a sip. Sit in respectful silence for a moment before setting the cup down.

5. Once you feel ready, begin divining. Go about your reading as you usually would, by the light of the candle if possible.

6. If you're outdoors, pour the rest of the cup of wine onto the earth as an offering. If you're working indoors, take the time to tip at least some of it onto the ground outside after you're done divining.

))) ● JOURNAL PROMPTS ● (((

- What is divination for? Are there things it shouldn't be used for?

- Do we determine our own destiny? Or are some things set in stone? How do you know?

- What does divination look like in your practice? If you haven't performed divination before, is it something you could see yourself doing as part of your practice? Why or why not?

- What divination systems are you already familiar with, and what category would they fall into? Do you have several methods that could be employed together or in different situations?
- Is there an imbalance between the methods of divination that you study or practise? Which areas of divination do you have yet to explore?

Further Reading

A Curious Future: A Handbook of Unusual Divination and Unique Oracular Techniques by Kiki Dombrowski

The Book of Primal Signs: The High Magic of Symbols by Nigel Pennick

"Ogham Symbol Gallery" by Patti Wigington

"Divination vs. Decision Making Strategies" by Jason Miller

CHAPTER 12
Herbs and Plant Magic

Herbalism and plant magic have been synonymous with the image of the witch for centuries, and this includes witchcraft's modern iterations. This chapter is an introduction to growing, harvesting, or working with herbs. Anyone who is interested can incorporate these practices into their witchcraft. And before you feel the need to start labelling yourself as any particular type of witch, remember that it's the quality and depth of your craft that matters, not how you explain or justify it to the rest of the world.

The best books about plants are not always written by witches. I recommend looking into scholarly gardening and horticulture books before dropping loads of money on a pretty, witchy book about herbs. Gardening books are typically written by people who studied horticulture or a related field at the university level. Titles in this genre can also often be picked up fairly cheaply secondhand.

Before we dive in, here are some things to remember about working with herb and plant matter:

Always research an herb or plant before you burn it, ingest it, or rub it on your skin for the first time. Many herbs become toxic when burned. Some irritate the skin or eyes; others have side effects like sickness or even death if consumed.

Seek consent before exposing another person to any herb or plant for magical purposes.

Keep herbs away from children and pets. Store them safely and out
of reach. If you're growing herbs, keep poisonous or dangerous herbs
in a separate part of the garden, and do not allow children or pets (and
maybe even certain adults) to play in that spot.

Growing Herbs

Growing your own herbs for cooking, brewing, or magical workings is beneficial in a number of ways. You can save a lot of money and, if all goes well,
you'll end up with a product of a higher quality than what you'd get at a shop.
Also, when you use herbs or plants you've grown yourself in a magical working, you're imbuing a part of yourself into it as well—consider all the time
and energy you spent planting, watering, caring for, harvesting, and drying
throughout the process.

Many herbs are easy to grow. Lots thrive in pots and planters, but some are
a bit trickier or fussier. Some grow a little *too* well and will take over your garden! Here are some other things to keep in mind when it comes to growing
your own herbs:

**Good soil and good drainage are essential for the success of
most plants.** Most grow best in neutral or slightly alkaline soil; a pH
level of six to seven-and-a-half is ideal.

Find a sheltered spot out of the wind for new plants. This is especially important for tender seedlings.

Most annuals will grow quickly and easily from seeds. Annuals
are plants that grow, go to seed, and then die within a year, drying out
and leaving seeds. Annuals can be cut and used all summer but die in
colder months.

Most perennials can be grown from root divisions. Some wood-
ier herbs (like rosemary) can be grown from cuttings.

Keep indoor plants in a sunny spot. Make sure to keep them away
from heaters and radiators, as they will dry out very quickly. Dry roots =
dead plant. Indoor herbs need new potting mix every six months or so.

Do not overwater your garden. Or underwater, for that matter. Try
to get into a routine of watering regularly, doing it at the same time
of day. Unless you live in a warm climate, avoid watering in the late
afternoon or evening: it can cause plants to rot.

Practise good garden hygiene. When pruning, always disinfect secateurs (garden shears) when moving between different plants. Carefully wipe the blades with a rag and straight methylated spirits, or try using a solution no stronger than one part tea tree oil to ten parts water. Dip equipment into the solution for around thirty seconds. This will stop any diseases from spreading from plant to plant. Use this same mixture on your watering can, which should be thoroughly washed out every few months.

Dreaming of putting in a herb garden of your own? Before your spade hits the dirt—and more importantly, before you spend any money or otherwise acquire any plants—take into account how much time and energy you can actually put into a garden. Start small—very small—and expand later if you feel the need. Look at the soil, the space, and the light, and work within your means.

Some Popular and Easy-to-Grow Herbs

Try one or two of these options if you're new to growing stuff.

Plant in Full Sun: Parsley, basil (summer only), thyme, lemon balm, chives, rosemary (permanent shrub), culinary sage

Plant in Partial Shade: Bay (small tree), honeysuckle (clumping bush), wild strawberries, rocket/arugula

Plant in Full Shade: Violets, hellebore, valerian

Plants That Should Be Confined to Pots: Borage, comfrey, coriander (partial shade), mint (partial shade)

Some of the easiest-to-grow herbs are the ones that can be used in the kitchen. These also have magical associations.

Culinary Herbs Grown for Their Leaves: Basil (annual), bay (perennial tree/bush), borage (annual), burnet (biennial), chervil (biennial), chives (perennial), garlic (perennial), lovage (perennial), marjoram (perennial), mint (perennial), sage (perennial), tarragon (perennial), thyme (perennial)

Culinary Herbs and Spices Grown for Their Seeds: Anise (annual), carraway (biennial), coriander (annual), dill (annual), fennel (biennial)

EXERCISE
Groundwork

Choose a species or family of herbs and research all you can about it, including its botanical name and its meaning, different varieties, healing properties (or other properties, if applicable), how to propagate and grow it, magical correspondences, etc.

Harvesting Herbs

It feels pretty darn witchy to stroll through your herb garden to gather ingredients you've grown yourself. (I like to go full "mediaeval peasant" and carry a basket on my arm, too.)

To keep your garden and herbal supplies healthy and productive, remember to:

Harvest herbs on sunny or dry days when there is no dew or moisture on the grass or plants. This will help the drying process and reduce the risk of mould forming.

Use a clean pair of scissors to snip off fresh, green leaves. Make sure the scissors are fairly sharp and don't leave behind frayed or snapped limbs on the plant; these will die back and limit new growth.

Make sure secateurs are clean before you start using them. For the most effective cut, place the branch or stem in the jaws at a forty-five-degree angle. Ensure the branch is as deep as possible in the jaw, as this gives you more leverage when cutting. I recommend watching some YouTube videos about pruning if you're new to it.

Drying and Storing Herbs

Herbs need warm, very dry conditions in order to dry out without rotting or growing mould. Back in the day, herbs were dried inside rooves or on the floors of warm, dry attics for weeks at a time. Very few of us have attics these days (I'm terribly jealous of those who do), but there are still a range of ways to dry your herbs ready for use:

Dry herbs in a warm and well-ventilated space. I recommend hanging small bunches upside down in a dry corner out of direct sunlight or above a heater/radiator in a very dry room. Drying herbs by this method can take anywhere between two days and two weeks. Check and turn herbs every few days to ensure even drying. In cooler, damper weather, make sure none of your herbs are touching to avoid them going mouldy.

Dry herbs in the oven. Lay them on an ungreased baking tray in a single layer. Place in the oven at the lowest setting for ten to fifteen minutes, or as long as it takes for the leaves to become dry to the touch. I like to line my tray with baking paper or foil because it makes it easier to catch any fallen bits.

Store completely dried herbs in clean, dry airtight containers or jars. Some folks like to sterilise their jars (as you would for making jams or preserves) before the herbs go in. Even dried herbs won't last forever, and they need to be kept in a very dry, dark spot. Always label things clearly, and never rely on guesswork if you aren't sure about something that's missing a label.

Sourcing Herbs and Plants

Growing your own plants is the preferable option, whether it's a full garden, a potted garden, or a small indoor garden. But not everything is growable in every part of the world, nor does every witch has a knack for—or even an interest in—gardening.

No garden? No worries. Some herbs are easier (not to mention cheaper!) to get than others. Just as it is with any of the other material "stuff" associated with witchcraft, having a witchy herb cupboard is not like collecting Pokémon: there is no obligation to have absolutely every plant. Just figure out what you need and what you'll be using the most of, and build up a basic herbal cabinet from there.

Here is a list of ideas for finding or buying herbs, ordered from the cheapest option to the most expensive.

Try Wildcrafting

This is just a fancy, witchier word for ethical scrumping or foraging. Many useful botanicals grow on roadsides, in parks and on public land, but it's important to know what to look for. Do your research and have a printout or a good book on herbs that you can bring along with you to make sure you're picking what you think you're picking.

Be respectful of local laws around foraging for food, and respect the plants and other creatures (humans and otherwise) who might rely on these plants and trees later. Never take more than you need, and use everything you take.

If you're planning on consuming wildcrafted herbs or plants or using them on your body in any way, *always* bring a qualified, experienced herbalist or horticulturalist with you; some poisonous and edible plants are almost identical. People have fallen seriously ill or died because they mistook one plant for another.

Be sure to wash foraged leaves and fruit well before you use them.

Covet Thy Neighbour's Grass

If you spot something groovy growing in a local garden, politely ask for a cutting, if you feel comfortable doing so. People are often happy to oblige if it means someone is showing an interest in their garden. Plus, this approach often works much better than saying, "Hello! I'm a witch! Can I have a cutting from your laurel tree for my spells?"

Similarly, you can raid the gardens or supplies of friends and family. With permission, of course.

Find a Produce Swap or "Food Is Free" Initiative

Many community gardens and neighbourhood centres host produce swaps where people can share and trade produce they've grown, including herbs. If you can't find one, consider organising one with Pagan friends, or ask your local meetup facilitators if they would mind if you organised one at the next meet.

Watch for Farmers' Markets and Roadside Stalls

This one is probably more for the country and regional folks, but farmers' markets can be a great place to pick up seedlings for not much coin. Similarly, some of my most interesting plant finds were purchased from some bloke selling plants on the roadside in one iteration or another.

Buy from Supermarkets and Other Shops

You can buy dry or fresh herbs from supermarkets, health food stores, and other shops, though you might need to try a witchy or new age shop for the more exotic or inedible ones. Only do this if you've exhausted your other options. When buying dried herbs, always buy food grade and irradiation free. Once again, don't feel as though you need to spend oodles of money to be a better witch.

EXERCISE
The Nine Herbs Charm

Investigate the "Nine Herbs Charm." What was it? Where did it originate? Which herbs were involved? Could it be replicated today? What for?

Some Common Plants and Their Correspondences

Magical correspondences—the qualities we associate with things we use magically—vary hugely across cultures and geographic location. There is no "right" correspondence for anything. This section has some general ideas to get you started, but really, what's important is figuring out what works for you, as well as *why* it works.

Aconite (*Aconitum napellus*): Also known as *monkshood*, *wolfsbane*, *blue rocket*, or *helmet flower*. Grows in mountainous areas of Europe and North America. Grow it for its beauty in semi-shade. The element of water; calming; enchantment; fear; protection; relationships; skills; strength. Poisonous.

Agrimony (*Agrimonia eupatoria*): Also known as *stickwort*, *cocklebur*, or *church steeples*. Sleep and relaxation; protection; banishing; dreams and dreamwork; gratitude; harmony; healing; breaking hexes.

Allspice (*Pimenta officinalis*): Also known as *buffalo herb*, allspice is the seed of an evergreen tree native to Central and South America and the West Indies. The element of fire; attraction; business; communication; friends and friendship; healing; kindness; good luck; prosperity; strength.

Aloe (*Aloe* spp.): Best known varieties are *Aloe vera, Aloe ferox*, and *Aloe socratina*. The juice of aloe leaves is fantastic for cooling sunburnt skin. The element of water; the afterlife; healing; beauty; friends and friendship; love; protection; purification.

Amaranth (*Amaranthus* spp.): Also known as the *flower of immortality and unwithering*, amaranth is a flower thought to symbolise immortality. In several occult traditions, a crown of these decorative blooms is thought to bestow supernatural gifts upon the wearer.[120] The element of fire; passage between life and death; protection; purification; divination and psychic power.

Angelica (*Angelica archangelica*): Also known as *archangel and angel herb*, angelica is a common garden plant that should *never* be wild-crafted, as many poisonous plants are almost identical to it. The element of fire; the sabbat of Imbolc; the sabbat of Beltane; healing; attraction; banishing; consecrating, blessing and purification; spirituality.

Anise (*Pimpinella anisum*): Also known as *sweet cumin* or *aniseed*, anise is native to the Middle East and the Mediterranean. The element of air; protection; psychic power; divination; spirits; clairvoyance; dreams and dreamwork; psychic ability.

Apple (*Malus* spp.): The element of air; the element of water; the sabbat of Samhain; the underworld; birth and rebirth; immortality; offerings; the afterlife; attraction and beauty; rebirth and renewal; sex and sexuality.

Ash (*Fraxinus* spp.): Considered a magically powerful tree in many European cultures and their folklore.[121] The Winter Solstice; death; passage and journeys; protection; health; prophecy; insight and intuition; dreams.

120. Drury, *The Watkins Dictionary of Magic*, 15.

121. Pennick, *Elemental Magic*, 33.

Aster (*Aster novi-belgii*): The element of water; the autumn equinox; calming; happiness and mental health; love; memory; release; stress; truth and truth-telling.

Basil (*Ocimum basilicum*): The element of fire; the sabbat of Imbolc; love; money; the afterlife; power; confidence and assertiveness; friends and friendship; blessing; purification; sex and sexuality.

Bay (*Laurus nobilis*): The leaves of an evergreen tree in the laurel family, bay was used in rituals during the Middle Ages to keep away and resist witchcraft.[122] The element of fire; the winter solstice; the sabbat of Imbolc; the sun; healing; psychic powers; strength; victory/success; release; banishing; purification, especially ritual purification.

Belladonna (*Atropa belladonna*): Also known as *deadly nightshade*, *banewort*, or *witch's berry*. The sabbat of Samhain; death; psychic powers; darkness; the imagination; the night and night magic; witches and witchcraft. All parts of the plant are poisonous.

Bergamot (*Monarda didyma*): Also known as *bee balm*, *Indian plume*, and *Oswego tea*. This is what gives Earl Grey tea its flowery flavour. The element of air; authority; calming; focus and concentration; courage; dreams and dreamwork; power/energy; support.

Blackberry (*Rubus* spp.): Also known as *bramble* and *brambleberry*. A bundle of nine thorny blackberry branches wrapped together at one end make what the author Nigel Pennick calls a "sprite flail," used to spiritually cleanse little-used paths.[123] The element of water; the sabbat of Lammas; money; hunters; protection; communication; death and rebirth; grounding; the mind; purification of people and spaces; prosperity.

Blackthorn (*Prunus spinosa*): Also known as *sloe*, *fairy tree*, *sloe plum*, or *wishing thorn*. Folklorically, a very significant plant. Blackthorn wands are thought to be able to direct magical power.[124] Defence; protection; revenge; the otherworld; destruction and ruin; truth and truth-telling; hexes and cursing.

---

122. Rose, *Herbs & Things*, 41.

123. Pennick, *Elemental Magic*, 34, 97–99.

124. Pennick, *Elemental Magic*, 34.

Borage (*Borago officinalis*): Also known as *starflower* and *bee bread*. The element of air; courage; calming; business and money; power; purification; psychic power; divination; beginnings; skills.

Broom (*Sarothamnus scoparius*): Also known as *besom*, *broom tops*, *Irish broom*, or *Scotch broom*. The element of air; the sabbat of Samhain; the sabbat of Imbolc; divination; purification; creativity; concentration and focus; harmony, especially harmony in the home/family; strength; wisdom. Poisonous.

Burdock (*Arctium lappa*): Also known as *beggar's buttons*, *bur*, and *great burdock*. The element of water; banishing; purification; protection; calming; energy/power; healing; negativity.

Cardamom (*Elettaria cardamomum*): The element of water; focus and concentration; courage; confidence; calming the mind; creativity and the arts; sex, sexuality, and sexual desire; healing; love, especially lustful love; sex magic; strength.

Carnation (*Dianthus carophyllus*): Also known as *gillies*, *giles*, *gilly-flower*, *Jove's flower*, or *pinks*. The element of fire; protection; power; health and well-being; regeneration; awareness; balance; calming; communication; blessing and consecration; rebirth and renewal; strength.

Catmint (*Nepeta cataria*): Also known as *catnip*. The element of water; beauty; happiness; dreams and dreamwork; animals and animal magic; courage and strength; attracting love and prosperity; nightmares and sleep disorders; spirits; friends and friendship.

Chamomile (*Matricaria chamomilla* and *Anthemis nobilis*): Known for its medicinal and mythic associations. In ancient Egypt, it was included in offerings to the sun god Ra. Some Germanic tribes associated the herb with the god Baldur, while in Prussia, wreaths of the flowers hung in the home were thought to protect it from lightning and storms.[125] The element of water; the winter solstice; the summer solstice; love; purification; relaxation and sleep.

Chrysanthemum (*Chrysanthemum morifolium*, *Dendranthema grandiflorum*, and Others): The element of fire; the autumn equinox;

---

125. Drury, *The Watkins Dictionary of Magic*, 54.

cheerfulness and good humour; protection; innocence; love, romance and relationships; problems; protection; strength; truth and truth-telling.

Cinnamon (*Cinnamomum zeylanicum*): Also known as *sweetwood*, cinnamon sticks are actually the bark of an evergreen tree native to Sri Lanka. The element of fire; action and decision making; attraction, especially sexual attraction; sex, sexuality, and sex magic; purification; divination; health and vitality.

Cloves (*Eugenia carophyllus* and *Eugenia aromatica*): Cloves are the dried flower heads of a tree originally native to the Molucca Islands.[126] The element of fire; banishing; protection; offerings; authority; creativity; divination; debt collecting; the weather; sex and sex magic; power / energy; the mind and mental health.

Comfrey (*Symphytum officinale*): Also known as *knitbone, boneset, ass-ear, healing herb,* or *blackwort.* Protection of people; deflection; purification; health and healing; balance, especially healthy balance; banishing; binding; control; memory; divination and psychic abilities.

Coriander (*Coriandrum sativum*): A sixteenth-century formula holds that incense made from coriander seeds, parsley root, and other ingredients will summon minor devils.[127] The element of fire; community and community building; blessing and consecrating; fertility; magic, especially sex magic; peace and harmony; harmonious relationships; health and longevity; protection and security; sleep, dreams and dreamwork.

Cumin (*Cuminium cyminum*): The element of fire; balance, especially balance in the spiritual life; banishing; the hearth and home; health and longevity; cleansing and purification; luck and prosperity.

Cypress (*Cupressus sempervirens*): Also known as the *tree of death* due to often growing in or around cemeteries.[128] The element of earth; banishing; binding; death; rebirth; immortality; eternity; the underworld; transition and transformation; the afterlife.

---

126. Little, *The Complete Book of Herbs and Spices*, 54.

127. Rose, *Herbs & Things*, 265.

128. Kynes, *Llewellyn's Complete Book of Correspondences*, 153.

Daffodil (*Narcissus pseudonarcissus*): Also known as *daffy-down-dilly* or *fleur de coucou*. The element of water; the sabbat of Imbolc; fertility; luck; the afterlife; beauty and strength; love, especially unrequited love; friends and friendship; magic; spirits.

Dandelion (*Taraxacum officinale*): Also known as *priest's crown*, *piss-a-beds*, or *tell-time*. There are several different folkloric "cures" for warts involving juice of dandelion.[129] The element of air; the spring equinox; divination and seeing the future; psychic power; the otherworld; prophecy; psychic protection.

Dill (*Anethum graveolens*): Also known as *dillseed*, *dillweed*, or *dilly*. Dill is associated with magic powers in the herbal folklore of several different parts of Europe.[130] The element of fire; defence, security, and protection; hexes and cursing; desire; the hearth and home; justice and truth-telling; dreams and nightmares; willpower and mental health; protection from witches and witchcraft.

Dittany of Crete (*Origanum dictamnus*): The element of water; astral travel and the astral realm; spirit communication; pathworking; beginnings; control, especially inner control; manifestation; spirits; divination; visions.

Elder (*Sambucus nigra*): Also known as *lady tree*, *bourtree*, or *scaw*.[131] Folklorically, elder is thought to absorb and eliminate harmful energies wherever it is planted.[132] The summer solstice; the sabbat of Beltane; banishing; release; revenge; blessings; the otherworld; protection; visions; spirit contact; occult/spiritual learning; healing.

Elm (*Ulnus procera*): Also known as *ellum* or *elvin*. The element of air; protection; attraction; energy; ruin; hexing and cursing; empathy and compassion; strength and endurance; death, rebirth, and renewal; pregnancy and childbirth.

Fennel (*Foeniculum vulgare*): Also known as *sweet fennel*, *wild fennel*, and *fenkel*, this tough perennial appears in the folklore of Europe, Asia, and

129. Rose, *Herbs & Things*, 56.

130. Rose, *Herbs & Things*, 56.

131. Latham-Jones, *Village Witch*, 193.

132. Pennick, *Elemental Magic*, 35.

Egypt.[133] The element of fire; the summer solstice; healing; purification; banishing; fertility; sight and vision; protection of the home and family.

Foxglove (*Digitalis purpurea*): Also known as *fairy's thimbles* and *dead men's bells*. The element of water; defence; protection; protective magic; challenges/struggles; power and energy; release and banishing. Poisonous.

Garlic (*Allium sativum*): Since ancient times, valued for its health and restorative properties across many cultures. The element of fire; protection of the home; protection from negativity; healing; health and vitality; anxiety and mental health; security; stability; growth.

Geranium (*Geranium* spp.): Easy to grow from cuttings. Some Mediterranean folkloric beliefs hold that geraniums grown by doors or windows will protect the home and bring health and happiness.[134] Grown near a grapevine, geraniums will repel pests from grapes. The home; prosperity; health; balance; beginnings; structure and routine; forgiveness; emotions and emotional stability.

Ginger (*Zingiber officinale*): Native to hot, humid climates. Australia has its own native ginger, *Alpinia caerulea*. The element of fire; psychic power; protection; spirits and ancestors.

Hawthorn (*Crataegus* spp.): Also known as *whitethorn*, *mayflower*, *bread and cheese*, or *bird eagles*.[135] Very unlucky if brought on a journey. In parts of the British Isles, it was traditionally used as a protective charm for houses and cow sheds.[136] In traditional Chinese medicine, the berries (haws) are associated with heart health when properly prepared. The sabbat of Beltane; happiness; protection; power; the otherworld; fairies.

Hazel (*Corylus avellana*): The element of water; luck; power over evil; the otherworld; divination and psychic power; pathworking and spiritual journeys; creativity and the arts; manifesting.

Heather (*Calluna vulgaris*, *Erica cinerea*, and Others): The element of water; the sabbat of Samhain; the sabbat of Imbolc; the sabbat of Lammas; luck; adaptability and versatility; messages and omens; love

133. Kynes, *Llewellyn's Complete Book of Correspondences*, 174.

134. Little, *The Complete Book of Herbs and Spices*, 80.

135. Little, *The Complete Book of Herbs and Spices*, 88.

136. Pennick, *Elemental Magic*, 34.

and romance; family, especially non-blood family; spirituality; trust, truth, and truth-telling.

Holly (*Ilex aquifolium*): The element of fire; the winter solstice; energy; strength; power; intuition; protection and security; blessing and consecrating; courage and confidence; dreams and dreamwork. Poisonous.

Honeysuckle (*Lonicera caprifolium*): Hung around doors and windows on May Day, honeysuckle can be a charm for good luck and prosperity. The element of earth; the spring equinox; the autumn equinox; the sabbat of Beltane; psychic powers.

Hops (*Humulus lupulus*): Cultivated in many countries for use in the manufacturing of beer. Several old herbal remedies include hops as an ingredient in a preparation to relieve the pain of a constant erection.[137] Healing; relaxation and sleep; balance; calming; dreams and dreamwork.

Iris (*Iris versicolor*): Also known as *flag* or *flag lily*. The element of water; the spring equinox; authority and figures of power; awareness and clarity; creative energy; inspiration; death; faith; freedom; divination and psychic ability.

Ivy (*Hedera helix*): Also known as *English ivy* or *true ivy*. The element of earth; the sabbat of Beltane; defence against psychic attack; protection for animals; fertility; prosperity; marriage; messages and omens; transition and transformation.

Jasmine (*Jasminum grandiflorum*): Folklorically, dreaming of jasmine often points to a marriage or new love.[138] The element of water; the spring equinox; the moon; divination; dreams; insight and intuition; friends and friendship; hidden messages and ideas; treachery; sex and sexuality; happiness; grace.

Lavender (*Lavandula officinalis*): Native to hilly areas of the Mediterranean. The element of air; the summer solstice; love; luck; peace and harmony; protection of people; purification; relaxation and sleep.

---

137. Little, *The Complete Book of Herbs and Spices*, 90.

138. Rose, *Herbs & Things*, 71.

Lilac (*Syringa vulgaris*): The element of water; the sabbat of Beltane; exorcism; protection; cleansing; spirits and land spirits; egregore and spirit of place; creativity; inspiration; love and relationships; memory.

Lily (*Lilium* spp.): The element of water; the moon; death; endings; the afterlife; communication; negativity; the otherworld and the underworld; relationships; willpower; pride; quests; manifestation. Many varieties are poisonous.

Lovage (*Levisticum officinale*): Also knowns as *smellage* in parts of rural England due to its reputation as a deodorant.[139] Old herbalists used to associate lovage with eyesight. The element of fire.

Magnolia (*Magnolia grandiflora*): The element of earth; attraction; clarity and truth; dreams and dreamwork; fidelity; relationships; divination, visions and psychic ability; meditation and pathworking; cleansing and purification.

Maidenhair Fern (*Adiantum capillus-veneris*): Also known as *Venus hair* or *rock fern*. A well-known houseplant that can nevertheless be difficult and fussy to grow. The element of air; beauty and superficial appearances; confidence and courage; protection from hexes; purification; release; spirits; wealth; health and well-being.

Marigold (*Calendula officinalis*): There are dozens of different flowers known as marigold the world over. The element of fire; the sabbat of Beltane; the sun; psychic powers; divination; dreams. Some varieties are poisonous.

Marjoram (*Origanum majorana*): Also known as *mountain mint* or *joy of the mountains*.[140] There are many different varieties, including dittany of Crete. The element of air; health and well-being; death and the afterlife; focus and concentration; sleep and sleep disorders; calming; witches and witchcraft.

Mint (*Mentha* spp.): There are around forty different varieties, and not all are edible. Mint will overrun your garden if planted in the ground, so stick to pots. The element of air; the sabbat of Samhain; healing.

---

139. Little, *The Complete Book of Herbs and Spices*, 111.
140. Little, *The Complete Book of Herbs and Spices*, 116.

Mullein (*Verbascum thapsus*): Also known as *moly*, *blanket herb*, *lady's foxglove*, *hag's taper*, *beggar's blanket*, *cow's lungwort*, *bullock's lungwort*, or *our lady's flannel*. In Homer's *Odyssey*, it is "moly" that protected Ulysses from Circe's magic. Courage; divination; protection.

Nettle (*Urtica dioica*): Used in food and medicine all over the temperate regions of the world for thousands of years. The most well-known varieties were introduced to the British Isles by the Romans.[141] The element of fire; protection, especially psychic protection; courage; banishing; communication and messages; defence and security.

Oak (*Quercus* spp.): The element of fire; the winter solstice; the summer solstice; strength; power; purification; charms, especially charms against lightning and storms.[142]

Parsley (*Petroselinum crispum*): Folklorically speaking, parsley seeds must go to the devil and back seven times before the plant will grow.[143] The element of air; purification and cleansing; messages and communication; clarity; truth and honesty.

Peony (*Paeonia* spp.): Associated with Asklepios, the healer son of Apollo, the peony was considered a healing plant by the ancient Greeks. Peony is named after Paeon, a student of Asklepios who was saved by Zeus when Asklepios became jealous of his student's skill in healing and medicine. Many versions of the myth have Zeus turning Paeon into a flower so that he can escape Asklepios's wrath.[144] The element of fire; the sun; protection; healers and healing.

Pomegranate (*Punica granatum*): The mystic fruit of the Eleusinian rites. Also known as *grenadier*.[145] The element of earth; the sabbat of Samhain; the underworld; journeys; hidden/unexpected wealth; prosperity; protection; hidden knowledge; wisdom.

Poppy (*Papaver* spp.): Opium poppies (*Papaver somniferum*) are illegal to grow in many parts of the world. The element of fire; the sabbat of Lam-

141. Little, *The Complete Book of Herbs and Spices*, 130.

142. Pennick, *Elemental Magic*, 32.

143. Little, *The Complete Book of Herbs and Spices*, 135.

144. Winter, *Fire Magic*, 129.

145. Kynes, *Llewellyn's Complete Book of Correspondences*, 162.

mas; the moon; fertility; luck; money; the astral self; the astral realm; dreams and dreamwork; messages and omens, especially from dreams.

Rose (*Rosa* spp.): A formula dated 1600 calls for rosewater and marigold water to be mixed with several other ingredients as a means of seeing fairies.[146] The element of water; the sabbat of Beltane; beauty; love; romance; marriage; attracting love; friends and friendship; dedication and devotion; softness/gentleness; self-care; self-work; emotions, especially emotional protection.

Rosemary (*Rosmarinus officinalis*): Also known as *dew of the sea*. The element of fire; the winter solstice; the sun; healing; mental powers; courage; protection; purification; memory; dreams; health; strength; cleansing; the otherworld.

Rowan (*Sorbus* spp.): Also known as *care*.[147] There are around one hundred species of rowan trees. In Europe, Asia, and some parts of North America, they are commonplace in parks and nature reserves. The element of fire; protection of the home; strength; binding; divination; psychic power. The berries are poisonous.

Rue (*Ruta graveolens*): Also known as *common rue*. It has been traditionally thrown onto midsummer fires in many cultures.[148] The element of fire; the sun; warding; revenge; memory. Poisonous.

Sage (*Salvia officinalis*): Difficult to dry unless dried very slowly. Only use dried sage that is a strong green colour. White sage (*Salvia apiana*) is burned as part of the sacred ceremonies of some Native American peoples. Its sale is exploited by new age and occult wholesalers. Do not buy white sage unless you grow your own.[149] The element of air; the sabbat of Samhain; the winter solstice; the spring equinox; the autumn equinox; immortality; wisdom; protection; offerings; the otherworld; purification.

---

146. Rose, *Herbs & Things*, 257.

147. Latham-Jones, *Village Witch*, 189.

148. Frazer, *The Golden Bough*, 213.

149. I discuss some alternatives to white sage in my book *Fire Magic*.

Snapdragon (*Antirrhinum majus*): The element of fire; business and money; protection; plain speaking; singing and the voice; prosperity; strength; truth and truth-telling.

Strawberry (*Fragaria × ananassa*): The element of water; adaptability; attraction and desire; beauty and grace; divination and psychic skill; friends and friendship; peace and harmony; attracting love and good luck.

Sunflower (*Helianthus annuus*): Native to Central America and grown commercially for their seed in similar climates. The element of fire; the summer solstice; the sun; luck; magic; money.

Tansy (*Tanacetum vulgare*): Also known as *bachelor's buttons*. Do not work with tansy in any capacity if you are pregnant. The element of water; the sabbat of Imbolc; the spring equinox; the otherworld; immortality. Poisonous.

Thistle (*Carduus benedictus*): Also known as *blessed thistle*, this is another herb that has been used in various remedies for centuries, and in many parts of the world. The element of fire; the winter solstice; the autumn equinox; protection of the home; strength; warding negativity; luck; ancestors.

Thyme (*Thymus* spp.): Native to the Mediterranean, where it still grows wild on rocky hillsides. Very easy to grow, and hardy, but can take over an herb garden if left to its own devices. The summer solstice; courage; health; psychic powers; healing; purification.

Valerian (*Valeriana officinalis*): The element of water; purification; relaxation and sleep; power; release; protection; anger and upset; love and sex; dreams and dreamwork; reconciliation after sizeable disagreements.

Vervain (*Verbena officinalis*): Also known as *Druid's weed* or *enchanter's plant*. Used as a protective talisman well into the eighteenth century in places such as England and Wales.[150] The summer solstice; peace and harmony; relaxation and sleep; purification; cleansing; psychic power; strength; creativity; guidance; divination; dreams; the otherworld.

Violet (*Viola odorata*): The element of air; the sabbat of Imbolc; healing; money; good news; sex and sexuality; love and romance; guidance and messages from unexpected sources; changes and transitions.

---

150. Little, *The Complete Book of Herbs and Spices*, 187.

Wattle (*Acacia* spp.): There are almost 1,000 species of wattle in Australia alone, all vastly different and flowering at different times of year.[151] The sabbat of Lammas; the sabbat of Imbolc; inspiration; protection; rites of passage; psychic power. Many are poisonous.

Wheat (*Triticum aestivum*): The element of earth; the sabbat of Lammas; abundance; animals; harvest and harvest blessings; life, death, and rebirth; food supply; rebirth and renewal; cycles, especially the Wheel of the Year; fertility; wealth and prosperity.

Wisteria (*Wisteria* spp.): The element of fire; the sabbat of Imbolc; the summer solstice; love; enchantment; sexual power; storytelling; power and power struggles; the otherworld; dreams and dreamwork.

Wormwood (*Artemisia absinthium*): The element of fire; the sabbat of Samhain; love; psychic powers; binding; divination and psychic skills; dreams and dreamwork; magic and sex magic. Poisonous.

Yarrow (*Achillea millefolium*): Also known as *arrowroot*, *bloodwort*, or *thousand-leaf*. This herb was named after Achilles and was traditionally brought to weddings for good luck and prosperity.[152] The element of air; attraction; power and authority; energy; health and well-being; emotional strength; animal magic; marriage.

EXERCISE
Herbs in the Scottish Play

Read act IV, scene I in Shakespeare's *Macbeth*, in which the witches concoct a magic brew from horrid-sounding ingredients. It's been suggested that many of these names are actually folk names or archaic names for herbal ingredients, and that the witches are rattling off a genuine list of magical herbs and correspondences. Research this theory, including which herbs are named.

---

151. "Wattles – Genus *Acacia*."

152. Rose, *Herbs & Things*, 116.

Ethics and Herbs

Not every herb is the same in terms of its origins, uses, or the means required to grow, harvest, and process it. It's important to consider the steps that needed to be taken to get an herb or other ingredient from nature onto your altar. Aim to minimise harm at every turn.

Getting Frank about Frankincense

The name frankincense comes from the Old French *franc* ("true," i.e., pure/of the highest quality) *encens* ("incense"). This fragrant gum resin has been used in sacred ritual for millennia, and it has been traded since ancient times.[153] The frankincense we and many other faiths use in ritual is the dried, resinous sap of different species in the *Burseraceae* family.

Frankincense is farmed by slashing the bark of the trees and allowing the sap that bleeds out to dry naturally. The resin is sorted by hand and is sold according to its quality. Generally, the more opaque frankincense resin is, the higher the quality.

Burning frankincense is thought to be very good protection for anyone undertaking magical or ritual workings, and it is commonly used in mosques and churches the world over.[154] The Catholic church purchases most of their quality frankincense by the tonne from Somalia, where in some places the sap is still tapped from the trees using methods dating back to biblical times.[155]

In many parts of the world, *Boswellia* trees are in decline because of high demand and habitat loss due to human-generated climate change. An independent study revealed a rapid decline of the trees in Somaliland's Cal Madow, one of the world's premier frankincense growing regions. The demand for frankincense has increased markedly over the last decade, and a kilo of resin now costs more than six times what it did a few years ago. The increased price, along with increased populations in these growing areas, has kicked off a scramble for resin that is more or less unregulated.[156]

153. *Online Etymology Dictionary*, s.v. "frankincense (n.)," accessed April 5, 2023, https://www.etymonline.com/word/frankincense#etymonline_v_11877.

154. Illes, *The Element Encyclopedia of 5000 Spells*, 140.

155. Patinkin, "World's Last Wild Frankincense Forests Are Under Threat."

156. "Frankincense Decline."

Overharvesting the sap is causing the trees to die, as they simply aren't given the time they need to recover.[157] This is leading to the early harvesting and decline of immature trees, and improper and unsustainable harvesting techniques altogether, such as completely stripping the bark and killing the trees in one fell swoop.

Despite what some suspect labelling would have you think, there is not currently a way to determine whether frankincense has been sourced sustainably or by using one of the methods mentioned above.[158] Put simply, it is not possible to purchase frankincense and be sure that you aren't contributing to an ecological disaster. Because there are entire communities that rely on the frankincense trade, this poses an ethical dilemma, to say the least.

Before you purchase frankincense again, I recommend you check out the organisations dedicated to frankincense sustainability. Read about the problems and challenges faced by those living and working in the frankincense trade, as well as the posed solutions. Keep them in mind before purchasing and using this resin.

White Sage and "Smudging"

It's become very trendy over the last couple of decades for people to cleanse their homes and other spaces of "bad energy" by burning white sage or other herbs, often called *smudging*. This is a term that originated in North America. Smudging is a practice sacred to some (but not all) Indigenous tribes from that region. Traditionally, the leaves of sacred plants are burned in a special container, with the smoke being wafted by hand (or with an eagle feather) to cleanse, protect, or heal a person or place.

In the United States, it was illegal for Native Americans to practise their religion until the late 1970s—even later in some areas. Many were incarcerated or murdered just for working to keep their traditions and ceremonies alive; smudging was often a practice included in these.[159]

As such, smudging is not something to be taken lightly, nor is it a trendy and fun thing to do to rid your home of "bad energy." When non-Native people

157. Patinkin, "World's Last Wild Frankincense Forests Are Under Threat."

158. "Certifiable Resin Supply Chain."

159. Burton and Polish, "The Ethics of Burning Sage, Explained."

burn sage or palo santo to "smudge" their homes, they are minimising the cultural and ceremonial significance of this ritual. This also has a disastrous effect on how these herbs are grown, harvested, and supplied.

If you love cleansing spaces with smoke, that's fine. But practise ethical witchcraft by purchasing one of these alternatives to white sage or palo santo:

- Mugwort or wormwood (use sparingly!)
- Juniper
- Pine
- Mint
- Rosemary

And instead of saying "smudging," try using the phrase *smoke cleansing*, the Anglo-Saxon word *recaning*, the Scottish word *saining*, or just the word *censing*.

EXERCISE
A New Friend

Choose and acquire a plant mentioned in this chapter that is easy to grow in your area. Study it for at least a month. Really get to know it, care for it, interact with it, and read about its history, uses, and growing habits.

❭ ❭ ❭ ● JOURNAL PROMPTS ● ❬ ❬ ❬

- What do you already know about herbalism? How do you believe herbalism interacts with witchcraft? Is it an essential component of witchcraft?
- How do you view plants and your relationship to them? Do you engage in any herbal practices already? Do you have an affinity for any plants?
- What steps could you take to work with a plant?
- If you could only work with one plant for an entire month, which would you choose?

Further Reading

Blackthorn's Botanical Magic: The Green Witch's Guide to Essential Oils for Spellcraft, Ritual & Healing by Amy Blackthorn

Natural Magic by Doreen Valiente

Sacred Smoke: Clear Away Negative Energies and Purify Body, Mind, and Spirit by Amy Blackthorn

The Real Witches' Garden: Spells, Herbs, Plants, and Magical Spaces Outdoors by Kate West

"Selecting Seedlings" by Tino Carnevale

"Getting to Know Poisonous Plants" by Denis Cox

"Growing Herbs Indoors" by Jane Edmanson

"Safe & Ethical Guidelines for Wildcrafting" by Rachel Berry

CHAPTER 13
Kitchen and Hearth Magic

Food really is magic. It's tied up in sensations of warmth and satiety, feelings of comfort and belonging, and memories with the people we love. Our sense of smell is one of the greatest triggers for memory, and it's the smells of food that I personally remember best.[160] If being well fed keeps us and the ones we love alive and happy, then preparing food is nothing short of a devotional act.

If I was to write a paragraph here about eating a fruit salad (watermelon, cantaloupe, grapes, blueberries, orange slices…) on a hot summer's day, chances are I would have conjured some pretty strong imagery in your brain. Even that first sentence has kicked things off a bit. Food sustains us. It brings us together. It can bring up any number of emotions and memories. See? Magic.

Recipe Favourites

The image of the witch working over bubbling brews in her little kitchen is just as iconic of that of the witch working with her herbs. This chapter is mostly made up of recipes and ideas, designed as introduction and inspiration for anyone interested in kitchen witchin'.

Anise and Sunflower Seed Biscuits

These lovely spiced biscuits make good cakes for rituals in the summer time. With the sunflower's correspondences to solar energy and anise's associations

160. Hamer, "Here's Why Smells Trigger Such Vivid Memories."

with divination and psychic power, these biscuits would also be great with a cup of tea as you read tarot or runes.

- 125 g (4.5 oz) unsalted butter or non-dairy spread
- 90 g (3 oz) fine sugar
- ½ cup sunflower seeds, lightly roasted[161]
- 3 cups wholemeal flour
- 2 teaspoons powdered anise
- 1 egg yolk, beaten (or 1 teaspoon of your preferred oil)
- Pinch of salt

1. Preheat oven to 180°C (356°F).
2. Cream the butter and sugar.
3. Add the sunflower seeds and beat in.
4. Sift the flour to remove the husks. Add anise powder.
5. Fold the flour into the butter and sugar mixture. If the mixture is too dry (i.e., it won't form into a dough), add the beaten egg yolk.
6. Roll the mixture into small balls, small enough to sit on a dessert spoon. Bake in the oven on an oiled flat tray for 25 minutes or so. The biscuits are done when they have just begun to brown.

Garlic Sauce

This is a great sauce to use with cooked veggies. Garlic has long had associations with health and vitality. Be careful with raw egg yolks, as they can cause illness. Use only fresh eggs, and make the sauce fresh when you need it rather than storing it for later.

- 4 garlic cloves
- 2 egg yolks (or 1 teaspoon of your preferred oil)
- Salt and pepper
- 1 teaspoon mustard powder

---

161. To roast the sunflower seeds, put them on a tray in the oven for 10 minutes or so, or toss them in a hot frying pan without adding oil.

- 165 mL (5.5 fl oz) olive oil
- A squeeze of lemon juice (about 2 teaspoons)

1. Crush the garlic cloves and remove the papery skin.
2. Beat the egg yolks and add salt, pepper, mustard powder, and crushed garlic. Mix well.
3. Add the olive oil slowly and carefully, whisking the whole time.
4. When the mixture is thick, add the lemon juice and whisk again.

Elderflower Wine

With a bit of forethought, this gorgeous drink can make a midsummer gathering extra special. Make in a large glass or ceramic bowl/container—don't use an aluminium container.

- 1 lemon
- 4 generous cups of elderflowers
- 700 g (1.5 lb) sugar
- 2 tablespoons white vinegar
- 4 litres (1 gallon) water

1. Grate the lemon rind and squeeze the juice into a bowl.
2. Add the elderflowers, sugar, and vinegar. Stir.
3. Add the water and stir again.
4. Cover the container and leave to stand for at least 24 hours.
5. Strain carefully, twice if necessary, and bottle. Make sure lids are firm.
6. Leave the bottle(s) in a dark place for at least 3 weeks before opening.

Mulled Wine

This recipe is my go-to for midwinter gatherings. It is certain to warm up your guests, body, and soul.

- 2 oranges
- 1 lemon
- 1 lime

- 1 cup caster sugar
- 3 large apples, chopped but not peeled
- 12 whole cloves
- 2–3 cinnamon sticks
- 1 whole nutmeg (to grate)
- 3–4 bottles of red wine
- 3 tablespoons honey
- 3 bay leaves
- 3 star anise

1. Use a potato peeler to remove large strips of skin from the oranges, lemon, and lime.

2. Put the sugar in a large saucepan and add the citrus peels and apples. Squeeze the juice of the oranges, lemon, and lime over the top.

3. Add the cloves and cinnamon sticks. Grate about half the nutmeg over the top. Store or compost the remaining nutmeg.

4. Add enough wine to cover the sugar mix. Warm gently.

5. Once the sugar has dissolved, bring to a boil.

6. Boil for a few minutes, stirring regularly until the mixture goes syrupy.

7. Once you have a thicker, syrupy mixture, turn down the heat and add the rest of the wine. Do not boil the mixture again, as this will cook off all the alcohol.

8. Add the honey, bay leaves, and star anise and simmer for 5 to 10 minutes.

9. Serve by ladling the heated wine into heatproof glasses or ceramic/ wood cups while still warm and delicious.

Herbs to Garnish Cooked Veggies

Vegetable dishes are a great option for any festival, particularly a fall harvest festival. A sprinkling of chopped fresh herbs can really liven them up, too. Here are my recommendations for herbs to add to basic veggie dishes:

Beetroot: Basil, caraway, coriander, or fennel seeds

Cabbage: Mint and lovage, caraway, or fennel seeds

Carrots: Mint, parsley, thyme, basil, sesame seeds, or allspice

Green Beans: Marjoram, sage, or dill seeds

Onions: Sage, tarragon, or thyme

Peas: Mint, tarragon, or sorrel

Potatoes: Basil, chives, mint, parsley, fennel, sage, or rosemary

Spinach: Marjoram, mint, or sorrel

Templates for Magical Baking

If food is magic, then recipes are just a procedure for making magic. These templates are for generic or "base level" types of food, with variations listed for each one, giving you a range of options and intentions. Have a play and see what works for you. When you get confident with these, investigate tastes, ingredients and their correspondences, and experiment. You might be surprised by what you come up with!

Template: Basic Pancake Batter

- 1 cup self-rising flour
- Pinch of salt
- 1 tablespoon of oil or melted butter
- ½ cup tepid water
- 1 egg

1. Sift flour into bowl with salt.
2. Make a well in the centre, then pour in oil or melted butter.
3. Stir into a batter, gradually adding the water. Beat well.
4. Mix the egg into the batter just before you use it.

NOTES

- The mixture needs to be beaten until smooth. Use a whisk or even a handheld mixer, if you have one. Beating the batter well also makes for lighter, fluffier pancakes.

- Allowing the batter to stand for some time before using softens the cellulose (fibrous molecules) in the mixture. With that being said, don't add the egg to the batter until you're ready to cook it.
- Cook your pancakes on a hot nonstick pan, oiled with a little bit of butter or your preferred cooking oil.
- Pancakes can be cooked, stacked between layers of plastic wrap, and frozen for up to three months.

Options and Variations

For Abundance and Prosperity: Serve with maple syrup and/or some walnuts fried in butter.

For Love, Beauty, and Sex: Add a dash of rosewater and/or vanilla essence to the batter. Serve cooked pancakes with stewed cherries and a dusting of icing sugar.

For Positivity and Good News: Serve with fresh strawberries or raspberries and a sprinkle of sugar.

For Protection: Add a ½ teaspoon of gin to the uncooked batter. Serve with fresh blackberries and icing sugar, or blackberry jam.

For Strength When Making Difficult Decisions: Add grated apple and a pinch of ground cinnamon.

To Have a Productive, Powerful Day: Serve with scrambled eggs or tofu, a pinch of thyme, and chopped spring onions. All the better if you can eat this where you can see the morning sun.

To Strengthen Divinatory Skills: Serve with hazelnut spread.

Template: Basic Cake Mix

- 2 tablespoons butter (or preferred dairy-free spread)
- 2 tablespoons caster sugar
- 1 egg (or ½ teaspoon of your preferred oil)
- 1.5 cups self-rising flour
- ½ cup of your preferred milk

1. Preheat oven to 180°C (356°F).
2. Beat the butter and sugar to a cream.

3. Add the egg and beat well.

4. Beat in the flour and milk until the batter is moderately stiff.

5. Bake in a greased 20 cm (8 in) square cake tin for about 15 to 20 minutes. To test if your cake is ready, run a skewer or toothpick through the centre. Bake until the toothpick comes out clean.

6. Allow your cake to stand in its tin for 5 to 10 minutes before turning it out onto a clean tea towel, a plate, or a cake cooler.

Notes

• When you make cakes, make sure all your ingredients are nearby before you start to mix. Having everything close at hand means you can focus on measurements and monitoring what you cook rather than trying to find some stray ingredient at the back of a cupboard while things burn or sink or dry out. It's also a pain to start cooking something only to find you're missing a key ingredient.

• It's also worth preheating the oven and preparing cake tins by lightly greasing, lining with baking paper, or dusting with flour.

• Sifting dry ingredients ensures for a more balanced, evenly cooked cake. Butter and sugar should be beaten to a creamy consistency.

• Eggs and milk at room temperature will mix and cook better and more evenly than when they are chilled.

Options and Variations

For Blessings and Good Luck: Add half a cup of walnuts to the uncooked batter. Decorate with a couple of borage flowers if you have them.

For Energy and Power: Add a cup of grated apple, a teaspoon of allspice, a teaspoon of cinnamon and a pinch of nutmeg to the uncooked mixture. Eat warm with butter.

For Improved Communication: Add a cup of fresh blackberries to the uncooked mixture.

For Initiations and Other Spiritual Transformations: Serve with pomegranate syrup and cream flavoured with a hint of vanilla.

For Success in Business and/or Financial Windfalls: Add a tablespoon of maple syrup and a small pinch of allspice to the uncooked batter. Before cooking, sprinkle a small handful of rolled oats on top of the cake.

To Attract a Lover: Add a teaspoon of vanilla essence, a pinch of cinnamon, and a cup of stewed, pitted dark cherries and to the uncooked mixture. You may need to add a little more sugar if the cherries are sour. Decorate with geranium petals if you have them.

To Diffuse a Heated Situation: Brew a cup of chamomile tea and add a spoonful to the uncooked cake mixture.

To Increase Psychic Power: Add a tablespoon of food-grade poppyseeds and the juice of 1 or 2 oranges.

Samhain Apple Cake: Before baking, cover the top of the cake with slices of apple. Sprinkle with ¼ cup sugar and 2 teaspoons of cinnamon before baking.

Hearth Magic

For centuries, the hearth was the centre of the home in many countries, which is why the word *hearth* can also be used to refer to someone's household. This is an idea kept in some forms of modern Asatru, where the words *hearth* or *kindred* are sometimes used to refer to a local group of worshippers.[162] This section contains spells, tips, and recipes for the home and family.

Herbal Teas

There are many, many herbs that make a pleasant-tasting cup of tea. If you understand herbs and their correspondences and are willing to experiment, you can brew teas with any number of magical intentions and properties.

How to Make a Decent Pot of Tea

Before I share my herbal tea recommendations, I want to share how I make tea.

1. Boil some fresh, cold water.
2. Warm your teapot by running it under hot water for 20 to 30 seconds. Tip out any excess water.

162. Paxson, *Essential Asatru*.

3. Add ingredients to your teapot. For herbal teas made with dried herbs, the typical ratio is one heaped teaspoon of tea per cup (250 mL/8.5 fl oz) of water. You might need to tweak this depending on your taste preferences and the type of tea.

4. Add boiling water to the teapot and steep for 3 to 7 minutes. This may also take some tweaking and experimentation.

5. Pour the tea into a cup, using a strainer to catch the herbs. Dispose of the herbs. (Omit the straining part of the process if you're planning on reading the tea leaves for divinatory purposes.)

6. Add sweetener, honey, lemon, milk, etc. to taste.

7. Cover your teapot with a cosy to keep it warm.

Try not to drink more than 4 or 5 cups of tea per day. Most teas have diuretic qualities, and some herbs are not healthy in large doses.

Some Herbal Tea Ingredients to Get You Started

If you're new to herbal teas, a good way to introduce yourself to them is to add a few fresh sprigs to a conventional pot of tea. You could also use a pinch of dried herbs. Lemony and minty herbs are lovely for beginners.

Always research and understand a herb before putting it in or on your body. Leaves and flowers can be drunk as infusions; these can be made by covering the leaves and flowers with boiling water and steeping for a few minutes before enjoying. Roots, bark, and seeds need to be boiled to extract their flavour.

Ancestors and Spirits: Agrimony, rosemary, or leaves

Balance: Chamomile or mint

Banishing Negativity: Rosemary leaves or agrimony

Beauty: Catmint, chamomile, or ginseng

Calming: Borage, chamomile, or ginseng

Communication: Rosemary leaves or chamomile

Creativity: Rosemary leaves or chamomile

Dreams and Dreamwork: Agrimony, catmint, chamomile, or rosemary leaves

Endings: Rosemary leaves

Energy and Power: Agrimony, borage, catmint, chamomile, ginseng, or rosemary leaves

Fertility: Catmint or ginseng

Grounding: Chamomile

Healing: Rosemary leaves, agrimony, alfalfa, lime flowers, or mint

Love: Chamomile, ginseng, lime flowers, mint, rosemary leaves, or lemon verbena

New Beginnings: Borage

Peace and Harmony: Agrimony, borage, catmint, or chamomile

Prosperity, Luck, and Abundance: Alfalfa, borage, chamomile, or mint

Protection: Agrimony, lime flowers, or mint

Psychic Ability: Borage, catmint, or ginseng

Purification: Borage, chamomile, mint, rosemary leaves, or lemon verbena

Skills: Borage

Strength and Courage: Borage, catmint, or mint

Tasseomancy

If you are interested in tasseomancy, a divination method that involves reading tea leaves (see chapter 11), here is a suggested method.

1. Querant (person receiving the reading) drinks almost all of the tea in their cup while focusing on a question or problem. They should leave the tea leaves in the cup.

2. Querant swirls remaining tea and leaves in the cup, turns it upside down on the saucer, and hands it to the reader.

3. The reader holds the cup with the handle facing the querant and examines leaves for symbols. Some symbols to get you started:

   Acorn: Youth, strength, man, small start for large accomplishment

   Anchor: Voyage, rest, problem solved, stability

   Boat (or Car/Plane/Other Vehicles): Discoveries, travel, companionship, a journey or undertaking

   Book, Computer, or Scroll: Wisdom, knowledge, learning, communication

Bull: Agriculture, strength, steadfastness, leadership, the otherworld, power

Cat: The afterlife, luck, magic, independence, witchcraft

Cow: Protection, spirituality, the home, death, funerals

Dog: Friendship, loyalty, magic, the otherworld, secrets

Fan, Especially an Open Fan: Indiscretion, disloyalty, things hidden, sleights, insults

Flame or Fire: Passion, sex, purification, creativity, destruction

Flower: Marriage, the fragility of life, unhappy love affair, passing joy

Goat: Beginnings, independence, security, sight, watchfulness

Hare: Creativity, witchcraft, dreamwork, messages and omens, spirits

Knife, Sword, or Dagger: Complications, logic, truth, dangers, power, skill

Shell: Communication, emotions, healing

Skull: Consolation, comfort, personal hurts, endings and a new life

Stag: Rebirth, quests and journeys, knowledge, messages

Wheel: Completion, eternity, a year, season/life cycles, progress, rebirth

4. Read symbols clockwise from the handle, with the fastest timing being at the left side of the handle. Items closest to the rim are read as instances or occurrences that are farther from the querant, while those closest to the bottom of the cup are nearest or most immediate.

Herbal Face Washes

A strong "tea" of certain herbs makes a great natural face wash. As with all herbs you put in or on your body, research them first, buy food-grade/irradiation free if you're buying dried herbs, and test the herb on a small patch of skin to make sure you're not allergic before using.

To make an herbal face wash, simply brew the tea, leave until cool, and strain. If you're using fresh leaves, you'll need to use about three times more than you would use for dried leaves. Here are some suggestions:

For Normal Skin: Fenugreek or marigold

For Dry Skin: Rosemary or parsley

For Oily Skin: Raspberry leaves, elderflower, or mint

For Breakouts: Alfalfa sprouts, hawthorn leaves or berries, marigold, lovage, nasturtium, parsley, or sorrel

To use herbal face washes, first rinse your face with water, then pour a little of the wash into your cupped hands. Hold your hands against the skin of your face as you lean over the basin/sink. Do this a few times as the tea drains away. Pat dry.

Do not store these washes for more than three or four days.

Sleep Bags

Sleep bags consist of dried herbs stitched into a pouch and placed under or near your pillow. They can bring about a number of positive, beneficial effects while you sleep. Never put sleep bags or other small objects in the beds of babies or children, as they pose a choking or suffocation hazard.

To make a sleep bag, cut a natural, breathable fabric like calico, cotton, or linen into two small (maybe 10 cm) squares. Place one square on top of the other and stitch three sides closed to make your bag. Stuff with dried herbs, then stitch closed. Here are some herbal combinations I recommend:

For Better Sleep: Rose petals, cloves, mint leaves, and geranium leaves/ petals

For Dreams: Mugwort, star anise, and dill

For Energy: Rose petals, mint, rosemary, and cloves

For Sensuality: Rose petals, rosemary, and patchouli

Experiment with the quantities and ratios of the herbs listed to find a fragrance that is pleasing and not overpowering.

> **EXERCISE**
> **A Witch's Brew**
>
> Experiment with some of the tea recipes in this chapter, as well as any others that interest you. Layer some tasseomancy into this practise. Take notes as you go. What factors change the outcomes of the reading? Once you're confident in basic tea magic skills, try adding planetary or solar timings, or integrate the dark moon toast in chapter 11.

))) ● JOURNAL PROMPTS ● (((

- What could be the drawback of using a label like "kitchen witch" to describe your practice in modern times?
- What kitchen implements would you consider most important for performing magic in the kitchen? What are their correspondences with more "traditional" tools?

Further Reading

Blackthorn's Botanical Brews: Herbal Potions, Magical Teas, and Spirited Libations by Amy Blackthorn

Sabbat Entertaining: Celebrating the Wiccan Holidays with Style by Willow Polson

The Magick of Food: Rituals, Offerings & Why We Eat Together by Gwion Raven

The Real

Witches' Kitchen: Spells, Recipes, Oils, Lotions and Potions from the Witches' Hearth by Kate West

"Tea Leaf Dictionary" by Flo Saul

"How to Make Tea" by T2

"Protection Magic Basics" by Patti Wigington

"Why I Am a Hearth Witch and What Is Hearth Witchery Anyway?" by Bekah Evie Bel

CHAPTER 14
Talismans

Special objects have been used by magical practitioners in countless ways over the years. Talismans are one of those magics that made their way into fiction and, later, pop culture—and have stayed there ever since. I can't even count how many books and movies include a person who carries an object that gives them special powers. Pop culture has also incorporated the idea of enchanted or cursed jewellery, statuettes, or weapons. But outside of books and films, how might these items be employed?

Examples of Amulets and Talismans

The words *amulet* and *talisman* are often used interchangeably, usually for a small object that is worn or carried for apotropaic purposes. That is, as protection against evil or misfortune. Think the stereotypical lucky rabbit's foot for luck.

Amulets and talismans can be simple, something natural like a stone or leaf, or they can be more detailed, made of precious metals, clay, or wood. The ancient Egyptians used a wide variety of amulets, with motifs such as the eye of Horus or the backbone of Osiris, called a *djed*.[163] Here are some examples of ancient amulets and talismans:

> **Almadel:** In mediaeval magic, this was a wax talisman inscribed with the names of deities and spirits. Almadels were made from wax so that

163. Drury, *The Watkins Dictionary of Magic*, 15.

they could easily be melted down, destroying the secret information or keeping it hidden from prying eyes.[164]

Eye of Horus: A popular amulet amongst the ancient Egyptians was the Eye of Horus, which could face left or right, depending which eye was being depicted. These were usually made of gold, silver, granite, lapis lazuli, or ceramic. Egyptologist Wallis Budge claimed that these could represent either the sun (right eye) or moon (left eye).[165]

Hand of Glory: In mediaeval magic, this was made from the severed right hand of an executed murderer, ideally cut from the corpse while the body was still hanging on the gallows. The hand was hung and drained of blood, then pickled and dried before being bitted with candles between the fingers. Hands of Glory were thought to be able to freeze people in their tracks, so they were sometimes used as a deterrent against thieves. Don't try this at home, obviously.

Katadesmoi: In ancient Greece, these were binding or cursing tablets used to bind another person to one's will. They were usually thin sheets of lead or slate on which the victim's name had been scratched before being thrown into graves, pits, or wells. The Roman equivalent was called *defixiones*. In 2020, archaeologists discovered more than thirty of these in a 2,500-year-old well in Athens.[166]

Common Talisman Correspondences

There are many reasons people make talismans, and as we know by now, every intention has its own correspondences. Some common correspondences are listed here to inspire you as you craft your own talismans. Keep in mind that there is no "right" correspondence for every person, culture, or geographic location in the world. Try to find what works for you, and challenge yourself to think about *why* they work.

164. Drury, *The Watkins Dictionary of Magic*, 13.
165. Drury, *The Watkins Dictionary of Magic*, 96–97.
166. GCT, "Ancient 'Curse Tablets' Discovered Down a 2,500-Year-Old Well in Athens."

Energy / Power

Colours: Blue, brown, copper, grey, green, orange, red, silver, yellow

Materials: Elder, fir, hawthorn, holly, juniper, oak, palm, pine, sycamore, bamboo, mistletoe, brass, copper, gold, silver, steel, tin

Element(s): All

Moon Phase(s): Full

Number(s): 5

Planet(s): The sun, the moon, the earth

Healing

Colours: Brown, gold, green, pink, purple, red, silver, turquoise, white

Materials: Alder, apple, ash, aspen, birch, cedar, cypress, elder, elm, hazel, holly, chestnut, juniper, laurel, oak, olive, palm, pine, rowan, spruce, walnut, willow, witch hazel, amber, jet, lodestone, petrified wood, quartz, salt, brass, copper, gold, iron, silver, steel, coral, abalone, ironstone

Element(s): All

Moon Phase(s): Full

Number(s): 1, 3, 7, 9

Planet(s): The sun, the earth, the moon

Love

Colours: Green, mauve, pink, red, white

Materials: Wattle/acacia, apple, cherry, chestnut, elder, helm, hawthorn, juniper, magnolia, maple, olive, pomegranate, sycamore, willow, clamshell, cockleshell, cowry, mother-of-pearl, copper, gold, silver, quartz

Element(s): Fire

Moon Phase(s): Full, waxing

Number(s): 2, 3, 5, 6, 7, 9

Planet(s): The moon, Venus, Mercury

Luck

Colours: Blue, green, orange, purple

Materials: Apple, ash, cedar, chestnut, hawthorn, hazel, holly, linden, oak, palm, pomegranate, rowan, quartz, obsidian, pyrite, copper, silver, tin, pearl

Element(s): All

Moon Phase(s): Waxing

Number(s): 3, 4, 5, 8, 9

Planet(s): Jupiter

Protection

Colours: Black, blue, brown, gold, green, purple, red, silver, white, yellow

Materials: Wattle/acacia, alder, ash, beech, birch, blackthorn, cypress, elder, elm, fir, hawthorn, hazel, holly, laurel, linden, magnolia, oak, olive, palm, pomegranate, rowan, spruce, sycamore, walnut, willow, witch hazel, amber, obsidian, jet, brass, copper, gold, iron, silver, steel, mother-of-pearl

Element(s): All

Moon Phase(s): All

Number(s): 3, 4, 5, 8, 9

Planet(s): The sun, the earth, the moon, Neptune

Psychic Abilities/Divination

Colours: Black, blue, purple, silver, white, yellow

Materials: Wattle/acacia, cedar, juniper, laurel, magnolia, palm, rowan, sandalwood, water lily, wormwood, iron, silver, snakeskin

Element(s): Air, fire, water

Moon Phase(s): Full, new, waxing

Number(s): 3, 9

Planet(s): The moon, Neptune

EXERCISE
Make a Wax Talisman

To make a modern almadel or wax talisman, collect candle wax. Lots of posh cheese comes coated in wax, which you could easily keep and fashion into any manner of magical bits and pieces. Modern solutions and all that.

Your talisman might be a simple, flat disc, or a more complicated shape or figure. You could mark your talisman with a sigil, a meaningful rune or symbol, or even an image or word that represents your intention. Almadels can also contain the name of a god or spirit.

A talisman can be activated in several ways. Some folks imbue their talisman with energy in a ritual context and keep it close by. Others activate theirs by ritual burning or destruction. No matter how you choose to activate your talisman, you will need to raise energy of some kind. This is a magical working, after all.

For my example, I'd activate my talisman by burning it because I like to light shit on fire. Working in a quiet spot or in my sacred space, I would ground myself and really focus on my intention. Then I would pick up the talisman and look at it—*really* look at it. I'd look at it until I could see it with my eyes closed. I'd think about why I chose it and what being successful in this undertaking will look like. Then, when I'm ready, I'd place it in a fireproof container (such as a cauldron) and set it alight. I would watch it destroy, and as I did, I'd "see" the talisman in my mind also being destroyed. Once the physical talisman has turned to ash, it's time to let go of its mental vision too.

Some people like to place protective talismans around the home.

EXERCISE
Sign Design

Put some energy into creating one of the talismans outlined in this chapter, meeting as many correspondences as possible, including materials, colours, elemental associations, magical timings, etc. Create your talisman in a magic circle. Wear it for several months or until you think it has performed its purpose.

☽ ☽ ☽ ● JOURNAL PROMPTS ● ☾ ☾ ☾

- Sigil magic has become very popular in the last decade or so. Why do you think that is?
- How would you go about creating sigils and talismans for others? Which do you think would be better suited for their needs? Why? Give examples of specific people, their needs, and your reasoning.

Further Reading

Practical Sigil Magic: Creating Personal Symbols for Success by Frater U.:D.:

Sigil Witchery: A Witch's Guide to Crafting Magick Symbols by Laura Tempest Zakroff

The Ancestral Power of Amulets, Talismans, and Mascots: Folk Magic in Witchcraft and Religion by Nigel Pennick

"Episode 75–Ritual Building Protection" on *The Folklore Podcast*

"Talisman, Amulet, Charm. Oh My!" by Gwyn

"The Magic of Sigils" by Patti Wigington

PART IV
Going Deeper

Further down the rabbit hole. A deep breath and tingling anticipation before a plunge. It's time to go deeper.

CHAPTER 15
Books, Study, and Magical Record-Keeping

Books and reading are how many of us pre-internet folks got our first taste of witchcraft. Even though many folks now learn their first tidbits about modern witchcraft online, pagan and witchcraft publishing is still very much a thing, as are recommended reading lists, study requirements (for some traditions), and personal exploration. This chapter looks at books, readings, and the "new" witch, as well as magical journaling and record-keeping.

Books Are Wonderful

...But books still fall into the "stuff" side of things. Don't get me wrong—as a literacy specialist with a teacher-librarian degree, I adore books. They're useful, and they can look pretty, but books alone won't improve your craft. And owning lots of books doesn't make you a better witch than someone who owns fewer or none. In this way, books are no different than any other witchy paraphernalia.

As a teacher, I would be more interested in hearing from somebody who is building a personal practice than someone who rattles off a list of the books they own. That sort of behaviour tends to broadcast how much money someone has or is willing to spend on books, rather than their intentions.

Reading and Study Are Wonderful

...*But* witchcraft isn't all about study. Reading and study can be a part of learning about witchcraft and improving your practice, but it's not the be-all and end-all. As witches seeking to improve our understanding of our craft—and we are all learning, always—what's important is how well we can consolidate our learning and put it to use in a practical sense. We need to be able to pause, reflect, and take stock before galloping on to the next book, course, tradition, whatever.

We need to be able to rest, too. By the time I've finished writing this book, I will have been writing for three years without a break. I wrote two books (not to mention launched and promoted one of them) during a pandemic and the worst bushfires in recorded history. All while having a full-time job, working on my own craft, teaching witchcraft, running a coven, scheduling and leading events, managing a nonprofit, and running a household. In terms of practice (even in terms of just being a functioning human), the best thing I can do for myself now is rest and recharge, not study more.

Study and Research Tips for Witches

Are you diving into witchy study or researching a particular facet of witchcraft? Congratulations. Study can be deeply rewarding, even nourishing. It can also be a headache and a pain, sometimes in equal parts.

Some folks who come to witchcraft haven't read or studied in some time, and that's okay. Here are some tips to help you start building a reading/studying practice that is sustainable and reflective, and that serves the practical side of your craft.

Be nice to yourself. Always. Especially if you are out of your comfort zone with reading and study. I know it's easier said than done, but try not to compare yourself to those who have been doing it longer, or who might have learned study and research skills as part of formal education that you weren't privy to. You're supposed to be doing this because you love and enjoy it, remember?

Start small. Focus on one text at a time. This might be a book, but it could also be a blog article, an encyclopedia entry, etc.

If you hit roadblocks or frustrations, stop. Rest, readjust, or look at other ways you can approach things. Don't punish yourself or feel you constantly have to force a state of "productivity." This is an interest, maybe even a passion, *not* your paid job.

Consider a note-taking method. If you are someone who needs to take written notes to learn, you aren't alone. This isn't appealing or useful to everyone, but if it interests you, you may find bullet journaling useful for note-taking and keeping track of resources. Other easy, useful note-taking methods include the Cornell method and the Outline method. A quick Google search on any of these should bring you up to speed on the basics of each.

Analysing Sources with CRAAP

Reading and research are great, and they can be really helpful and inspiring if you're a beginner, but they can also get overwhelming and confusing pretty quickly. There's a lot of information out there, and not all of it is helpful or reliable. Analysing sources means practising discernment about what you are reading and making decisions about the validity and reliability of a text.

In my work as a literacy specialist, one of my focuses is teaching information literacy to teens and young adults. I give them some tools for assessing how reliable or credible the information presented in a text is. Here is a condensed version of some of that, which should help you examine content you come across. The questions here are adapted from the CRAAP test, a strategy for critiquing text devised by librarian Sarah Blakeslee and her team.[167]

Currency

The C in CRAAP stands for currency. This refers to how recent a source is. In terms of witchy books, they were often written for the witchcraft of their time, and as such, they remain a product of society at the time they were written. Wicca and witchcraft in the 1990s were very different than Wicca and witchcraft in 2010, and again, that is different than what many witches are doing right now. This isn't to say that the only books we should be reading are the ones published now, but understanding context is important.

167. Blakeslee, "The CRAAP Test."

Witchy Books through the Decades

There is a lot to discover about the witchy books and decades of the past, but as a general guide, here are some things to remember about where witchcraft was focused at certain times, and how it was received by wider society.

1960s AND EARLIER

At this time, witchcraft laws had only just been overturned in some countries. Gerald Gardner's *Witchcraft Today* was first published in 1954. Society as a whole remained quite conservative until the late 1960s. Approaches to witchcraft were mostly academic, often informed or influenced in some way by Gerald Gardner, Margaret Murray, or others.[168]

1970s

By the seventies, as interest in Paganism and the occult grew—working hand-in-hand with society's more progressive values—new age publishing started to become more popular and lucrative.

Interest in Wicca and witchcraft started to grow significantly in America after the late 1960s, and books on magic and Paganism started to emerge for a wider, less academic audience. For the next few decades, many of these books would continue to make romantic, unsubstantiated claims about Paganism and its origins, especially its relationship to ancient societies and "Celtic" culture.

Paganism and pagan events are very much counterculture affairs that reject stuffy mainstream values and embrace growing movements like women's liberation, sexual liberation, political awareness, and so on. Starhawk's *The Spiral Dance* was first published in 1979, very much influenced by these concepts. It remains a classic text for many in witchcraft, feminist craft, and ecofeminist spaces.

1980s

Many countries experienced rapid socioeconomic change as the Western world embraced capitalism and the rise of the computer. The second half of this decade saw tensions escalate across the world as relationships soured between several countries involved in the new iteration of the Cold War.

---

168. O'Brien, "NeoPaganism."

The AIDS epidemic was first recognised in 1981 and went on to kill millions, including gay men and other marginalised people who had found their spiritual homes and chosen families in Pagan and witch communities.

The 1980s also saw the rise of the outer court (magical working or study groups that are more open and accessible to interested parties than a traditional Wiccan coven), with American writer Ed Fitch releasing books that popularised the idea that witchcraft didn't have to be coven-based or oathbound.[169] There were many other books like this around the second half of the decade: Raymond Buckland's *Complete Book of Witchcraft* first hit shelves in 1986, and Scott Cunningham's *Wicca: A Guide for the Solitary Practitioner* was first published in 1988. Both titles are still widely available today.

1990s

Satanic panic, a moral panic made up of over twelve thousand unsubstantiated cases of Satanic ritual abuse of children, started in the US in the early 1980s and had spread to the rest of the world by the 1990s. Some of the accused "Satanists" lost their jobs, were forced out of their neighbourhoods, or even went to jail.[170] Many witches and occultists who had been practising somewhat openly went underground; practice became a lot more private for many. Pagan and witch publications during this time often put an emphasis on how harmless modern witchcraft was and explicitly distanced it from Satanism or devil worship. Satanic panic also saw the rise of many Pagan and witch organisations (such as the Pan-Pacific Pagan Alliance) dedicated to educating the general public on what paganism was and was not.

As the internet became more accessible to people, witchcraft and Pagan spaces started expanding more rapidly than ever before. The mid-to-late nineties also saw a trend of witches on TV and in movies. Witchy books specifically for teens and young people started to come to the fore, including Silver Raven Wolf's *Teen Witch*, first published in 1998.

169. Mooney, "The Benefits of Outer Courts and Training Circles."
170. Wilkinson, "Let's Talk About Sects 1."

2000s

The boom of witches in popular culture continued throughout the 2000s, and with it came a publishing boom. Internet use became more and more prevalent, which contributed greatly to the globalisation of witchcraft as a whole. By the mid 2000s, social media had arrived, and it changed the way humans communicated in general. It certainly affected the way witches and Pagans accessed their spiritual communities.

Climate change and global warming became a much more common concern, and the US's War on Terror began after the September 11 attacks in 2001. Ultimately, the decade culminated in a global financial crisis and an economic recession in many countries the world over. This recession impacted the publishing landscape and, in turn, witchcraft in general.

2010s

The financial crisis took its toll on businesses all over the world, and Pagan and witchy publishing companies weren't spared from this. Larger publishing houses slowed their production, and many smaller ones—including niche publishers outside America, such as Capall Bann—closed their doors forever. This led to a market dominated by larger, American-based publishers, who often released quite US-centric books—which, as I've already mentioned, aren't always of much use to people living outside the US (especially if they also happen to be in the Southern Hemisphere!). This decade also saw the rise of tablets and smartphones, and they continue to affect the way we use and consume media.

2020s

The late 2010s and early 2020s have seen the rise of the online witchy "influencer." More than ever, witchcraft is an aesthetic, a trend, a look. While in-person Pagan and witch spaces are still going strong, e-Occultism—occult communities and practices that are largely online—has gained popularity, especially with the lockdowns and social-distancing laws of the early 2020s. Many areas of witchcraft and Paganism are less taboo than they were in the early years, and publishing reflects that. Many titles are available through large, mainstream literary retailers.

Questions to Ask Yourself about a Text's Currency

When was this content written? When was it published? For
books, you can find publication information on the first couple of
pages. Look for the original date a book was published and note any
reprints or new editions. For websites, you can usually find this information when you "view page source." Think about what was happening
in the world (and in pagan publishing specifically) and how that might
affect the content of the text.

Is there an updated version of this content? Newer editions of
books often have additional content added, or author/contributor
commentary on what was printed before. For online articles, look
for revisions or additions by using the "view page source" option.

Relevance

The R in CRAAP stands for Relevance. Once you've established a text's currency, decide whether that text actually provides what you're looking for. A
simple way to determine this is to know exactly what it is you're looking for.

Questions to Ask Yourself about a Text's Relevance

Why am I reading this? Devise and write down some questions or
statements to help guide your research before you begin. For example,
if you want to learn about celebrating the seasons as a modern solitary
Druid, you certainly wouldn't pick up texts on covens in British Traditional Wicca, or even on seasonal practice for groups of Druids, if you
could help it. Note that this only applies to texts you're reading for
study/research, as opposed to reading for pleasure, because you don't
need a reason to read anything you enjoy!

Authority

The first A in CRAAP is for Authority. Things can get a bit murky here when
discussing witchcraft texts; the CRAAP test was designed for academic texts
and articles, after all. While pagan and witchy books fall under the umbrella of
nonfiction, most of them aren't considered academic in the traditional sense.

In academia, the first A in CRAAP is a prompt to think about the author's
qualifications, degree(s), and experience in the field of study, as well as their

approach to subject matter. In many ways, this is a valuable approach for pagan and witchy texts too.

Questions to Ask Yourself about a Writer's Authority

Look into a writer's background, either in the "about the author" section of the book, or via a quick internet search.

What is their level of experience and participation in witch-craft and pagan spaces? How long have they been practising? Do they even practise? What groups, communities, traditions, or events are they connected to? If an author's bio focuses mainly on what was achieved in the 1980s, what are they doing now? How might their approach to their craft changed over time?

Do they have any qualifications that are recognised in the com-munity? This is where that aforementioned murkiness starts. There are folks out there—and some of them are authors in new age and witchy spaces—whose "qualifications" don't really hold water. There are places on- and offline where one can procure a cheap and very dodgy PhD qualification, for example. If a witchy or new age author goes to the trouble of rattling off titles like "PhD" or "Doctor," *especially on the cover of their books*, look into that.

There are other qualifications a writer might have that are rec-ognised in their community but not necessarily elsewhere: initiations into specific traditions or to certain degrees within those traditions, for example. Remember that these titles and initiations do not hold much meaning outside of the specific traditions; a high priestess of a coven isn't the high priestess of all witches everywhere.

Do they have any other formal qualifications? Some authors have real-world formal qualifications that translate into the content and context of their work. Good examples of this are witches who write books about teaching the craft who also happen to be teachers in the real world, or folks who have a degree in the performing arts who write about, say, ritual design. While these qualifications are certainly not mandatory in this field, knowing this about an author (especially one whose work or experience is unknown to you) can add gravity to what they have to say.

Accuracy

The second A is for Accuracy. This relates to whether or not the author has cited their sources. Again, this is more straightforward in academia—sources are considered scholarly and academic, or they aren't.

Witchcraft books, especially the more "mass market" ones, have a history of making claims without backing them up with evidence. This has improved somewhat, but it's still worth thinking about.

Questions to Ask Yourself about a Text's Accuracy

Keep an eye out for citations, either in the form of foot- or endnotes, or as a bibliography at the back of the book/end of the article.

Has the author cited their sources? Not everything in a witchy book warrants citation. Things that do would be things that are stated as fact: names, dates, statistics, figures, historical events, scientific/empirical concepts, etc.

Is there a bibliography? Generally, there tends to be a list of works cited or recommended for further study at the end of the article or in the back of the book. Pay attention to it to get an idea of what research went into the main text. Bibliographies can also lead you down some pretty fantastic reading rabbit holes of your own.

Purpose

The P in CRAAP stands for Purpose. Thinking about the purpose of a text—why it was written in the first place—is a higher-order skill and can require you to think quite deeply. It is a useful exercise nonetheless.

Questions to Ask Yourself about a Text's Purpose

Why was this text written? Is this to inform you about something? If it's an article online, is the author trying to sell you something? Convince you of something?

Who is the target audience? Think about who this book or article is written for and marketed to. How do you know who this is? If you aren't part of the target audience, what is appealing to you?

In what ways is this author biased? Unless the text you are reading is an academic text—which most witchy texts are not—it's likely some bias will exist in the writing. Once you've looked into the author's background, experience, and qualifications, you should have some idea of what topic(s) might be closer to them than others, and why that matters.

Just look at this book, for example. I'm an Alexandrian Wiccan who works in education, specifically disability education and language advocacy. While I've tried to keep things as eclectic as possible in most places, you will still see that most of the witchcraft I've discussed has been Wiccan-based in some way. I've also gone out of my way to explain key terms, to provide tips and workarounds if learning or doing something in the "traditional" sense doesn't work for you, and so on.

Bias isn't always a bad thing. Regardless, it's important to acknowledge it, and to approach the text you're reading with the understanding that it is one person's view and one person's way, not necessarily the *only* way.

EXERCISE
Practising the Witch's CRAAP

Use the CRAAP test to evaluate a witchcraft text that was published more than ten years ago.

Magical Record-Keeping

Now that we've discussed why it is important to practise discernment when it comes to the work of others, it's time to get your own house in order in terms of writing and record-keeping. One of my biggest regrets is that I didn't take any notes or write anything down during my first decade exploring witchcraft. I suspect I would have figured out a few things much quicker if I had.

By regularly jotting down some notes—however simple—you're laying the groundwork for learning for your future self.

Your Book of Shadows

One of the fancier options for magical record-keeping is a Book of Shadows. Sounds mystical and ancient, right? Nope. The term *Book of Shadows* is less than a century old. It was coined by the founder of Wicca, Gerald Gardner, in the early 1950s, and it was originally used to describe the handwritten book of oathbound material given to Gardnerian witches once they were initiated.[171] In her book *The Rebirth of Witchcraft*, Doreen Valiente, one of Gardner's priestesses, claimed that he found the term in a 1949 occult magazine; it was the title of an article next to an advertisement for Gardner's novel *High Magic's Aid*.[172]

Just as witchcraft has evolved and expanded in the decades since, the definition for a Book of Shadows (or BoS, for short) has grown to include a witch's more personalised books of magical instructions and records, spells, dream journals, and more. In traditional Wicca, *Book of Shadows* is still a term usually reserved for a book of oathbound material.

What to Put in Your Magical Journal

Keeping a magical journal will give you a better chance of replicating good results, and it will also help you examine why something didn't work.

In order to be of use to you later, and to help you paint a bigger picture of your practice as you go along, your journal/notebook should include details of any spell, ritual, working, or practical thing that you do. Include details like the date, moon phase, intention (what it is you're setting out to do), any ingredients or components used, etc. Try to be as scientific as possible. You don't have to write huge wodges of text. Provide some succinct, detailed points on what you did, how you did it, and why.

As you get more accustomed to doing this, you might add notes on books you're reading, correspondence notes, diary entries, etc. This is your book, so make it your own.

---

171. Mankey, *The Witch's Book of Shadows*, intro.
172. Valiente, *The Rebirth of Witchcraft*, 51.

EXERCISE
Keeping a Magical Journal

Starting with just a sentence or two, begin your own magical journal.

The idea of journaling can be daunting, especially if it's not something you're familiar with. As with most things I've discussed in this book, sustainability of practice is far more important than anything overly showy and Instagrammable.

Your journal might be a plain notebook in which you jot down details of rituals and magical workings, or it might be something fancier, if that interests you, but always, *always* aim for sustainability. Your magical journal should be something you can manage regularly without it becoming a chore.

))) ● JOURNAL PROMPTS ● (((

- How would you define a grimoire versus a Book of Shadows, in your own words?

- Is it appropriate to apply analytical tools such as the CRAAP test to books about witchcraft? Why or why not?

- What are some simple steps you can take to evaluate a book's accuracy and reliability as a seeker of witchcraft?

- Review the timeline earlier in this chapter. What would you say are the five defining moments that have shaped books about witchcraft and paganism over the last fifty years?

Further Reading

Grimoires: A History of Magic Books by Owen Davies

"Information Privilege and Poverty in Paganism" by Ash

The Bullet Journal Method: Track the Past, Order the Present, Design the Future by Ryder Carroll

CHAPTER 16
Doing Witchcraft

By now, hopefully you've had a go at some of the practical exercises in this book, or you've at least been inspired to do or make something mentioned in previous chapters. One of my main motives for writing this book was to get people to actually *do* witchcraft, rather than just thinking about it, talking about it, or posting about it online.

I know that in an ideal world, many of us would be living our best witch lives 24/7, maybe in a groovy little cottage in the forest or a rambling old mansion à la *Practical Magic*, with no cares in the world outside of our craft and the people we love. But modern life doesn't work that way. And the cost of participating in modern life is often a lot more than we'd like to pay in terms of time and energy. It's my hope that the suggestions in this chapter will help you live your craft in an authentic, achievable way that prevents it from becoming an afterthought.

Being a Witch around Non-Witchy People

Practising and learning about witchcraft can be exciting and joyous, especially when you're just starting out. But not everyone is going to understand it the way you do, and it's not necessarily your job to enlighten them. I get that it can be tempting, but unless someone specifically asks you about it (and you feel comfortable discussing it), witchcraft is not something folks are going to care about in the way you do. How would you feel if someone started discussing their deeply held spiritual beliefs without being prompted?

If you keep wandering down this path, you might also feel a bit of a disconnect from the "old" you and from the non-witchy world at large. Christmastime here in Australia still feels pretty odd, even alienating at times, for me. What's important to remember is that picking up the witch's broom doesn't mean you have to shun the rest of the world. Witches still exist in the same world as everyone else.

Witchcraft and Kids

I have some pretty strong feelings about indoctrinating kids into *any* kind of spirituality or religion. If you're a parent and you want to share your path with your kids, that's your business. But it's probably more ethical to keep the focus on nature and the seasons and spare them the heavier stuff until they're old enough to make their own informed choices. There are some great resources for pagan parents on the website Little Pagan Acorns.

When it comes to other people's kids, I think it's a similar set of circumstances to being a witch around non-witches: it's not your job to influence the spiritual lives of other people's children.

Life Rites

Scratch the surface of many secularised life rites—marriages, funerals, baby namings, what have you—and you'll discover that they are, unsurprisingly, Christocentric for the most part. If witches and pagans want to keep insisting that our practices have hit the mainstream, then as a community, we need to do better with how we mark and celebrate certain life rites, as well as how we prepare, celebrate, and grieve our dead. We need to know our witchy loved ones' wishes when it comes to how they'd like things handled in their old age, and at the end of their lives.

Seek out registered Pagan and witchy celebrants near you if you want legal ceremonies that reflect and respect your beliefs. If you choose to celebrate baby namings, coming-of-age ceremonies, and other events that don't require legal documentation, consider writing your own or reaching out to likeminded friends and elders.

Talk to the Pagans and witches close to you about their wishes for after they die. Many a Pagan or witch has received a generic funeral from well-meaning family members because their wishes weren't known or communicated. Think about what arrangements you would like when you die and discuss them with people you trust. If you live in a country that has them, consider formalising this in legal documentation such as a Final Directive.

It's worth mentioning here that no two witches or pagans will celebrate any of these things in the same way. A funeral for a traditional Wiccan might look very different than a funeral for an eclectic witch or a heathen; it might not. This is why communication is so important. For an excellent overview of the ways different Pagans deal with death, dying, and bereavement, read Mortellus's fantastic book *Do I Have to Wear Black?*

Keeping Yourself Nice

Self-care is one of those terms that's thrown around a lot these days, particularly in spaces where modern witchcraft intersects with various "wellness" movements. There is a place for self-care in witchcraft, absolutely, but what frustrates me about some of the discourse out there on witchcraft and self-care is that witchcraft can be *so much more*. Witchcraft is deeply personal, but at the same time, witchcraft isn't necessarily always about you. It's a difficult line to walk.

Self-indulgent ranting aside, self-care is still very important to the modern witch. If our minds and bodies are the most valuable tools we own—and they are; see chapter 8—then it follows that maintaining those tools is only common sense and in the best interests of our craft, whatever it might be.

If a plane is going down, you put on your own oxygen mask before you help others. If you don't attend to yourself, anyone you intended to help perishes anyway. Likewise, if your witchcraft involves service to people, to deities, to spirits, to the land, or to yourself in any way, then it makes sense that you should look after yourself so you can do the best job possible. In this way, self-care is an act of devotion and reverence; it's not to be sneezed at.

So, don't always put your needs behind those of others. Find a balance and learn that the word "no" can be both a complete sentence and a very powerful spell all on its own. Sleep. Be nicer to your body; it's awesome, and it carries around the electricity and gut bacteria that make you *you*. Drink more water.

Witchcraft in Troubled Times

Witchcraft is just one tool that we can use when times are tough. It is also, in many instances, borne out of troubled times. For instance, as things got worse for Londoners during World War II, people were moved out of the city and into the country. Gerald Gardner was among those people. One day, while riding his bike around country lanes, Gardner came across a certain Rosicrucian theatre company. In time, this chance meeting would lead Gardner to Wicca, and it ultimately changed the face of witchcraft for the next hundred years or more.[173] So, without World War II, there wouldn't *be* modern witchcraft. Not in a way we would recognise, anyway. Of course we wish troubled times weren't ours, but as Gandalf says, "All we have to decide is what to do with the time that is given us." Witchcraft was borne out of troubled, awful times, and in troubled times, we survive, we love and support those around us, and we love and support ourselves.

When I first read Lora O'Brien's book *A Practical Guide to Pagan Priesthood* in 2019, I was challenged to improve my practice and think about the way I served my community. But the one thing about that book that I kept sticking on was the way she talked about "crisis care" and the importance of being prepared for that.[174] It was something that, at the time, I couldn't get my head around. Now, as I'm writing this, it's 2021, and I've written this book during stressful global times. There are members of my community I haven't seen in over two years, and the few people I do see are like me: exhausted, scared, and stressed the fuck out. I'm learning firsthand—and very much on the fly—what it is to be a priestess during a time of monumental change and widespread uncertainty, when around me people are losing their minds, their jobs, or their lives.

This isn't to say I'm zooming around like a superhero helping people out of burning buildings. These unprecedented times have required an unprecedented amount of aforementioned self-care. My metaphorical aeroplane oxygen mask has slipped off more than once, and I've had to stop and readjust, or even just breathe. It's only then that I've been able to do what I can for the people around me. It floors me to think that this is the crisis care that Lora

173. Mankey, *Transformative Witchcraft*, chap. 1.

174. O'Brien, *A Practical Guide to Pagan Priesthood*, 109–21.

O'Brien talked about, and that was unrecognisable to me twelve months ago, but that's what it is.

Witchcraft and Community

If you're new to witchcraft and Paganism, you may not have looked much into community. Now, community is by no means crucial to your path as a witch. There are many who prefer to remain solitary, and they are no more or less valid witches than those who choose to participate in community, be it through public rituals and meetups, larger public organisations/traditions, or more private covens, outer courts, teaching circles, groves, and so on.

But, when it's done right, community of any kind can be one of the greatest teachers and boons in your life. I would not be the person or the witch I am today if it wasn't for the communities around me, the experiences we've shared together, and the friendships and chosen family I've gained along the way.

It's important to remember that, like literally any other special interest group you may dip your toe into, there is always the potential for drama and disaster. This is not unique to witch community, and the witch community is not any more or less prone to this sort of behaviour. If we were dog breeders, students in a drawing class, or part of a roller derby league, we would be faced with the same odds. Community consists of those who show up, not those who whine about community without participating. If you come across groups or individuals you don't gel with, politely move on and look elsewhere, but don't give up. Humans are humans whatever they happen to be doing, and you shouldn't let one or two jerks—or, worse, someone else's opinion—turn you off the entire idea of community. There is so much potential friendship and growth that can be gained from participating in its healthier forms.

What to Look For in a Witchy Group

Whether you're a clover-green newbie attending your first public meetup or an old hand dipping your toe into a new group, there are a few things to think about when assessing if this is a healthy group, and one that is right for you.

Does this group's tradition or "flavour" of witchcraft suit your needs and path? This is probably most relevant for covens or groves, but it's worth asking of more eclectic, less formal meetups too.

Do you feel safe here? Witchcraft groups are like any other social or special interest group. Pay attention to your gut feelings about a group and the people in it. Don't attend events at a private residence unless you've met folks in person somewhere public first. Always tell someone where you're going if you're going there for the first time. Bring a friend, if you have one so inclined. If something doesn't feel right or if you don't feel safe attending a meetup or public event, politely take your leave.

How are guests—especially newcomers—treated? Is everyone treated the same, and welcome to participate? Is the atmosphere more cliquey and intimidating to outsiders?

Are marginalised people welcome? Are people with disabilities welcome? What about queer, trans, or gender-diverse people? What about people of different racial, cultural, or socioeconomic backgrounds? How do you know?

Does the established group get along and work well together? Are their obvious fractures or tension in certain parts of the group dynamic? How are issues dealt with, if they arise?

Are they well organised? If you're attending a public ritual, does everyone know what they're doing? Are they on time, with everything they need? Are things properly explained?

Are their priorities in the right order? Are they genuine and earnest in their approach/discussion of witchcraft, or are things too flippant and blasé? A bit of silliness is good for the soul, but there is a balance to be struck here. Mirth is a fantastic thing, but look for reverence, too.

What are the group's expectations of new members? Will you have to pay money? If so, what does that money pay for, exactly? In the context of an outer court, coven, or grove, what study will you be expected to complete? What is the time commitment? How often will you need to turn up?

BASIC SKILLS
Visualisation IV

We haven't done a visualisation exercise in a while, so if you need a refresher, refer back to the others or the appendix at the end of the book. This exercise uses the visualisation skills you have developed so far, and it's a good way to energise yourself as you go about your work as a witch.

1. Stand, sit, or lie in a comfortable position. Relax, find stillness, and begin 4:4 breathing when you're ready.

2. Once you feel totally comfortable, start to visualise a silver spark in the air, above your head. Watch it glitter and grow, slowly, with your breath, until it is the size of a beach ball or balance ball.

3. Let it hover, sparkling and silver, above your head for a few seconds. Then visualise it moving slowly—always controlled, not falling—down your head and body, becoming transparent as your body moves through it, before disappearing into the ground beneath you.

4. As the silver ball passes, imagine it leaving behind a sparkling sheen on your skin. Visualise this radiant silver energy soaking into your skin. With the next breath you take, feel yourself becoming stronger, sturdier, and more energised.

5. Breathe in stillness for another minute or so before opening your eyes and continuing on with your day.

Repeat this whenever you have need of a bit of a boost. This is a good one to do in the shower before a busy day.

))) ● JOURNAL PROMPTS ● (((

- What would your ideal witchy group look like? What would they do? What would their values be? How often would they meet? How would seekers find them, and what would they have to do to join? Do you think a community like this exists? Why or why not?

- Have you ever been totally burnt out? How did you know? What are some warning signs you can look for in the future to avoid getting that run-down?

- What is self-care to you? What makes you feel rejuvenated? How do you know you are rejuvenated?

Further Reading

All Acts of Love and Pleasure: Inclusive Wicca by Yvonne Aburrow

Weave the Liminal: Living Modern Traditional Witchcraft by Laura Tempest Zakroff (especially chapter 6)

Wicca: A Comprehensive Guide to the Old Religion in the Modern World by Vivianne Crowley (especially chapters 7, 11–14)

"Amici Mortem: Transforming Our Cultural Experiences with Death" by Elizabeth Autumnalis

"Do We Need Pan-Pagan Clergy? (I Don't Think So)" by Jason Mankey

"Should I Join This Pagan Group or Not?" by John Beckett

CONCLUSION
So Now What?

It is my sincere hope that you have gotten something out of this book that has helped you understand witchcraft a little more deeply, even if that understanding is that it is perhaps not for you.

Witchcraft is the most nourishing and wonderful and, well, magical part of my life. It's also really hard sometimes, and it seems the more you learn and grow in these spaces, the more you realise just how much learning and growth you haven't done yet. But it's always, *always* worth these wobbles and occasional freak-outs. It's worth it for my relationship with my gods, and for the people I've met, and known, and loved.

When I was writing this book, I tried to share a good variety of information with lots of rabbit holes to explore on your own, and now's the time to do that exploring: you should have enough of a framework by now to understand (and practise) a lot of the magic discussed here. Reading is all very well, but for the most part, this stuff has to be *experienced* to make sense.

I could write another hundred thousand words and still not be able to capture the exact feeling of standing under the moon with the people you love the most. I can't convey to you in words what a forest does when you cast a circle within it, or what it feels like to perform magic for another person.

So what are you waiting for? Get to it! The magic's in the doing, after all.

APPENDIX
Prompts to Aid Visualisation Skills

Visualisation is not something that comes naturally to everyone. If you are having trouble, try using these simple prompting questions for help. Using these regularly and in order can help to kickstart your brain into visualising things.

Introduce the first one or two questions when you begin. You should be able to answer each one silently, in a sentence. Use that sentence to focus and bring detail to the picture you create in your mind's eye. Once you're okay and confident answering the first one or two, introduce another one *in order*. Each time you get comfortable with the questions you've introduced, introduce another, in order.

To make this even more clear, I've included an example of what this could look like in italics.

1. What am I seeing? *(I can see a globe.)*
2. What is its size? How big is it? *(The globe is as big as a basketball.)*
3. What colour is it? *(The globe is blue.)*
4. How many things am I seeing? *(There is just one globe.)*
5. What shapes can I see? *(This is a three-dimensional, perfect globe.)*
6. Where is the thing I am seeing? *(The globe is sitting in the air in front of me.)*

7. Is the thing moving? How does it move? *(The globe shimmers slightly from time to time.)*

8. What does the object feel like? *(The globe feels cool to the touch. It is smooth.)*

9. What is going on in the background of what I am seeing? *(The globe is floating in midair in a field of flowers. Behind it is a brilliant sunrise.)*

10. When is this taking place? *(It must be spring or summer here, judging by the flowers.)*

11. What sounds can be heard? *(I can hear the wind blowing gently through the grass around my feet.)*

12. What smells are there? *(I can smell the fresh, dewy grass and the flowers.)*

13. What is the mood or atmosphere of what I am seeing? *(Looking at the circle makes me feel hopeful. This scene feels very peaceful.)*

Glossary

almadel: A wax talisman inscribed with the names of deities or spirits.

altar: A surface or raised structure on which gifts or sacrifices to a god are made.

altered state: A state of consciousness that is different from normal, everyday consciousness. An altered state of consciousness usually minimises the external world, which allows subconscious imagery to rise into the conscious mind. Altered states can include some dreams, trance states, out-of-body experiences, dissociative ritual experiences, and hallucinations. Experiences had in an altered state are almost always considered unverified personal gnosis (see *UPG*).

animism: The belief that natural features of the world (such as trees, mountains, rivers, etc.) possess their own spirit. Sometimes this is extended to include inanimate objects, with the belief that they have their own life force or energy that is distinct from their physical form and that is capable of existing without a physical "shell."

apotropaic: Capable of warding off evil or negative influences.

asperging: Cleansing sacred space using salted water.

athame: A ritual knife.

besom: A ritual broom used to purify sacred space.

cakes and ale/cakes and wine: Eating and drinking food/beverages that have been ritually consecrated.

censer: A ritual incense burner. Sometimes used in circle casting.

censing: Cleansing a sacred space using smoke.

ceremonial magic: Magic that employs rituals, symbols, and ceremony as a way to represent the supernatural and mystical forces that link the universe and humanity.

chalice: A ritual cup.

chaos magic: A contemporary magical practice initially developed in England in the 1970s, drawing heavily from the philosophy of artist and occultist Austin Osman Spare.

circumambulation: To walk around something three times.

closed practice: A practice that is limited to certain people. Closed practices may require an invitation or initiation before an outsider can participate.

cone of power: The ritual act of visualising a "cone" of energy and directing it toward the goal or task at hand.

consecration: In Wicca and ritual magic, this is the ceremonial act of dedicating a tool, object, or space as special and sacred.

cross-quarter days: The four sabbats that are not solar-related (that are not equinoxes and solstices). They are Imbolc, Beltane, Lammas, and Samhain.

cultural appropriation: The unacknowledged or inappropriate adoption of an element or elements of one culture/identity by members of another culture. This can be seen as especially controversial when members of a dominant culture appropriate from minority cultures and/or cultures historically or currently oppressed by the dominant culture.

decolonise: The act of reversing, lessening, and trying to remedy the impact of colonisation.

deity: A supernatural being that is worshipped by people who believe it controls or exerts force over some aspect of the world.

deosil: The direction the sun is seen to be travelling. Counterclockwise in the Southern Hemisphere; clockwise in the Northern Hemisphere.

devotional: An exercise—such as a ritual or prayer—expressing reverence for a deity.

divination: The idea that a person can see the future by supernatural means. Fortune-telling.

eclectic witchcraft: Witchcraft that doesn't necessarily follow a certain tradition, or that follows many traditions.

equinox: The instant in time when Earth's equator passes through the geometric centre of the sun. This occurs twice each year.

esbat: A coven meeting. Some covens call full moon get-togethers esbats; some use the word to refer to meetings that are not on a full moon or sabbat.

Freemasonry: Fraternal organisations originally formed to regulate the qualifications and business of stonemasons.

gatekeeping: The activity of controlling (and usually limiting) general access to something.

Gnosticism: A general term often applied to belief systems of certain religious sects that appeared around the same time as Christianity and which were condemned as heretical by many orthodox church leaders. Followers of these sects are known collectively as Gnostics—people who believed in and sought *gnōsis*, the Greek term for "knowledge." In this case, the knowledge was considered hidden spiritual knowledge.

grounding: The ritual act of connecting the body's energy with the earth.

guardian spirit: A personal, protective spirit thought to oversee a person's day-to-day activities and watch for impending danger or misadventure.

hard polytheism: Belief that the gods are all individual deities.

Hermetic: Of or related to Hermes Trismegistus, a legendary figure from ancient Greece thought to originate from the gods Hermes and Thoth.

horoscope: In astrology, this is a map or figure of the heavens in a 360-degree view around the earth, to show the positions of the planets and the sun in different signs of the zodiac. These are often done for the moment of an individual's birth, but they can be drawn up for other times and dates too, including dates in the future.

idol: An object or image representing a god or spirit. These are often seen as having divine or magical powers.

libation: The act of pouring a liquid offering (especially wine) onto the ground or into an offering bowl as a religious or devotional act.

monotheism: Belief in one god.

open practice: A practice that is openly available and workable by anyone. Does not require a formal initiation or invitation.

operative witchcraft: Rituals and workings done with the intention of altering the external universe in some way: spells, charms, curses, blessings, divination, etc.

pantheon: All the gods of a single belief system or tradition.

pathworking: Any visualised journey, usually undertaken in a meditative or altered state of consciousness. The term was originally used to describe the process of mentally or astrally journeying along the paths of the Qabalistic Tree of Life.

polytheism: Belief in multiple gods.

primary phase: A phase of the moon that takes place at a specific time, calculable to the minute. The primary phases are new/dark moon, first quarter, full moon, third/last quarter.

quarters: In circle casting, these are the four cardinal points (north, east, south, west) of a circle.

raising energy: Building up energy to direct toward magical goals. This can be done in a number of ways, including dancing, drumming, or singing.

ritual witchcraft: Rituals and workings done to bring one closer to deity, to benefit deity, or to otherwise alter the relationship between human and deity (or spirits) in some way: prayers, devotionals, seasonal celebrations, etc.

sabbat: Witches' holy day.

soft polytheism: Seeing all gods as aspects of one god.

solstice: An event that occurs when the Sun appears to reach its most northerly or southerly excursion relative to the celestial equator on the celestial sphere. Two solstices occur annually.

statement of intent: A few sentences, often spoken aloud at the beginning of the ritual, to explain the purpose and/or observance of the ritual.

theistic: Relating to the belief/worship in one or more deity (god). Nontheistic refers to practices that do not involve deities.

Thelema: An esoteric philosophy originally developed in the early 1900s by Aleister Crowley.

Theosophist: A follower of the teachings of the Theosophical Society.

traditional Wicca: Wiccan traditions directly related to the one originating in the New Forest region of England, and with initiatory lineage traceable back to it. E.g., Gardnerian or Alexandrian Wicca.

unverified personal gnosis (UPG): A term used in religious discussions to preface or qualify a particular statement on metaphysical reality.

wand: A magical tool—usually a stick or length of wood—sometimes used in circle casting.

Wheel of the Year: The calendar that many witches use to mark a year's worth of celebrations.

widdershins: In circle casting, the opposite direction to deosil.

Witches' Rede: Also known as the Wiccan Rede. A statement used by some witches to provide moral guidance (*An it harm none, do what ye will*). Thought to be adapted from Aleister Crowley's "Do what thou wilt shall be the whole of the Law."

Bibliography

Aburrow, Yvonne. *All Acts of Love & Pleasure: Inclusive Wicca*. New York: Avalonia, 2014.

————. "What Is Theology?" *Dowsing for Divinity* (blog), January 1, 2013. https://dowsingfordivinity.com/2013/01/01/what-is-theology/.

Adler, Margot. *Drawing Down the Moon: Witches, Druids, Goddess-Worshippers, and Other Pagans in America Today*. Boston: Beacon Press, 1981.

Albertsson, Alaric. *To Walk a Pagan Path: Practical Spirituality for Every Day*. Woodbury, MN: Llewellyn Publications, 2013. Scribd.

Alden, Temperance. *Year of the Witch: Connecting with Nature's Seasons through Intuitive Magick*. Newburyport, MA: Weiser Books, 2020.

Applewhite, Courtney. "Author Interview." *Reading Religion*, July 2018. https://readingreligion.org/9780300229042/.

Aradia, Sable. "Seekers and Guides: An Elemental Journey." *Agora* (blog), March 3, 2014. https://www.patheos.com/blogs/agora/2014/03/seekers-and-guides-an-elemental-journey/.

————. *The Witch's Eight Paths of Power: A Complete Course in Magick and Witchcraft*. San Francisco: Weiser Books, 2014.

Ash. "Information Privilege and Poverty in Paganism." *The Gardnerian Librarian* (blog), December 1, 2020. https://www.patheos.com/blogs/the gardnerianlibrarian/2020/12/information-privilege-and-poverty-in -paganism/.

Ashcroft-Nowicki, Dolores. "The Gypsy Runes." *The Golden Dawn Journal: Book I: Divination*, edited by Chic Cicero and Sandra Tabatha Cicero, 231–38. St. Paul, MN: Llewellyn Publications, 1994.

Autumnalis, Elizabeth. "Amici Mortem: Transforming Our Cultural Experiences with Death." Hawthorne and Rose (blog), February 24, 2019. https://www.patheos.com/blogs/hawthorneandtherose/2019/02/amici-mortem-on-transforming-our-cultural-experiences-with-death/.

Barber, Shannon. "Black Magic, Black Skin: Decolonizing White Witchcraft." *Ravishly*, October 23, 2017. https://ravishly.com/black-magic-black-skin-decolonizing-white-witchcraft.

Beckett, John. "Eight Essential Elements of Good Pagan Ritual." *Under the Ancient Oaks* (blog), October 15, 2019. https://www.patheos.com/blogs/johnbeckett/2019/10/8-essential-elements-of-good-pagan-ritual.html.

———. *The Path of Paganism: An Experience-Based Guide to Modern Pagan Practice*. Woodbury, MN: Llewellyn Publications, 2017. Scribd.

———. "Should I Join This Pagan Group or Not?" *Under the Ancient Oaks* (blog), October 29, 2019. https://www.patheos.com/blogs/johnbeckett/2019/10/should-i-join-this-pagan-group-or-not.html.

———. "UPG: Why Unverified Personal Gnosis Is Good and Necessary." *Under the Ancient Oaks* (blog), March 14, 2018. https://www.patheos.com/blogs/johnbeckett/2019/03/upg-why-unverified-personal-gnosis-is-good-and-necessary.html.

Bel, Bekah Evie. "Why I Am a Hearth Witch and What Is Hearth Witchery Anyway?" *Hearth Witch Down Under* (blog), July 17, 2017. www.patheos.com/blogs/hearthwitchdownunder/2017/07/hearth-witch-hearth-witchery-anyway.html.

———. "Witchcraft 101 – Sometimes You Have to Follow the Rules." *Hearth Witch Down Under* (blog), October 25, 2017. https://www.patheos.com/blogs/hearthwitchdownunder/2017/10/witchcraft-101-sometimes-follow-rules.html.

Berry, Rachel. "Safe & Ethical Guidelines for Wildcrafting." *Sierra Botanica* (blog), January 20, 2015. https://sierrabotanica.com/2015/01/safe-ethical-guidelines-for-wildcrafting/.

Blackthorn, Amy. *Blackthorn's Botanical Brews: Herbal Potions, Magical Teas, and Spirited Libations*. Newburyport, MA: Weiser Books, 2020.

————. *Blackthorn's Botanical Magic: The Green Witch's Guide to Essential Oils for Spellcraft, Ritual & Healing*. Newburyport, MA: Weiser Books, 2018.

————. *Sacred Smoke: Clear Away Negative Energies and Purify Body, Mind, and Spirit*. Newburyport, MA: Weiser Books, 2019.

Blake, Deborah. *Circle, Coven & Grove: A Year of Magickal Practice*. Woodbury, MN: Llewellyn Publications, 2017.

————. *Everyday Witchcraft: Making Time for Spirit in a Too-Busy World*. Woodbury, MN: Llewellyn Publications, 2015.

————. *Witchcraft on a Shoestring: Practicing the Craft without Breaking Your Budget*. Woodbury, MN: Llewellyn Publications, 2010.

Blakeslee, Sarah. "The CRAAP Test." *LOEX Quarterly* 31, no. 3 (Fall 2004): 6–7. https://commons.emich.edu/loexquarterly/vol31/iss3/4.

Boardman, John, Jasper Griffin, and Oswyn Murray, eds. *The Oxford History of the Classical World*. 3rd ed. New York: Oxford University Press, 1993.

Brison, Todd. "Three Elements Required for a Successful Ritual." *Medium*, October 3, 2017. https://toddbrison.medium.com/3-elements -required-for-a-successful-ritual-3d3af89e5a2e.

Burton, Nylah, and Jay Polish. "The Ethics of Burning Sage, Explained." *Bustle*. Updated February 24, 2022. https://www.bustle.com/wellness/is -burning-sage-cultural-appropriation-heres-how-to-smoke-cleanse-in -sensitive-ways-18208360.

Campanelli, Pauline. "The Wheel of the Year." *Llewellyn's Magical Sampler: The Best Articles from the Magical Almanac*, edited by Ed Day, 329–335. Woodbury, MN: Llewellyn Publications, 2015.

Carnevale, Tino. "Selecting Seedlings." *Gardening Australia*. Broadcast July 29, 2016. https://www.abc.net.au/gardening/how-to/selecting -seedlings/9438016.

Carroll, Ryder. *The Bullet Journal Method: Track the Past, Order the Present, Design the Future*. New York: Portfolio/Penguin, 2018.

"Certifiable Resin Supply Chain." Save Frankincense. Accessed February 20, 2020. https://www.savefrankincense.org/certifiable-resin-supply-chain.

Connor, Kerri. *Ostara: Rituals, Recipes & Lore for the Spring Equinox*. Woodbury, MN: Llewellyn Publications, 2015. Scribd.

Cox, Denis. "Getting to Know Poisonous Plants." Sustainable Gardening Australia. Accessed February 8, 2023. https://www.sgaonline.org.au /getting-to-know-poisonous-plants/.

Crowley, Vivianne. *Wicca: A Comprehensive Guide to the Old Religion in the Modern World*. London: Element, 2003.

Crowther, Patricia. *Lid Off the Cauldron: A Handbook for Witches*. London: Frederick Muller Limited, 1981.

Davies, Owen. *Grimoires: A History of Magic Books*. Oxford: Oxford University Press, 2010.

d'Este, Sorita, and David Rankine. *Circle of Fire: A Practical Guide to the Symbolism & Practices of Modern Wiccan Ritual*. London: Avalonia, 2008.

———. *Wicca Magical Beginnings: A Study of the Possible Origins of the Rituals and Practices Found in This Modern Tradition of Pagan Witchcraft and Magick*. London: Avalonia, 2008.

Dombrowski, Kiki. *A Curious Future: A Handbook of Unusual Divination and Unique Oracular Techniques*. 2nd ed. Dallas, TX: Witch Way Publishing, 2021.

Dominguez, Ivo, Jr. *The Four Elements of the Wise: Working with the Magickal Powers of Earth, Air, Water, Fire*. Newburyport, MA: Weiser Books, 2021.

Dorsey, Lilith. *Orishas, Goddesses, and Voodoo Queens: The Divine Feminine in the African Religious Traditions*. Newburyport, MA: Weiser Books, 2020.

———. *Water Magic*. Woodbury, MN: Llewellyn Publications, 2020.

Drury, Nevill. *The Watkins Dictionary of Magic: Over 3,000 Entries on the World of Magical Formulas, Secret Symbols, and the Occult*. London: Watkins Publishing, 2005.

Drury, Nevill, and Gregory Tillett. *The Occult Sourcebook*. London: Routledge & Kegan Paul, 1978.

Duncan, Hal. "An thread: if you want to know why some of us hated Harry Potter liberal centrism even before Rowling destroyed her own standing among the moderately progressive." Twitter, August 9, 2020. https:// twitter.com/hal_duncan/status/1292560296503054338.

DuQuette, Lon Milo, and David Shoemaker, eds. *Llewellyn's Complete Book of Ceremonial Magick*. Woodbury, MN: Llewellyn Publications, 2020.

Edmanson, Jane. "Growing Herbs Indoors." *Gardening Australia*. Broadcast August 16, 2019. https://www.abc.net.au/gardening/how-to/growing -herbs-indoors/11413846.

Enodian, River. "How Do I Get in Touch or Communicate with a God or Daimon?" *Tea Addicted Witch* (blog), May 10, 2018. https://www.patheos .com/blogs/teaaddictedwitch/2018/05/how-do-i-get-in-touch-with-a -god/.

"Episode 75 – Ritual Building Protection, with Guest James Wright." Podcast. *The Folklore Podcast*, May 15, 2020. MP3 audio, 50:00. http://www .thefolklorepodcast.com/season-5/episode-75-ritual-building -protection-with-guest-james-wright.

Farrar, Janet, and Stewart Farrar. *A Witches' Bible: The Complete Witches' Handbook*. London: Robert Hale, 1996.

"Frankincense Decline." Save Frankincense. Accessed February 20, 2020. https://www.savefrankincense.org/frankincense-decline.

Frazer, James George. *The Golden Bough: A Study in Magic and Religion*. 3rd ed. London: Macmillan, 1976.

GCT. "Ancient 'Curse Tablets' Discovered Down a 2,500-Year-Old Well in Athens." *Greek City Times*, February 6, 2020. https://greekcitytimes .com/2020/02/06/ancient-curse-tablets-discovered-down-a-2500 -year-old-well-in-athens/.

Gottlieb, Kathryn. "Cultural Appropriation in Contemporary Neopaganism and Witchcraft." Honors thesis, University of Maine, 2017. https:// digitalcommons.library.umaine.edu/cgi/viewcontent.cgi?article=1303 &context=honors.

Green, Marian. *A Witch Alone: Thirteen Moons to Master Natural Magic*. London: The Aquarian Press, 1991.

———. *Elements of Ritual Magic*. Dorset, UK: Element Books, 1990.

Gruben, Michelle. "Circle-Casting Basics: All You Need to Know about Magick Circles." Grove and Grotto, July 13, 2017. https://www .groveandgrotto.com/blogs/articles/circle-casting-basics-all-you -need-to-know-about-magick-circles.

Gwyn. "Talisman, Amulet, Charm. Oh My!" *3 Pagans and a Cat* (blog), October 21, 2019. https://www.patheos.com/blogs/3pagansandacat/2019/10/talisman-amulet-charm-oh-my/.

Hale, Amy. "On Paganism, Fakelore, and Tired Conversations about Authenticity." *Medium*, November 18, 2018. https://medium.com/@amyhale93/on-paganism-fakelore-and-tired-conversations-about-authenticity-10ab0c9537d0.

Hamer, Ashley. "Here's Why Smells Trigger Such Vivid Memories." *Discovery*, August 1, 2019. https://www.discovery.com/science/Why-Smells-Trigger-Such-Vivid-Memories.

Heselton, Philip. *Witchfather: A Life of Gerald Gardner*. Loughborough, Leicestershire: Thoth Publications, 2012.

Hocken, Vigdis. "Friday: Frigg's and Freya's Day." Time and Date. Accessed April 5, 2023. https://www.timeanddate.com/calendar/days/friday.html.

———. "Monday: The Moon's Day." Time and Date. Accessed April 5, 2023. https://www.timeanddate.com/calendar/days/monday.html.

———. "Thursday: Thor's Day." Time and Date. Accessed April 5, 2023. https://www.timeanddate.com/calendar/days/thursday.html.

———. "Tuesday: Tiw's and Mars' Day." Time and Date. Accessed April 5, 2023. https://www.timeanddate.com/calendar/days/tuesday.html.

———. "Saturday: Saturn's Day." Time and Date. Accessed April 5, 2023. https://www.timeanddate.com/calendar/days/saturday.html.

———. "Sunday: The Sun's Day." Time and Date. Accessed April 5, 2023. https://www.timeanddate.com/calendar/days/sunday.html.

———. "Wednesday: Odin and Wodan's Day." Time and Date. Accessed April 5, 2023. https://www.timeanddate.com/calendar/days/wednesday.html.

Holmyard, E. J. *Alchemy*. Harmondsworth, UK: Penguin Books, 1957.

"How to Make Tea." T2. Accessed February 9, 2023. www.t2tea.com/en/au/how-to-brew/how-to-brew-tea.html.

Huson, Paul. *Mastering Witchcraft: A Practical Guide for Witches, Warlocks & Covens*. London: Rupert Hart-Davis, 1970.

Hutton, Ronald. *The Stations of the Sun: A History of the Ritual Year in Britain.* Oxford: Oxford University Press, 1996.

Illes, Judika. *The Element Encyclopedia of 5000 Spells: The Ultimate Reference Book for the Magical Arts.* London: Element Books, 2004.

Jaynes, Julian. *The Origin of Consciousness in the Breakdown of the Bicameral Mind.* Toronto: University of Toronto Press, 1976.

Kelden. "A Brief History of Modern Traditional Witchcraft." *By Athame and Stang* (blog), January 18, 2018. https://www.patheos.com/blogs /byathameandstang/2018/01/introduction-traditional-witchcraft-pt-2/.

Kelly, Aidan. "About Naming Ostara, Litha, and Mabon." *Including Paganism with Aidan Kelly* (blog), May 2, 2017. https://www.patheos.com/blogs /aidankelly/2017/05/naming-ostara-litha-mabon/.

Kynes, Sandra. *Llewellyn's Complete Book of Correspondences: A Comprehensive & Cross-Referenced Resource for Pagans & Wiccans.* Woodbury, MN: Llewellyn Publications, 2016.

———. *A Year of Ritual: Sabbats & Esbats for Solitaries and Covens.* St. Paul, MN: Llewellyn Publications, 2004.

Latham-Jones, Cassandra. *Village Witch.* London: Troy Books, 2011.

Lipp, Deborah. *Magical Power for Beginners: How to Raise & Send Energy for Spells That Work.* Woodbury, MN: Llewellyn Publications, 2017.

Little, Brenda. *The Complete Book of Herbs and Spices.* Frenchs Forest, NSW: Reed Books, 1986.

Lyte, Fire. *The Dabbler's Guide to Witchcraft: Seeking an Intentional Magical Path.* New York: Tiller Press, 2021.

MacLir, Alferian Gwydion. *The Witch's Wand: The Craft, Lore & Magick of Wands & Staffs.* Woodbury, MN: Llewellyn Publications, 2015.

MacMorgan, Kaatryn. *All One Wicca: A Study in the Universal Eclectic Tradition of Wicca.* Lincoln, NE: Writers Club Press, 2001.

Mankey, Jason. "The Charge of the Goddess: A History." *Raise the Horns* (blog), April 6, 2015. www.patheos.com/blogs/panmankey/2015/04/the -charge-of-the-goddess-a-history/.

———. "Do We Need Pan-Pagan Clergy? (I Don't Think So)." *Raise the Horns* (blog), May 27, 2019. https://www.patheos.com/blogs/panmankey /2019/05/do-we-need-pan-pagan-clergy-i-dont-think-so/.

———. *Transformative Witchcraft: The Greater Mysteries.* Woodbury, MN: Llewellyn Publications, 2019. Scribd.

———. *The Witch's Athame: The Craft, Lore & Magick of Ritual Blades.* Woodbury, MN: Llewellyn Publications, 2016.

———. *The Witch's Book of Shadows: The Craft, Lore & Magick of the Witch's Grimoire.* Woodbury, MN: Llewellyn Publications, 2017. Scribd.

———. *Witch's Wheel of the Year: Rituals for Circles, Solitaries & Covens.* Woodbury, MN: Llewellyn Publications, 2019.

McKay, Dodie Graham. *Earth Magic.* Woodbury, MN: Llewellyn Publications, 2021.

Michelle, Heron. "My Quest to Find the Elemental Guardians of the Watchtowers." *Witch on Fire* (blog), February 26, 2018. https://www.patheos .com/blogs/witchonfire/2018/02/quest-elemental-guardians/.

Mierzwicki, Tony. *Hellenismos: Practicing Greek Polytheism Today.* Woodbury, MN: Llewellyn Publications, 2018. Scribd.

Miller, Jason. "Divination vs. Decision Making Strategies." Strategic Sorcery (blog). Accessed February 7, 2023. https://www.strategicsorcery.net /divination-vs-decision-making-strategies/.

Mooney, Thorn. "The Benefits of Outer Courts and Training Circles." *Oathbound* (blog), January 24, 2020. https://www.patheos.com/blogs /oathbound/2020/01/the-benefits-of-outer-courts-and-training-circles/.

———. "Why Worship." *Oathbound* (blog), July 26, 2017. https://www .patheos.com/blogs/oathbound/2017/07/why-worship/.

———. *The Witch's Path: Advancing Your Craft at Every Level.* Woodbury, MN: Llewellyn Publications, 2021.

NASA. "Sun." Solar System Exploration. Updated March 22, 2023. https:// solarsystem.nasa.gov/solar-system/sun/overview/.

Nat's What I Reckon. "Sin Bin Soup." Uploaded April 8, 2020. YouTube video, 3:45. https://www.youtube.com/watch?v=wIwhdOx9BL0.

O'Brien, Lora. *A Practical Guide to Pagan Priesthood: Community Leadership and Vocation.* Woodbury, MN: Llewellyn Publications, 2019.

————. "NeoPaganism: A Brief History of Our Modern Pagan Religion." *Lora O'Brien—Irish Author & Guide* (blog), October 27, 2018. https://loraobrien.ie/neopaganism-a-brief-history-of-our-modern-pagan-religion/.

Opie, Iona, and Moira Tatem, eds. *A Dictionary of Superstitions.* New York: Oxford University Press, 1992.

Patinkin, Jason. "World's Last Wild Frankincense Forests Are Under Threat." *Yahoo! Finance*, December 24, 2016. https://finance.yahoo.com/news/worlds-last-wild-frankincense-forests-084122152.html.

Paxson, Diana L. *Essential Asatru: Walking the Path of Norse Paganism.* New York: Citadel, 2006.

————. *Taking Up the Runes: A Complete Guide to Using Runes in Spells, Rituals, Divination, and Magic.* Boston, MA: Weiser Books, 2005.

Pennick, Nigel. *The Ancestral Power of Amulets, Talismans, and Mascots: Folk Magic in Witchcraft and Religion.* Rochester, VT: Destiny Books, 2021.

————. *The Book of Primal Signs: The High Magic of Symbols.* Rochester, VT: Destiny Books, 2014.

————. *The Complete Illustrated Guide to Runes.* London: HarperCollins, 2003.

————. *Elemental Magic: Traditional Practices for Working with the Energies of the Natural World.* Rochester, VT: Destiny Books, 2020.

Phillips, Matthew, and Julia Phillips. *The Witches of Oz.* Berkshire, UK: Capall Bann Publishing, 1994.

Polson, Willow. *Sabbat Entertaining: Celebrating the Wiccan Holidays with Style.* New York: Citadel, 2002.

Rankine, David, and Sorita d'Este. *Practical Elemental Magick: Working the Magick of the Four Elements in the Western Mystery Tradition.* London: Avalonia, 2008.

————. *Practical Planetary Magick: Working the Magick of the Classical Planets in the Western Esoteric Tradition.* London: Avalonia, 2007.

Rasbold, Katrina. "Ritual Crafting: Creating Rituals That Work (Part 1)." *Witch at the Crossroads* (blog), June 8, 2015. https://www.patheos.com/blogs/energymagic/2015/06/rituals1/.

Raven, Gwion. "Casting a Circle – Creating Sacred Space." *The Witches Next Door* (blog), July 12, 2016. www.patheos.com/blogs/thewitchesnextdoor/2016/07/casting-a-circle-creating-sacred-space/.

————. *The Magick of Food: Rituals, Offerings & Why We Eat Together*. Woodbury, MN: Llewellyn Publications, 2020.

Rose, Jeanne. *Herbs & Things: Jeanne Rose's Herbal*. New York: Grosset & Dunlap, 1972.

"S1 Ep16: How to Cast a Witchcraft Circle." Podcast. *Seeking Witchcraft*, December 25, 2019. MP3 audio, 34:01. https://www.podbean.com /media/share/dir-qsxsq-789d156?utm_campaign=w_share_ep&utm _medium=dlink&utm_source=w_share.

Saul, Flo. "Tea Leaf Dictionary." Aunty Flo. Accessed February 9, 2023. https://www.auntyflo.com/tea-leaf-dictionary.

Swiss, Tom. "Energy in the Art of Magic." *The Zen Pagan* (blog), May 21, 2021. https://www.patheos.com/blogs/thezenpagan/2021/05/energy-in-the -art-of-magic/.

Taylor, Astrea. *Air Magic*. Woodbury, MN: Llewellyn Publications, 2021.

Tuan. "The Working Tools of the Witch: The Sword." *Esoterica* (1995): 42–44.

U.:D.:, Frater. *Practical Sigil Magic: Creating Personal Symbols for Success*. Woodbury, MN: Llewellyn Publications, 2012.

Valiente, Doreen. *Natural Magic*. London: Robert Hale, 1975.

————. *The Rebirth of Witchcraft*. London: Robert Hale, 1989.

Waite, Arthur Edward. *The Book of Ceremonial Magic*. New York: Citadel Press, 1989. Scribd.

————. *The Pictorial Key to the Tarot: Being Fragments of a Secret Tradition Under the Veil of Divination*. Wiltshire, UK: Paragon, 1993.

"Wattles – Genus *Acacia*." Australian National Botanic Gardens. Updated December 24, 2015. https://www.anbg.gov.au/acacia/.

West, Kate. *The Real Witches' Garden: Spells, Herbs, Plants, and Magical Spaces Outdoors*. Woodbury, MN: Llewellyn Publications, 2010.

————. *The Real Witches' Kitchen: Spells, Recipes, Oils, Lotions and Potions from the Witches' Hearth*. Woodbury, MN: Llewellyn Publications, 2016.

"What Is Paganism?" *Tasmanian Pagan Alliance* (blog). Accessed January 18, 2023. https://taspainc.com/what-is-paganism/.

Wigington, Patti. "Blessed Be." *Learn Religions*. Updated June 25, 2019. https://www.learnreligions.com/what-is-blessed-be-2561872.

————. "History of the Wiccan Phrase 'So Mote It Be.'" *Learn Religions*. Updated March 29, 2018. https://www.learnreligions.com/so-mote -it-be-2561921.

————. "I Don't Care Where You Get Your Tools: You Do You, Boo." Patti Wigington, June 23, 2019. www.pattiwigington.com/i-dont-care-where -you-get-your-tools-you-do-you-boo/.

————. "The Magic of Sigils." Patti Wigington, June 20, 2020. https:// www.pattiwigington.com/the-magic-of-sigils/.

————. "Ogham Symbol Gallery." *Learn Religions*. Updated June 25, 2019. https://www.learnreligions.com/ogham-symbol-gallery-4123029.

————. "Protection Magic Basics." Patti Wigington, June 1, 2021. www .pattiwigington.com/protection-magic-basics/.

Wilkinson, Lili. "Let's Talk About Sects 1: Satanic Panic." Uploaded June 13, 2016. YouTube video, 6:17. https://youtu.be/jL477uwaJjs.

Williams, Brandy. "Is the Term Black Magic Racist?" *Star & Snake* (blog), May 14, 2018. https://www.patheos.com/blogs/starandsnake/2018/05 /is-the-term-black-magic-racist/.

————. "White Light, Black Magic: Racism in Esoteric Thought." Brandy Williams. Accessed June 1, 2021. https://brandywilliamsauthor.com /white-light-black-magic-racism-in-esoteric-thought/.

Willow. "Decolonizing Witchcraft: Racism, Whitewashing, and Cultural Appropriation in Witchcraft and How to Decolonize your Practice." *Flying the Hedge* (blog). Updated July 27, 2020. https://www.flyingthehedge .com/2020/06/decolonizing-witchcraft.html.

Winter, Josephine. *Fire Magic*. Woodbury, MN: Llewellyn Publications, 2021.

Zai, Dr. J. *Taoism and Science: Cosmology, Evolution, Morality, Health, and More*. Brisbane: Ultravisum, 2015.

Zakroff, Laura Tempest. *Sigil Witchery: A Witch's Guide to Crafting Magick Symbols*. Woodbury, MN: Llewellyn Publications, 2018.

————. *Weave the Liminal: Living Modern Traditional Witchcraft*. Woodbury, MN: Llewellyn Publications, 2019.

To Write to the Author

If you wish to contact the author or would like more information about this book, please write to the author in care of Llewellyn Worldwide Ltd. and we will forward your request. Both the author and publisher appreciate hearing from you and learning of your enjoyment of this book and how it has helped you. Llewellyn Worldwide Ltd. cannot guarantee that every letter written to the author can be answered, but all will be forwarded. Please write to:

Josephine Winter
℅ Llewellyn Worldwide
2143 Wooddale Drive
Woodbury, MN 55125-2989

Please enclose a self-addressed stamped envelope for reply,
or $1.00 to cover costs. If outside the U.S.A., enclose
an international postal reply coupon.

Many of Llewellyn's authors have websites with additional information and resources. For more information, please visit our website at http://www.llewellyn.com.